Mental Health Care

Mental Health Care

A Care Worker Handbook

Tina Tilmouth with Erica Pavord

HODDER
EDUCATION
AN HACHETTE UK COMPANY

Orders: please contact Bookpoint Ltd, 130 Milton Park, Abingdon, Oxon OX14 4SB. Telephone: (44) 01235 827720. Fax: (44) 01235 400454. Lines are open from 9.00 – 5.00, Monday to Saturday, with a 24 hour message answering service. You can also order through our website www.hoddereducation.co.uk

If you have any comments to make about this, or any of our other titles, please send them to educationenquiries@hodder.co.uk

British Library Cataloguing in Publication Data

A catalogue record for this title is available from the British Library

ISBN: 978 1 444 18379 5

First Edition Published 2013

Impression number   10 9 8 7 6 5 4 3 2 1

Year   2016 2015 2014 2013

Copyright © 2013 Tina Tilmouth, Erica Pavord

Cover photo © Chris Schmidt/iStockphoto

Illustrations by Barking Dog Art

Typeset by Datapage (India) Pvt. Ltd.

Printed in Italy for Hodder Education, an Hachette UK Company, 338 Euston Road, London NW1 3BH

Contents

Acknowledgments

Acknowledgments

Every effort has been made to trace and acknowledge ownership of copyright. The publishers will be glad to make suitable arrangements with any copyright holders whom it has not been possible to contact.

Photo credits

The authors and publishers would like to thank the following for the use of images in this volume:

page 10 © Fancy / Alamy; page 38 © Samaritans; page 56 (left) © Paula Solloway – Photofusion Pictures; (right) © Sheila Terry/Science Photo Library; page 86 © ZUMA Wire Service / Alamy; page 93 © Alvaro German Vilela – Fotolia.com; page 104 © Crown Copyright; page 113 © Cultura Creative / Alamy; page 150 © Monkey Business – Fotolia.com; page 187 © David J. Green / Alamy; page 196 © Science Photo Library / Getty Images.

Walkthrough

We want you to succeed!

This book has been designed to include all the topic knowledge, assessment support and practical advice you will need for the following qualifications:

- NCFE Level 1 Award in Mental Health Awareness (501/0253/9)
- NCFE Level 2 Award in Understanding Working with People with Mental Health Issues (500/9956/5)
- City & Guilds Level 3 Diploma in Mental Health Care (600/5241/7)

The book has been written with the work-based learner in mind. Everything in it reflects the assessment criteria and evidence based approach that is applied to this vocational qualification.

In the pages that follow you will find up-to-date resource material which will develop your knowledge, rehearse your skills and help you to gain your qualification.

Prepare for what you are going to cover in this unit, and prepare for assessment:

The reading and activities in this chapter will help you to:

1. Identify possible causes of mental health problems.
2. Identify examples of mental health problems.
3. Identify the key strengths and limitations of the psychiatric classification system and alternative frameworks for understanding mental distress.
4. Understand how mental ill health may be indicated through an individual's emotions, thinking and behaviour.
5. Identify the common sources of information on mental health issues.

Understand how your learning fits into real life and your working environment:

Case study

John

John, 76, was a widower living in a small rural village. He had a part time job as a gardener for local people. He ate well, growing most of his own food, and usually slept soundly, although he did not feel particularly rested on waking. Recently he had begun to wake in the early hours and found it difficult to get back to sleep.

Reflect on how learning relates to your own experiences

Time to reflect

Discuss with a partner what boundaries are and why they are so important for a worker in a mental health care setting.

Generate evidence for assignments:

Evidence Activity

 Activity 2.1

Research the causes of mental illness and make notes for your portfolio. Reflect on the potential causes and contributing factors for two of your own clients with respect to their mental health issues. Be sure to respect confidentiality and use pseudonyms.

Reinforce concepts with hands-on learning

Research and investigate

 Activity 1.2

Using Dahlgren and Whitehead's social determinants of health model, plot the factors that have influenced your own and a colleague's mental health across your lifespan.

Each unit begins with a guide to which parts of each qualification are covered and where to find the knowledge you need and activities to test your understanding.

City & Guilds Level 3 Diploma in Mental Health Care (QCF) (600/5241/7)		
Promote communication in health, social care or children's and young people's settings (J/601/1434)		
Learning Outcome 1 Understand why effective communication is important in the work setting		
Assessment Criteria	Page reference	Activity
1.1 Identify the different reasons people communicate		
1.2 Explain how communication affects relationships in the work setting		

Develop an awareness of mental health across the lifespan

What are you finding out?

In this chapter we will look at what constitutes mental health and ill health and address some of the factors that can influence an individual's mental condition.

Our mental health is fundamental not only to our general health, but also to our quality of life. With growing recognition worldwide that there is a social and economic impact across the lifespan for those suffering with mental ill health, the importance of mental health and wellbeing to overall health has been widely studied and reported upon.

But understanding what's considered normal mental health can be problematic. For example, a person who reports that they hear voices might have schizophrenia, but what about somebody who drinks a lot of alcohol? Is that also a sign of mental illness? The distinction between mental health and mental ill health doesn't always appear obvious. If you feel sad at times or fed up, would it be true to say you were depressed? People with stress may say they feel depressed, but perhaps they just mean they are feeling down at that moment, and how does that feeling differ from other times in their life? What constitutes a true sign of mental ill health?

Mental health is about balance. An expectation of being happy and satisfied throughout our lifespan is unrealistic and we will all at some point experience anxiety, sadness and other negative emotions within our lives.

An awareness of mental health and what constitutes illness can greatly enhance your work as a carer of those with mental health issues and this chapter will help clarify this for you.

The reading and activities in this chapter will help you to:

1. Define the terms 'mental health' and 'mental ill health' and evaluate two different views on the nature of mental wellbeing and mental health.
2. Understand the different views on the nature of mental wellbeing and mental health and the factors that may influence both across the lifespan.
3. Discuss and evaluate a range of factors that may influence mental wellbeing and mental health problems across the lifespan, including biological, social and psychological factors.
4. Explain how the following risk factors and protective factors influence levels of resilience in individuals and groups in relation to mental wellbeing and mental health:
   - risk factors including inequalities, such as poor quality social relationships, and
   - protective factors such as socially valued roles, social support and contact.
5. Explain the steps that an individual may take to promote their mental wellbeing and mental health and key agencies that can help.
6. Identify strategies for supporting an individual in promoting their mental wellbeing and mental health.
7. Evaluate a strategy for supporting an individual in promoting their mental wellbeing and mental health.
8. Show the key aspects of a local, national or international strategy to promote mental wellbeing and mental health within a group or community/settings.

Assessment criteria covered in this chapter

Reading this unit and completing the activities will provide you with the knowledge, understanding and skills required to meet the assessment criteria listed below.

City and Guilds Level 3 Diploma in Mental Health Care (QCF) (600/5241/7)		
Understand mental wellbeing and mental health promotion (F/602/0097)		
Learning Outcome 1 Understand the different views on the nature of mental wellbeing and mental health and the factors that may influence both across the life span		
Assessment Criteria	Page reference	Activity
1.1 Evaluate two different views on the nature of mental wellbeing and mental health	pp. 3–4	Evidence activity 1.1, p. 7
1.2 Explain the range of factors that may influence mental wellbeing and mental health problems across the life span, including: a. biological factors b. social factors c. psychological factors	p. 7	Research and investigate activity 1.2, p. 10
1.3 Explain how the following types of risk factors and protective factors influence levels of resilience in individuals and groups in relation to mental wellbeing and mental health: a. risk factors including inequalities, poor quality social relationships b. protective factors including socially valued roles, social support and contact	p. 10	Evidence activity 1.3, p. 12
Learning Outcome 2 Know how to implement an effective strategy for promoting mental wellbeing and mental health with individuals and groups		
2.1 Explain the steps that an individual may take to promote their mental wellbeing and mental health	p. 15	Time to reflect activity 1.5, Activity 2 p. 18
2.2 Explain how to support an individual in promoting their mental wellbeing and mental health.	p. 18	Time to reflect activity 1.6/1.7, p. 19
2.3 Evaluate a strategy for supporting an individual in promoting their mental wellbeing and mental health	p. 19	Time to reflect activity 1.6/1.7, p. 19
2.4 Describe key aspects of a local, national or international strategy to promote mental wellbeing and mental health within a group or community	p. 20	Research and investigate activity 1.8, p. 23
2.5 Evaluate a local, national or international strategy to promote mental wellbeing and mental health within a group or community	p. 20	Research and investigate activity 1.8, p. 23

NCFE Level 1 Award in Mental Health Awareness (501/0253/9)		
Develop an awareness of mental health (K/600/6596)		
Learning Outcome 1 Be aware of what is meant by mental health		
Assessment Criteria	Page reference	Activity
1.1 Define the terms 'mental health' and 'mental ill health'	p. 3	Evidence activity 1.1, p. 7
1.4 List common sources of information on mental health issues	p. 16	Evidence activity 1.5, Activity 1, p. 16

(Continued)

(Continued)

Learning Outcome 2 Be aware of some of the social and personal effects of mental ill health		
2.2 Identify the effects that experiencing a mental health problem might have on an individual	p. 12	Evidence activity 1.4, p. 15
Learning Outcome 3 Be aware of some of the responses to mental health issues		
3.4 Identify where to refer people for further help or guidance about mental health issues	p. 16	Evidence activity 1.5, Activity 1 p. 16
3.5 Identify ways to promote positive mental health	p. 17	Time to reflect activity 2, p. 18

NCFE Level 2 Award in Understanding Working with People with Mental Health Issues (500/9956/5)		
Mental health and mental health issues (M/601/2948)		
Learning Outcome 1 Understand the background to mental health		
Assessment Criteria	Page reference	Activity
1.1 Define the term mental health	p. 3	Evidence activity 1.1, p. 7
1.2 Define the key components of mental wellbeing	p. 3	Evidence activity 1.1, p. 7
1.3 Explain the need for positive mental health	p. 7	Research and investigate activity 1.2, p. 10
1.4 Describe key risk factors in developing mental ill health	p. 12	Evidence activity 1.4, p. 15
1.5 Identify the effects that experiencing a mental health problem might have on an individual	p. 12	Evidence activity 1.4, p. 15
1.6 Give examples of the ways in which individuals may cope with their mental health problem	p. 15	Time to reflect activity 1.5, Activity 2 p. 18

1 Define the terms 'mental health' and 'mental ill health' and evaluate two different views on the nature of mental wellbeing and mental health

Having an understanding about how you view mental health and ill health is a good place to start your studies and your own definitions and answers to the question above will reveal either a positive or negative view of mental health.

The subject of health whether, physical or mental, is a difficult concept to get to grips with as the definition of health is a contested one and we all have our own views. Negative definitions describe health as simply 'the absence of illness or disease'. Townsend and Davidson (1982) provide us with:

'… freedom from ascertainable disease'.

A more positive definition is one that describes health as a more holistic notion.

You may recall the World Health Organization's definition of health as being

'a state of complete physical, mental and social wellbeing and not merely the absence of disease and infirmity'

(WHO, 1946).

This definition has been upheld as a more favourable description of health, with its multi-faceted view combining the social, mental and physical aspects of health. Critics have pointed to the problems there are with measuring and achieving this definition simply because it encompasses the whole of the human race. If we were to approach the many different societies around the globe with their different values, attitudes and norms, how much might this change the definition? In response to the critics the definition was revisited by the WHO some years later and in 1984 they came up with:

> 'the extent to which an individual or group is able, on the one hand to realise aspirations and satisfy needs; and, on the other hand, to change or cope with the environment. Health is, therefore, seen as a resource for everyday life, not an object of living; it is a positive concept emphasising social and person resources, as well as physical capabilities.'

(WHO, 1984)

Time to reflect

Consider the following question and reflect upon your answer. Keep your answer in a portfolio of work.

- What does mental health mean to you?

What does emerge from this last definition is just how multi-faceted the concept is. Holistic health incorporates several different facets including:

- physical
- intellectual/mental
- emotional
- social
- spiritual
- sexual.

(Ewles and Simnett, 1999)

Physical health refers to bodily functions and fitness and describes the ability of the body to function in an efficient way.

Intellectual and mental health concerns the sense of purpose we have in life and our ability to feel good and to cope. If we can think clearly and coherently then we are more likely be intellectually and mentally healthy. It also deals with the need to grow and learn and our capacity to become self-actualising. We can sense an emerging definition for mental health here, but it is more than just this.

Self-actualisation is worth mentioning since it is a term much used by psychologists. Referred to as a 'basic drive', and one which enables us to reach our full potential, you can see that Figure 1.1 Maslow's Hierarchy of Needs (1978) has 'self-actualisation' at the apex of the pyramid and this refers to creativity, motivation and problem solving as well as lack of prejudice as notions associated with this ability.

Emotional health is about our capacity to love and feel loved, and to be able to voice our emotions in a responsible manner in order to maintain relationships with others.

Being involved in these sorts of relationships and having a sense of support in our lives is all about **social health**. Our ability to make friends and to be involved in activities with others is incorporated here as well.

Spiritual health is often difficult to recognise because not all of us believe in a God or a religion. Some individuals have a strong need to belong to a group or organised religion and feel they

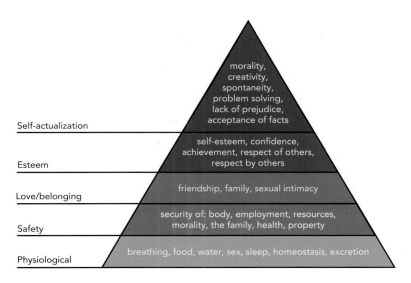

Figure 1.1 Maslow's hierarchy

are not complete without a belief of this kind. But spiritual health can also be about our moral principles and the way in which we live and have purpose in our lives.

Sexual health is about how we accept and express our own sexuality.

The above represent our individual dimensions of health, but clearly we are also affected by external influences and it is becoming increasingly accepted that mental health issues are as much about the environmental and social factors surrounding our lives as they are determined by biology and genetic factors. The wider society in which we live, where we live and the sort of environment we live in will all have influences on our mental health and wellbeing. This is referred to by the WHO and other writers in the field as the social determinants of health, or 'the conditions in which people are born, grow, live, work and age' (WHO) and we cover this in a later section.

In the government's New Horizons: Towards a Shared Vision for Mental Health (2009) publication, mental health is defined as:

> 'more than the absence or management of mental health problems; it is the foundation for well-being and effective functioning both for individuals and their communities.'

The document goes on to describe mental wellbeing as our 'ability to cope with life's problems and make the most of life's opportunities' and about 'feeling good and functioning well, as individuals and collectively'.

Another definition provided by the World Health Organization, along with its general health definition, refers to mental health as

> 'not just the absence of mental disorder … is defined as a state of well-being in which the individual realises his or her own abilities, can cope with the normal stresses of life, can work productively and fruitfully, and is able to make a contribution to his or her community.'

(WHO, 2003)

Both definitions speak of wellbeing as a multi-dimensional entity, much more than just being happy or satisfied. It includes health in social, physical, mental states and implies emotional, career and spiritual domains, and this view is supported in the definition by the government office for science in their Foresight Mental Capital and Wellbeing Project (2008):

'Mental wellbeing is a dynamic state in which the individual is able to develop their potential, work productively and creatively, build strong and positive relationships with others and contribute to their community. It is enhanced when an individual is able to fulfil their personal and social goals and achieve a sense of purpose in society.'

(Foresight Mental Capital and Wellbeing Project (2008) Final project report. London: The Government Office for Science)

So our state of mental health and wellbeing are moving, fluid concepts, subject to change and dependent upon various aspects of our lives. Our final definition supplied by the Health Education Authority (1997) (and you are now encouraged to see if you can find more definitions for your portfolio) refers to mental health as:

'the emotional and spiritual resilience that enables us to enjoy life and survive pain, disappointment, and sadness. It is a positive sense of wellbeing and an underlying belief in our own and other's self worth.'

(Health Education Authority, UK, 1997)

On the subject of mental ill health, would it be true to say that this is the opposite of mental health? In describing ill health of a mental nature the United Kingdom Network of the International Society for the Psychological Treatment of Schizophrenia and other Psychoses, or ISPS UK, makes the point that an individual might experience a mental health problem and yet still enjoy good mental wellbeing. How so? They make the comparison with physical health issues in which individuals may still be able to live a productive life and enjoy good wellbeing despite having a chronic or disabling conditions. They comment that:

'Equally, someone can have poor mental well-being, but have no clinically identifiable mental health problem.'

(ISPS, UK)

When we experience difficulties in our daily lives our mental wellbeing will be affected. The way we feel and think about the problem we are experiencing will inevitably affect the way in which we function for a while. But it does not mean we are mentally ill. If, however, our thinking becomes significantly changed and we start to experience feelings and thoughts which change our behaviour and distress us to the point that they start to affect how we function, then we may think about seeking help in terms of specialist mental treatment.

Life, and its demands upon our time and resources, brings challenges and difficulties at times. We experience changes in our feelings, thinking and behaviour, and it would be an oversimplification to say that at these times we all need additional help. Some individuals thrive on stress and challenge in their jobs and lives and without it would quickly become bored. Others experience stress which brings them to their knees and seek help by means of medication. The point is we are all different and experience the trials and tribulations in life differently. There is no clear cut-off between illness and health and an individual with problems that fit the definition of a mental illness may be mentally healthy in other ways and function in society. Our mental health can change as our circumstances change and doesn't always stay the same, particularly as we move through different stages of our life.

Mental ill health, though, is the emergence of a more serious mental health problem that may require treatment in specialist services.

The CMHA comments that:

'Mental illness is a term that describes a variety of psychiatric (emotional, perceptual, thinking and behavioural) problems that vary in intensity and duration, and may recur from time to time. Major mental illnesses include Anxiety, Mood, Eating, and Psychotic

Disorders. Mental illnesses are diagnosable conditions that require medical treatment as well as other supports.'

(www.cmha.ca)

Being mentally healthy means more than just *not* having a mental health problem, it is about making the most of our potential in life and career, coping with life and playing a full part in our family life, work life and social life.

Stress and fear are things we all experience at times and in general these pass. If they develop into a more serious problem then we may seek help from the mental health services that are on offer.

> **Evidence Activity**
>
> **Activity**
>
> Using the material from the above section and any additional reading you have undertaken, write down at least two definitions of 'mental health' and 'mental ill health' and evaluate the differences between the terms 'mental wellbeing' and 'mental health'.

2 Understand the different views on the nature of mental wellbeing and mental health and the factors that may influence both across the life span

In Activity 1.1, you will have started to think about your own views on mental health and wellbeing and these will be a subjective assessment. As you will now realise, the difficulty that arises in determining the nature of these two states is due to fact that we are all individuals and have very different ideas about what we think being mentally well really means.

One subjective view of mental wellbeing might be to say that we are happy or satisfied with our lives. However, the difficulty here is the fact that what makes you happy is unlikely to be the same for your clients or other care workers. How we feel and the emotions we have may be one part of mental wellbeing, but is it enough? As we showed above in the definitions supplied by various sources, feeling good and having a fulfilling life is bound up in the need to experience purpose and meaning in addition to positive emotions. As a therapist I see numerous people who have achieved a great deal in their lives and are in happy stable relationships with few worries and yet they tell me there is no meaning to what they do and they are seeking that meaning.

Carol Ryff, a psychologist, developed a clear model of psychological wellbeing that breaks it down into six key parts and these are:

- self-acceptance
- positive relations with others
- autonomy
- environmental mastery
- purpose in life
- personal growth.

(Kishida et al, 1989)

If we are to have a good understanding of the factors that influence our mental health and wellbeing in order to be able to better help our clients and patients, we need to be aware of the factors that can contribute to this and of how to promote social, emotional, cultural, spiritual and intellectual wellbeing.

So how might we measure the state of wellbeing to ensure that clients are getting their overall needs met and to provide us with a sense of how happy, and healthy, someone is? When things are not going well and our joy in life and general sense of calm is lacking we start to experience stress, worry and anxiety. Our mental wellbeing becomes compromised and this will inevitably lead to our quality of life being reduced. For the people in our care this can lead to depression and its subsequent effects on physical wellbeing and health.

Mental wellbeing is about enabling our clients to experience a well-rounded and balanced life with all the attendant emotions that go with this, and there are a number of factors that can affect this. By recognising these factors we may be in a better position to prevent mental ill health or at the very least to minimise its impact.

The Main Determinants of Health

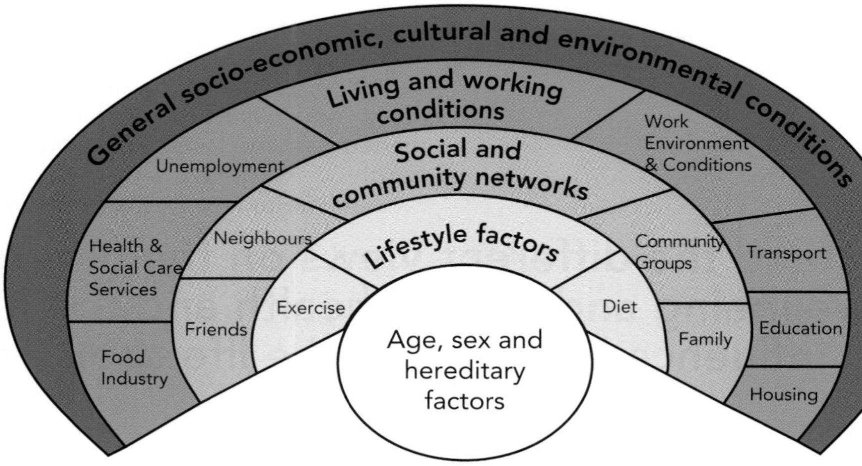

Figure 1.2 Social determinates of health

The Social Model of Health, as described by Dahlgren and Whitehead (1991, in Tilmouth et al (2010)) shows the layers of influence on health. Their social ecological theory of health maps the relationship between the individual and their environment and health. Although this model is more often applied to health in general, as we have shown our mental health is a complex entity and can be affected by the conditions in which we live and does not always have a biological or genetic cause.

At the centre of this particular model is the individual with their own attendant set of genes which will have an influence on that individual's experience of health. However, surrounding them are influences on health that can be changed to a certain extent. For example, the first layer describes personal behaviour and ways of living that can promote or damage health – for example we choose whether or not we wish to smoke and in the same way we can choose how we react to a stressful situation.

The next layer refers to the influences imposed by our social and community lives. If there is support for members of the community in unfavourable conditions then this will have a positive effect on an individual. Lack of support will evidently work the opposite way and have a negative one. The third layer includes structural factors such as housing and working conditions, and the services and welfare systems in place to support us in our society.

As we can see there are social, economic and environmental conditions that influence the health of individuals within our society and these are all shaped by government policy as well as the distribution of money, power and resources at global, national and local levels. The link between the social determinants of health and health inequalities is a fairly strong one.

The Government Office for Science published a report entitled The Influence of Social, Demographic and Physical Factors on Positive Mental Health in Children, Adults and Older People (2008) in which they completed a literature review on the determinants of mental health and the concepts of positive mental health.

That mental health is determined by biological, psychological, social, economic and environmental factors, interacting in complex ways, is strongly supported in the literature. The study determined that demographics such as age, gender and ethnicity are important determinants in the way in which they influence further exposure to risk factors such as poverty, discrimination, violence and sexual abuse. The recognition of these social determinants of mental wellbeing has led to an emphasis on models of mental health promotion that address:

- Strengthening individuals – through interventions designed to promote self-esteem.
- Strengthening communities – by increasing social support, and improving community safety and neighbourhood environments.
- Promoting childcare and self-help networks.
- Developing health and social services which support mental health.
- Improving mental health within schools and work places through anti-bullying strategies and work/life balance policies.
- Reducing structural barriers to mental health – through initiatives to reduce poverty, discrimination and inequalities and to promote access to education, meaningful employment and housing, as well as services and support for those who are vulnerable.

(Barry and Friedli, 2008)

Factors such as poverty are shown to affect mental health and wellbeing greatly. The Eurobarometer (2002), which surveyed 10,878 people over the age of 15 across 11 European countries, reported that the lowest income quartile had the poorest mental health status in all countries/regions (Lehtinen et al., 2005 cited in Barry and Friedli, 2008). Similar findings have been reported in the UK, as shown in the British Household Panel Survey which identified income, poverty (absolute and relative), health, employment, relationships and neighbourhood social contact as having an impact on positive mental health.

In addition, the influence of parenting, education and attachment and security for children has been shown to have a significant impact on good mental health in later life and the study highlighted several writers supporting this view.

> 'There is a complex and dynamic relationship between parenting style, the home environment and socioeconomic factors. Economic adversity has a significant influence on the risk of poor adjustment and there are marked socioeconomic gradients in social and emotional adjustment across childhood, with no evidence that the gradients narrow as children get older (Graham and Power, 2004). Socioeconomic status patterns anxiety, aggression, confidence, emotional and cognitive development, concentration and hence readiness for school (Sacker et al., 2002; Bartley, 2006).

(Barry and Friedli, 2008)

As a protective factor for children the study highlights the importance of 'early attachment, warm and affectionate parenting, a secure and safe home, and informal sources of community support'.

For adults, working conditions and unemployment are also factors affecting mental health.

A poor working environment, characterised by features such as high job demands together with low social support in the role and effort–reward imbalance, was seen to be responsible for a higher prevalence of depressive symptoms among workers in lower graded jobs (Stansfeld et al.,1999).

The mental health impact of unemployment is well documented, with effects such as a higher risk of suicide, higher levels of anxiety, depression, uncertainly about the future and loss of self-esteem.

In Breslin and Mustard's 2003 study the relationship between unemployment and mental health was researched, and the results suggested that among 31- to 55-year-olds, becoming unemployed led to increased distress and, in some, clinical depression.

Research and investigate

1.2 Activity

Using Dahlgren and Whitehead's social determinants of health model (Figure 1.2), plot the factors that have influenced your own and a colleague's mental health across your lifespan. Reflect on the differences and comment on how influential this has been to your life now.

Promoting mental health and wellbeing means society as a whole needs to address the challenges of those external factors that have been shown to be determinants for mental ill health. This section has highlighted how poverty, upbringing, work environment and unemployment may all impact upon an individual's mental health, and in future sections we will address more of these factors.

3 Explain the range of factors that may influence mental wellbeing and mental health problems across the life span, including biological, social and psychological factors

In this section we will look at various factors associated with the process of ageing that impact on our mental health and wellbeing.

We can all see the effects of ageing on the body (see Figure 1.3) and none of us are immune to the changes that happen within our bodies, however much we try to delay the process.

Whilst the changes we all experience are not necessarily harmful, they are perceived as a sign of decline and deterioration. Our hair may start to thin and even the younger population are surprised to find their first grey hair! Skin becomes thinner and loses elasticity resulting in wrinkles and sagging. With a slowing down of bodily functions the body's ability to absorb nutrition from food and to fight infection starts the decline, for some to the point of ill health. Our senses become less acute and we start to experience eye problems and hearing loss. Muscle mass decreases, and joints and bones start to wear and become less efficient, making exercise and movement more difficult the older we get. Yet, despite these physical changes, the mind of the individual can remain remarkably young and if you were to ask a group of elderly people how old they feel, invariably they would reveal a much younger age than their chronological one.

Figure 1.3 The ageing process

So ageing happens, but does it mean that mental health issues are an inevitable part of that process? Stereotypes may give the impression that the elderly person is confused, ill tempered and slow in their cognitive faculties. This leads to the assumption that elderly people are depressed and suffer with dementia, but what are the psychological effects of ageing?

Memory loss and absent mindedness are both common psychological effects of ageing and for many it is the short-term memory more than long-term that becomes more hazy. Whilst recalling what happened 20 years ago may be relatively easy, what happened at dinner last night may be an issue. Clear thought also becomes problematic and older people may find they start to repeat themselves in conversations or cannot recall doing certain things. This may be a sign of Alzheimer's disease or dementia, which are conditions associated with degeneration of mental function.

Physically there are changes going on in the brain which are the cause of these things happening, but might there also be other reasons for these changes?

Statistics support the notion that depression is the most common mental health problem in later life affecting quality of life and physical health but, with an ever increasing ageing population, should we be surprised by this fact? If we look at the potential causes of this particular illness we can start to see that social and economic factors are all hugely influential. The process of getting older brings with it emotional and social change. As we age, invariably people we love die and such loss will affect the individual emotionally and mentally. The grief felt at this time, whilst being a normal reaction, can lead to times in the person's life when their mental health is compromised. In addition, the loss of physical function and ability to move due to poor physical health can also cause a grief reaction, and the person's mental health can suffer because they mourn such losses. Ageing is also a period of readjustment. Changes in circumstances, such as where an individual will live – particularly if they need help with physical issues, retirement from work – with perhaps a change in income, can all have major effects on a person's mental health. With such readjustment there are inevitably effects on social activity, and this may cause the person to become socially isolated which can be a potential for depression and cause a marked decrease in quality of life.

However older people, like any age group, are not a uniform group who all share the same characteristics and traits and, like other age groups, not all will suffer mental health problems just because they have reached old age.

The factsheet produced by the Actively Ageing Well Project comments:

'The majority of older people enjoy good mental health and make valuable contributions to society. Many contribute to the economy as employees and volunteers, carers, grandparents, and as consumers.'

(Actively Ageing Well Project, 2007)

Evidence shows that having a role in society, good social networks, an adequate income and living in a supportive neighbourhood all have a positive effect on a person's wellbeing and their continued mental health (Moriarty, 2005) but this is not just an effect experienced by the older age group. All age groups are affected by these factors.

That the social and economic condition in which we live impacts upon our health throughout life is well documented, and the poorest individuals in our population experience worse health and on average die younger. This sort of disadvantage impacts upon our physical health, which in turn may lead to poor mental health (Wilkinson and Marmot, 2003). The link between physical health and mental health is clear and much literature supports this view.

'Good physical health is associated with good mental health, and poor physical health is associated with poor mental health.'

(Laventure, 2007)

Being physically healthy is an important factor at any point in the lifespan, and it would seem that it is increasingly important for our mental health as well. Wilkinson and Marmot, (2003, p. 9) comment that:

'It is not simply that poor material circumstances are harmful to health: the social meaning of being poor, unemployed, socially excluded or otherwise stigmatised also matters. As social beings we need not only good material conditions but, from early childhood onwards, we need to feel valued and appreciated. We need friends … more sociable societies … to feel useful … to exercise a significant degree of control over meaningful work. Without these we become more prone to depression, drug use, anxiety, hostility and feelings of hopelessness, [which all rebound on physical health]'.

Our mental health status is influenced by a range of physical, social and psychological factors including: income, employment, poverty and education as well as physical health. As we age, evidence from research suggests that physical activity can promote good mental health as well as being an effective measure in preventing and treating existing mental health problems. Exercise and keeping physically fit has been shown to enhance mood by decreasing symptoms of depression and improving wellbeing.

Evidence Activity

 Activity

In your placement, ask for permission to interview an elderly person.

Plan questions which will help you to find out how the process of ageing has affected the person physically, socially and psychologically.

Evaluate the process and write up a report to show your findings from the interview. Compare your notes with somebody else from your group.

Write a reflective account about what you have learned and keep it in your portfolio.

4 Explain how risk factors and protective factors influence levels of resilience in individuals and groups in relation to mental wellbeing and mental health

As we learned previously, physical and mental health is not simply the outcome of biological or genetic processes. Other influences known as the 'social determinants of health' create inequalities in social conditions, and this can lead to unequal outcomes for different social groups.

Our living conditions, the type of housing and environments in which we live, the health and education services we have access to, as well as the jobs we do and the incomes we have, all influence our health.

The World Health Organization [WHO], 2004) recognises these effects:

> 'The social conditions in which people live and work can help create or destroy their health. Lack of income, inappropriate housing, unsafe workplaces and lack of access to health care systems are some of the social determinants of health leading to inequalities.'

Much research supports the notion that those on low incomes or individuals who belong to socially excluded groups are more at risk of poor health outcomes since the effects of social determinants of health are not distributed equally.

For example, people on lower incomes, with poorer education, may live in poorer housing or less healthy environments than those people who are well off. Living in a damp housing environment can lead to the occurrence of respiratory disorders. This factor can indirectly affect the person's educational attainment due to absenteeism from school and thus later limit employment options with fewer higher paid job opportunities. This, in turn, raises the risk of poverty with its adverse impact on health. That social determinants of health are interconnected can thus be shown, for example, by the fact that poverty is linked to poor housing, access to health services or diet, which are in turn linked to health (see Figure 1.4).

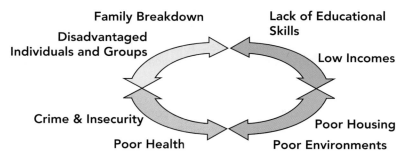

Figure 1.4 Cycle of deprivation

As we can see in the diagram the cycle of deprivation is a vicious circle, leaving individuals trapped in social exclusion.

The impact of this situation leads to stress and isolation and these are the risk factors that can increase the likelihood of experiencing poorer mental health.

The risk factors affecting the mental health of an individual were summarised in a report from the Scottish Government as:

1. The incidence or the impact of negative life events and experiences for individuals, e.g abuse, relationship breakdown, long-term illness or disability.
2. Social isolation and exclusion.
3. The impact of deprivation and structural inequalities in health.

(Scottish Government, 2005)

The mental distress that comes about as a result of these risk factors is because of the way people think and feel when in these situations. The feelings of distress at being unable to pay bills and thus experiencing debt, together with the hopelessness that comes with the inability to change the circumstances in which they live, all lead to expression of mental health problems of one kind or another. In addition the inequalities that arise due to the poverty caused by financial problems leads to the inability of the individual to take part in social activities, which then inevitably raises issues of isolation.

With respect to employment, the more beneficial option for mental health is to be in work since it is likely to offset some of the financial difficulties and social isolation felt by lack of contact with society. However, this also depends upon a range of factors. Whilst being unemployed tends to be detrimental to mental health, being in a job which is insecure, or where there is a lack of control in decision making, or negative relationships in the work place – including bullying and harassment – can also have detrimental effects of mental wellbeing. (Marmot et al., 1991). In addition those who suffer with mental health issues, whatever the cause, are more likely to be excluded from work and rely upon on income support or invalid benefits to live.

Other risk factors include early childhood experiences. Children who experience abuse, family breakdown or live in poverty are also at risk of mental health problems and may experience lower levels of educational attainment as a result. Poor attachment to the primary caregiver early in life can lead to feelings of loneliness and isolation with the child feeling unsafe and confused.

All the risk factors we have discussed can be influenced, and in some cases changed, by protective factors, such as strong relationships which give support, living a healthy lifestyle and possessing coping strategies to manage stress.

The Scottish Government's report cited above summarises the protective factors as:

1. Psycho-social life and coping skills of individuals, for example increasing a sense of self-esteem and autonomy.

2. Social support as a buffer against adverse life events, for example self-help groups, someone to talk to.
3. Access to resources and services which protect mental wellbeing, for example increasing benefit uptake and increasing opportunities for physical, creative and learning activities.

(Scottish Government, 2005)

Numerous self-help groups, in addition to government commissioned reports, highlight the role of resilience in mental and emotional health and provide guidance for individuals towards a healthier outlook in order to manage their mental health issues in a more positive way. We look at these in the next section.

This notion of resilience is an interesting one and is often used to describe an individual's ability to recover from difficult or stressful situations. It appears to be a quality that some people possess in abundance whilst others lack the basic ability to bounce back after certain events.

Psychologists have identified factors that make someone resilient:

● possessing a positive attitude
● being optimistic
● being able to regulate their emotions
● and being able see failure as constructive feedback rather than criticism.

So having good emotional health gives us the ability and the tools to cope with difficult situations and maintain a positive outlook. In traumatic circumstances we are able to remain focused and flexible enough to deal with adversity in a more positive way. This is resilience; the ability to recognise our emotions and express them appropriately and divert depression, anxiety or other negative moods. In addition to this, a protective factor that helps is a strong support network of people that we rely on for support and encouragement.

A study by Friedli (2009) entitled Mental Health, Resilience and Inequalities, explores the influence that mental health has on a wide range of outcomes for individuals and communities.

The influences she comments upon are:

'healthier lifestyles; better physical health; improved recovery from illness; fewer limitations in daily living; higher educational attainment; greater productivity, employment and earnings; better relationships with adults and with children; more social cohesion and engagement and improved quality of life.'

However the report further recognises the effects of inequality upon the mental wellbeing of communities and individuals and suggests that:

'Mental health is also the key to understanding the impact of inequalities on health and other outcomes. It is abundantly clear that the chronic stress of struggling with material disadvantage is intensified to a very considerable degree by doing so in more unequal societies. An extensive body of research confirms the relationship between inequality and poorer outcomes, a relationship which is evident at every position on the social hierarchy and is not confined to developed nations … What is also needed is a shift in consciousness and a recognition that mental health is a precious resource to be promoted and protected at all levels of policy and practice.

(Friedli, 2009)

The risks to our mental health include economic disadvantage, physical ill health and social exclusion, and these occur across different social groups. Protective factors include our resilience in dealing with difficult situations and maintaining a positive outlook. In the next section we look at the steps we need to take to promote mental health.

Evidence Activity

 Activity

Identify the risk and protective factors of two individuals in your place of work and describe how they how affect their mental wellbeing and mental health; include inequalities, such as deprivation and poor quality social relationships as well as social support and contact.

5 Explain the steps that an individual can take to promote their mental wellbeing and mental health

Without an environment that respects and protects basic human rights and allows individuals to access healthy lifestyles, mental health becomes an issue. Poverty, poor housing and low income increase disadvantage and increase risks to mental health. Such circumstances leave individuals feeling vulnerable and hopeless. In this section we look at how we as individuals can help ourselves to promote our own mental wellbeing and how we can support others to do likewise. We revisit the concept of resilience we touched on in Section 4. As care workers in mental health we need to be aware of the effects on carers of looking after a loved one with mental health issues and help them to identify strategies that might be useful for them.

As we mentioned in earlier sections, good mental health is about more than just the absence of a mental disorder, and an individual who is mentally healthy has a sense of wellbeing. This state is characterised by:

- the ability to cope with life's normal stresses
- taking part in productive work
- making a contribution to one's community
- resilience and emotional balance
- a sense of contentment
- being able to build and maintain healthy relationships
- self-confidence and high self-esteem
- good work–life balance
- a sense of meaning and purpose in life.

The Health Education Authority makes the point that:

'Mental health promotion can be seen as a kind of immunization, working to strengthen the resilience of individuals, families, organizations and communities, as well as to reduce conditions which are known to damage mental well-being in everyone, whether or not they currently have a mental health problem.'

(Health Education Authority, 1998, p.1)

So how can individuals make a positive impact on their own mental health to promote their mental wellbeing? Can we avail ourselves of this immunisation as mentioned above?

There are numerous organisations where individuals can access information about how they can help themselves and others to better mental health. Some of these are shown in the box below.

British Association for Behavioural and Cognitive Psychotherapies (BABCP)
tel. 0161 705 4304
web: www.babcp.com
Can provide details of accredited therapists

British Association for Counselling and Psychotherapy (BACP)
tel. 01455 88 33 16
web: www.bacp.co.uk
See website for details of local practitioners

The British Psychological Society
tel. 0116 254 9568
web: www.bps.org.uk
Publishes a directory of chartered psychologists across the UK

Carers UK
carers line: 0808 808 7777
web: www.carersuk.org
Information and advice on all aspects of caring

Food for the Brain
tel. 020 8788 3801
web: www.foodforthebrain.org
Promotes the link between food and mental health

The Institute for Complementary and Natural Medicine (ICNM)
tel. 020 7922 7980
web: www.i-c-m.org.uk
Provides information and a list of professional, competent practitioners

Relate
tel. 0300 100 1234
web: www.relate.org.uk
Offers counselling for adults with relationship difficulties

(Mind, 2010)

Evidence Activity

 Activity 1

Access information from two of the organisations in the box that are relevant to your own workplace.

Make notes and compile a fact sheet for individuals and their carers which highlights ways in which the organisation can help them.

In addition to the above organisations, the NHS and local PCTS, together with voluntary and charitable organisations such as MIND, also provide fact sheets which detail ways in which we are able to help ourselves to better mental wellbeing. Later on we will cover the government policies that are currently being implemented at a national level to improve access to mental health agencies.

MIND has produced a fact sheet which details suggestions for improving mental health and these include:

- Taking care of your physical health by eating and sleeping well, taking part in regular exercise and enjoying yourself.

- Valuing and accepting yourself.
- Recognising that mental distress is not compulsory. The way in which we think about what happens to us and how we interpret the bad times we all experience can be changed. Identify your negative thinking and recognise how this affects your mood. Seek help from others or self-help books.
- Talking about how you feel to others such as friends or a self-help group.
- Seeking help from a therapist or counsellor or asking your GP to recommend a course of treatment for you.
- Maintaining social networks.
- Not allowing stress and negative emotions to build up.

The NHS also supply the following guidance in their Five Steps to Mental Wellbeing.

Five steps to mental wellbeing:

- **Connect**. Connect with the people around you: your family, friends, colleagues and neighbours. Spend time developing these relationships.
- **Be active**. You don't have to go to the gym. Take a walk, go cycling or play a game of football. Find an activity that you enjoy, and make it a part of your life.
- **Keep learning**. Learning new skills can give you a sense of achievement and a new confidence. So why not sign up for that cooking course, start learning to play a musical instrument, or figure out how to fix your bike.
- **Give to others**. Even the smallest act can count, whether it's a smile, a thank you or a kind word. Larger acts, such as volunteering at your local community centre, can improve your mental wellbeing and help you build new social networks.
- **Take notice**. Be more aware of the present moment, including your feelings and thoughts, your body and the world around you. Some people call this awareness 'mindfulness', and it can positively change the way you feel about life and how you approach challenges.

(http://www.nhs.uk/Conditions/stress-anxiety-depression/Pages/improve-mental-wellbeing.aspx)

As we can see from the above guidance, mental wellbeing is about taking action and making small changes to our lives to increase our own resilience. In Section 4 we identified resilience as being an 'individual's ability to recover from difficult or stressful situations'. You will know people who always seem to bounce back from bad situations, who are able to be positive in adversity and carry on with their lives despite difficult times. It is possible that you will also be aware of people who become very stressed with hardship and believe they cannot cope.

The fact is we all experience hard times and painful situations. Disappointments, loss and change are a part of everybody's lives and they can cause stress and anxiety even in the healthiest individuals.

It is the individual who has good mental and emotional health who is able to cope with this anxiety and they do this by seeing the setback for what it is, and maintaining their emotional balance in dealing with it. Is this something we can teach ourselves and others to adopt as a strategy?

Figure 1.5 Being active

The American Psychological Association (APA) believes so and has suggested ten ways in which resilience may be improved.

1. Accept change and focus on the things that you can change.
2. Connect with others and recognise the importance of good relationships. Accept help, don't be afraid to ask for it.
3. Accept that a crisis need not be insurmountable. Whilst you may be unable to change what's happened, you can look toward the solution and act accordingly.
4. Act decisively, and even if you feel stressed, doing so will help build self-confidence and resilience.
5. Create realistic goals and take small steps to achieve them.
6. Embark upon self discovery. What might you learn from what has happened?
7. Start to view yourself positively. Developing your confidence and problem-solving ability helps to build resilience.
8. Be hopeful. Think about what you want and visualise it.
9. Take care of yourself and pay attention to your physical and mental caretaking.
10. Keep things in perspective and avoid blowing things out of proportion.

(Adapted from http://www.apa.org/helpcenter/road-resilience.aspx#)

Resilience, then, is not something that some people have and others lack. Rather it is a trait that involves actions, thoughts and behaviours that can be learned and developed by anybody.

Time to reflect

 Activity 2

Think about the last time something happened in your life that caused you distress and reflect on how you dealt with it. What thoughts and actions and behaviours did you display?

As a result of the ten points shown above, how might you change your actions next time to have a more positive outcome? Write a piece to show your learning here.

Time to reflect

'Health promotion is the process of enabling people to increase control over, and to improve, their health.'

(Ottawa Charter for Health Promotion. WHO, Geneva, 1986)

6 Explain how to support an individual in promoting their mental wellbeing and mental health

In the UK today there are around 1.5 million carers who are the main support for individuals affected by mental health problems, and as mental illness can strike at any time it is important that these people are supported. The BBC Health website gives some practical information to help carers in their support of those with mental health issues.

In the first instance it is all about gathering information and seeking professional help. Talking to members of the health team, such as GPs, psychiatrists, community nurses, social workers and psychotherapists in your local area will help.

Carers may need to be helped to make a list of the sorts of things they should find out. For example:

- Symptoms of the condition and how to handle them.
- The treatments available, such as talking therapies, complementary therapies and medication.
- The existence of local support groups.
- The warning signs of the condition worsening.
- Contact numbers if a medical emergency occurs.

(adapted from http://www.bbc.co.uk/health/support/support_giving.shtml)

Carers also need to know about the entitlement to a care programme approach (CPA) assessment, which is the process that identifies a person's health and social needs, from their home life and employment to personal safety, rights and financial issues.

There is a real concern for those diagnosed with mental health issues that this may cause others to treat them differently or to avoid them. Carers need to be aware that a calm approach is needed when dealing with this. Hallucinations and delusions, whilst they may be frightening for the person experiencing them, may also cause the carer some distress. Listening to their loved one without judgement or criticism is a more useful approach. In cases of depression and anxiety it would be easy to tell the person to 'snap out of it', or to 'pull themselves together' but this is something they are not able to do in this situation, and could increase the feeling of inadequacy and lack of self-confidence they already feel.

7 Evaluate a strategy for supporting an individual in promoting their mental wellbeing and mental health

Carers can be helped to encourage their loved one to engage with some of the strategies we have already identified, namely the ten steps to resilience as outlined in the previous section. By empowering them in this way they will be in a position to help someone who's mentally distressed regain some control of their life. By helping the person to think about what they want – from the carer, from others and from their life – they can start to build up a picture of their future.

Other strategies that can help the carer include understanding their own rights in the situation, and that they may need to engage with somebody to talk about what they are going through. They may also be worried that their loved one will harm themselves and knowing that their call for medical attention will be treated with sympathy is a great help.

 Time to reflect

  Activity

Discuss with a service user their experience of the support they had when either a) they were diagnosed with a mental health issue or b) a member of their family became mentally ill.

How would you as a care worker improve their experience? What would you do to make a difference for them?

Carers need to look after themselves properly and be aware that they will be able to give much more help to the person they are caring for if they are healthy themselves. By referring them to a support group for carers or friends and relatives they will be able to access much needed additional support from people who know what they are going through.

8 Describe the key aspects of a local, national or international strategy to promote mental wellbeing and mental health within a group or community

In this section we will look at some of the policies put forward to address the growing concern over mental illness and the promotion of wellbeing in the UK and we will set the scene by initially addressing the historical overview of the general reforms in health care. In Chapter 5 we address other aspects of the legal framework.

In 1998 the White Paper Modernising Mental Health Services: Safe, Sound and Supportive (Department of Health) was published and announced an investment of an additional £700 million for mental health services. In addition, the creation of a National Service Framework for Mental Health (NSF-MH) for working-age adults was also announced.

Major reforms to health and social services had already been published in various papers, namely:

- Our Healthier Nation (Department of Health, 1998b);
- The New NHS: Modern and Dependable (Department of Health, 1997);
- Modernising Social Services (Department of Health, 1998c);
- A First Class Service: Quality in the new NHS (Department of Health, 1998d).

It was the publication of the National Service Framework for Mental Health (Department of Health, 1999) which provided a breakthrough in terms of mental health because, for the first time, minimum standards for mental health services were laid out.

The publication of the NHS Plan in 2000 highlighted the NSF, brought attention to the emergence of new community teams being developed and made reference to the intention to raise the profile of mental health by making it one of the three priority areas alongside cancer and coronary heart disease. It also set specifications for crisis resolution, assertive outreach teams and early intervention teams.

Over the coming years much attention was given to the problem of funds for mental health not always reaching the services they were destined for. In 2004 the publication of the five-year review of the NSF-MH (Department of Health) revealed that while some progress towards some of the targets had been made, still more needed to be done. Inequality in provision was still an issue in some parts of the country.

As we mentioned earlier, social exclusion with respect to mental health, features as a continuing problem for some individuals and this has been addressed in policy.

In 2004 the Social Exclusion Unit reported on mental health, making recommendations for further change to the National Institute for Mental Health in England (NIMHE) for implementation. This body, set up in 2002, was charged with implementing government mental health policy. It is now part of the Care Services Improvement Partnership (CSIP).

The Mental Health Act (1983) also came under scrutiny in 2004 and has undergone reform and amendment, despite calls to revise the act completely. We cover this in more detail in Chapter 5.

The National Institute for Clinical Excellence, established in England and Wales in 1999, is also worthy of mention here as it was set up to provide guidance to the NHS on health technologies. In 2005 it combined with the Health Development Agency with the purpose of providing national guidance on the promotion of good health and the prevention and treatment of ill health. With respect to mental health, NICE provides technology appraisals of mental health treatments such as computerised cognitive behavioural therapy, ECT and antipsychotic drugs for schizophrenia and mania. There are also clinical guidelines which recommend appropriate treatment and care of people with specific mental health conditions including: anxiety, depression, schizophrenia, eating disorders, post-traumatic stress disorders and self-harm.

In addition to government policy there have also been a number of regional projects undertaken to research implementation and new ways of working within mental health reform. Some of these include the following.

- **Right Here Programme, England and Northern Ireland, 2009.**
  A five-year collaboration between the MHF and the Paul Hamlyn Foundation the aim of the which is to improve the wellbeing and mental health of young people aged 16–25 through the participation of this age group in developing new and innovative interventions in mental health.
- **Brighter Futures, Scotland, 2007–2011.**
  A project working with older people to deliver a peer mentoring service to improve the wellbeing and the mental health of more isolated older people by enhancing their social network's community engagement.
- **MyCare, England, Scotland, Wales, 2009–2010**
  This project, carried out in collaboration with the Princess Royal Trust for Carers, was concerned with the experiences and needs of young people aged 9–25 years old who are looking after parents with severe mental health needs (Mental Health Foundation, 2012).

In 2009 the Department of Health published their white paper: New Horizons: Towards a Shared Vision for Mental Health. Addressing the link between mental and physical health, this paper described some of the factors that affect wellbeing and highlighted everyday strategies for preserving it.

New Horizons confirmed the emerging view that:

'the greatest degree of effective recovery is gained from early identification and treatment … (and) that people with mental health problems are able to run their own lives, participate in the life of their families and communities, and work productively to earn their living and contribute to the economy, to varying degrees – just like people with physical health problems.'

A major breakthrough in the understanding of mental health within national policy was made with the publication of the government's 2010 public health white paper, Healthy Lives, Healthy People: Our Strategy for Public Health in England. In this publication there was more than a passing reference to the fact that inequality in social conditions leads to mental health as well as physical health issues. In section 1.9 the document states:

'We know that people suffer a substantial burden of ill health from living with conditions that give them pain, affect their mental health, or prevent them from doing their usual activities, making them dependent on the care of others.'

and in section 1.11:

'Wellbeing – a positive physical, social and mental state – is an important part of our health. Good wellbeing does not just mean the absence of mental illness – it brings a wide range of benefits, including reduced health risk behaviour (such as smoking), reduced mortality, improved educational outcomes and increased productivity at work.'

(DoH, 2010)

This publication moved the 'prevention 'agenda forward, emphasising the need to target the causes of ill health by addressing lifestyles and risk behaviour. By stopping smoking, eating a healthier diet, increasing physical activity and reducing alcohol consumption many premature deaths and illnesses could be avoided. As research has shown that people with mental ill health issues are much more likely to smoke and have alcohol or drug problems, addressing these factors would see improvements in mental and physical health and would be a positive outcome. Some critics, however, argued that the government's paper did not go far enough in its prevention agenda and argued that a more useful approach would be to determine why people become mentally ill rather than merely treating the illness once it had occurred. The RCN's responses pointed out that as:

> 'most mental health initiatives are "down-stream" (i.e. when someone is ill) so greater emphasis is needed on how we can incentivise "up-stream" awareness whilst retaining and improving investment in Improving Access to Psychological Therapies (IAPT) services.'

> (Royal College of Nursing, 2012)

In 2011 the government's mental health strategy, No Health Without Mental Health, was published. Public mental health was defined in this paper as:

> 'The art and science of promoting well-being and equality and preventing mental ill health through population-based interventions to: reduce risk and promote protective, evidence-based interventions to improve physical and mental well-being; and create flourishing, connected individuals, families and communities.'

This paper promised to mainstream mental health in England, improving the parity of esteem between mental and physical health services. Its intention was clear; to promote good mental health by early intervention particularly in childhood and teenage years, in order to prevent mental illness from developing and alleviate the effects when it does occur.

This white paper went much further than Healthy Lives, Healthy People, recognising that the foundations for wellbeing are laid down before birth. It was acknowledged that by protecting and promoting wellbeing through the early years, individuals would meet adulthood and old age with a strengthened outlook and resilience. As the document states:

> 'Only a sustained approach across the life course will equip us to meet the social, economic and environmental challenges we face and deliver the short- and long-term benefits we need.'

> (HMGOV, 2011)

Over the last 20 years there have been major reforms to the health service and within the last 10 years there has been growing evidence to show the positive impact of improving mental wellbeing on health, social and economic outcomes. This section has shown how government programmes, policies and projects have increased the emphasis on public mental health and wellbeing and how this has impacted upon the way in which the mental health service has developed in the UK.

Summary

This chapter has defined the terms 'mental health' and 'mental ill health' and has looked at different views on the nature of mental wellbeing. The factors that influence both across the lifespan have been demonstrated by looking at the social determinants of health according to Dahlgren and Whitehead.

Emerging evidence shows that having a role in society, together with good social networks, an adequate income and living in a supportive neighbourhood will all have a positive effect on a person's wellbeing and their continued mental health. Together with resilience, and the steps an individual can take to help themselves to enhance mental wellbeing, there is growing recognition in government policy that mental wellbeing is:

> 'a positive physical, social and mental state – is an important part of our health. Good wellbeing does not just mean the absence of mental illness – it brings a wide range of benefits, including reduced health risk behaviour (such as smoking), reduced mortality, improved educational outcomes and increased productivity at work.'

> (DoH, 2010)

The last word here goes to Friedli (2004):

> 'Mental health influences how we think and feel, about ourselves and others and how we interpret events. It affects our capacity to learn, to communicate and to form, sustain and end relationships. It also influences our ability to cope with change, transition and life events: having a baby, experiencing bereavement, going to prison …'.

Research and investigate

 1.8 **Activity**

Research one of the above policies to promote mental wellbeing and mental health within your setting and identify and evaluate the key aspects of it that are applicable to your own setting.

References

Bartley, M (Ed) (2006) *Capability and Resilience: Beating the Odds*. London, ESRC Human Capability and Resilience Research Network, UCL Department of Epidemiology and Public Health. Available at: www.ucl.ac.uk/cpabilityandresilience

Barry, M and Friedli, L (2008) *The Influence of Social, Demographic and Physical Factors on Positive Mental Health in Children, Adults and Older People*. Foresight Mental Capital and Wellbeing Project (2008) Final project report. London: The Government Office for Science.

Breslin, F C, Mustard, C (2003) Factors influencing the impact of unemployment on mental health among young and older adults in a longitudinal, population-based survey. *Scand J Work Environ Health* 29(1): 5–14.

Canadian Mental Health Association http://www.cmha.ca

DoH (1997) The New NHS: Modern and Dependable. London: Department of Health.

DoH (1998a) Modernising Mental Health Services: Safe, Sound and Supportive. London: Department of Health.

DoH (1998b) Our Healthier Nation. London: Department of Health.

DoH (1998c) Modernising Social Services. London: Department of Health.

DoH (1998d) A First Class Service: Quality in the New NHS. London: Department of Health.

DoH (2008) Foresight Report: Mental Capital and Wellbeing Project. London: Department of Health.

DoH (2009) New Horizons: Towards a Shared Vision for Mental Health. London: HM Government.

DoH (2010) Healthy Lives, Healthy People: Our Strategy for Public Health in England. London: The Stationery Office.

DoH (2011) No Health without Mental Health. London: The Stationery Office.

Ewles, L and Simnett, I (1999) *Promoting Health: A Practical Guide to Health Education*. 4th edition. Edinburgh: Harcourt.

Friedli, L (2009) *Mental Health, Resilience and Inequalities*. Copenhagen: World Health Organization.

Graham, H and Power, C (2004). Childhood Disadvantage and Adult Health; A Life Course Framework. London: Health Development Agency.

HM Gov (2011) *No Health without Mental Health A cross-government mental health outcomes strategy for people of all ages*. Available at: http://www.mentalhealth.org.uk/content/assets/PDF/publications/need_2_know_peer_support1.pdf?view=Standard

The International Society for Psychological and Social Approaches to Psychosis, www.ispsuk.org

Kishida, Y, Kitamura, T, Gatayama, R, Matsuoka, T, Miura, S, Yamabe, K (1989). Ryff's psychological well-being inventory: factorial structure and life history correlates among Japanese university students. Kuamoto: Department of Psychiatry, Kumamoto University School of Medicine.

Laventure, B (2007) Actively Ageing Well Project. Available at: http://www.ispsuk.org/ (accessed on 5/9/12).

Lehtinen, V, Sohlman, B and Kovess-Masfety, V (1997) *Promotion of Mental Health on the European Agenda*. Finland: National Research and Development for Welfare and Health.

Maslow, A H (1978) *Motivation and Personality*. New York, Harper and Row.

Mental Health Foundation (2012) The Right Here Programme. London: Mental Health Foundation

Marmot, M G, Davey Smith, G, Stansfeld, S A, Patel, C, North, F, Head, J, et al. (1991) Health inequalities among British civil servants: the Whitehall II study. *Lancet*; 337: 1387–93.

Mind (2010) *How to Improve your Mental Well-Being*. London: Mind. Available at http://www.mind.org.uk/help/diagnoses_and_conditions/mental_wellbeing.

Moriarty J (2006) Update for SCIE Best Practice Guide on Assessing the Mental Health Needs of Older People. London: Social Care Workforce Research Unit, King's College London.

NHS Confederation July 2009 A Future Vision for Mental Health. London: The Future Vision Coalition. Available at: http://www.nhsconfed.org/Publications/Documents/Future_vision_for_mental_health_FINAL.pdf

Psychology Today (n.d.) *Resilience*.

Royal College of Nursing (RCN) (2012) Response to Healthy Lives, Healthy People: Towards a Workforce Strategy for the Public Health System. Available at: http://www.nursingtimes.net/Journals/2012/06/29/d/w/w/RCN-response-PH-Workforce-Strategy-Consultation.pdf.

Sacker, A, Schoon, I and Bartley, M (2002) Social inequality in education achievement and psychosocial adjustment throughout childhood: magnitude and mechanism. *Social Science and Medicine*, 55: 863–80.

Scottish Government (2005): *National Programme for Improving Mental Health and Well Being: Addressing Mental Health Inequalities in Scotland – equal minds*. Available: http://www.scotland.gov.uk/Publications/2005/11/04145113/51151Protective factors (accessed 19/9/12).

Stansfeld, S A, Fuhrer, R, Shipley, M J, and Marmot, M G (1999) 'Work characteristics predict psychiatric disorder: prospective results from the Whitehall II Study', *Occupational and Environmental Medicine*, 56 (5): 302–7. (Abstract accessed online on 6/9/12: http://oem.bmj.com/content/56/5/302.abstract).

Tilmouth, T, Davies-Ward, E and Williams, B (2011) *Foundation Degree in Health and Social Care*. London, Hodder Education.

Townsend, P and Davidson, N (Eds) (1982) Inequalities in Health. The Black Report. London: Penguin Books.

World Health Organization (WHO) (1946) *Constitution: Basic Documents*. Geneva: WHO.

World Health Organization (1984) *Health Promotion: A Discussion Document on the Concept and Principles*. Copenhagen: WHO Regional Office for Europe.

World Health Report – A Vision for Global Health. Shaping the Future.

Wilkinson, R and Marmot, M (Eds) (2003) *Social Determinants of Health: The Solid Facts,* 2nd edn. Denmark: WHO.

Understand mental health problems across the lifespan

What are you finding out?

In this chapter we start to look at the possible causes of mental ill health and the ways in which they are diagnosed. The two main classification systems are described and the key strengths and weaknesses of this type of categorisation are addressed.

The effects of a mental health condition in terms of how the individual presents with certain signs and symptoms is followed by a discussion about the more far reaching societal effects of having a mental health problem. The impact of mental ill health on individuals and others in their familial, social or work network and the discrimination they experience due to misinformation, assumptions and stereotypes is further explored using research carried out by the Social Exclusion Unit and other writers in the field.

The reading and activities in this chapter will help you to:

1. Identify possible causes of mental health problems.
2. Identify examples of mental health problems – including describing the main types of mental ill health according to the psychiatric (DSM/ICD) classification system: mood disorders, personality disorders, anxiety disorders, psychotic disorders, substance-related disorders, eating disorders and cognitive disorders.
3. Explain the key strengths and limitations of the psychiatric classification system and explain two alternative frameworks for understanding mental distress.
4. Explain how mental ill health may be indicated through an individual's emotions, thinking and behaviour.
5. List common sources of information on mental health issues.
6. Explain how mental ill health may have an impact on the individual and those in their familial, social or work network including:
   a. psychological and emotional
   b. practical and financial
   c. the impact of using services
   d. social exclusion
   e. positive impacts.
   Explain how individuals experience discrimination due to misinformation, assumptions and stereotypes about mental ill health.
7. Outline how mental health is reported in the media and identify the negative effects media reporting can have on an individual and society.

Assessment criteria covered in this chapter

Reading this unit and completing the activities will provide you with the knowledge, understanding and skills required to meet the assessment criteria listed below.

NCFE Level 1 Award in Mental Health Awareness (501/0253/9)		
Develop an awareness of mental health (K/600/6596)		
Learning Outcome 1 Be aware of what is meant by mental health		
Assessment Criteria	Page reference	Activity
1.2 Identify possible causes of mental health problems	p. 27	Evidence activity 2.1, p. 29
1.3 Identify examples of mental health problems	p. 29	Evidence activity 2.2, p. 32
1.4 List common sources of information on mental health issues	p. 36	Evidence activity 2.5, p. 38
Learning Outcome 2 Be aware of some of the social and personal effects of mental ill health		
2.1 State the percentage of people in the UK that might experience mental health problems	p. 92	
2.2 Identify the effects that experiencing a mental health problem might have on an individual	p. 38	Evidence activity 2.6, p. 41
2.3 Outline how mental health is reported in the media	p. 38	Evidence activity 2.6, p. 41
2.4 Identify the negative effects media reporting can have on an individual	p. 38	Evidence activity 2.6, p. 41
2.5 Identify the negative effects media reporting can have on society	p. 38	Evidence activity 2.6, p. 41
2.6 Outline how stereotyping can affect people with mental health problems	p. 38	Evidence activity 2.6, p. 41
Learning Outcome 4 Be aware of cultural diversity in relation to mental health issues		
4.1 Identify possible causes of mental distress in different cultural groups	p. 29	Evidence activity 2.1, p. 29

City & Guilds Level 3 Diploma in Mental Health Care (600/5241/7)		
Understand mental health problems (J/602/0103)		
Learning Outcome 1 Know the main forms of mental ill health		
Assessment Criteria	Page reference	Activity
1.1 Describe the main types of mental ill health according to the psychiatric (DSM/ICD) classification system: mood disorders, personality disorders, anxiety disorders, psychotic disorders, substance-related disorders, eating disorders, cognitive disorders	p. 29	Evidence activity 2.2, p. 32
1.2 Explain the key strengths and limitations of the psychiatric classification system	p. 32	Research and investigate activity 2.3, p. 34
1.3 Explain two alternative frameworks for understanding mental distress	p. 32	
1.4 Explain how mental ill health may be indicated through an individual's emotions, thinking and behaviour	p. 35	Case Study activity 2.4, p. 36

(Continued)

(Continued)

Learning Outcome 2 Know the impact of mental ill health on individuals and others in their social network		
2.1 Explain how individuals experience discrimination due to misinformation, assumptions and stereotypes about mental ill health	p. 38	Evidence activity 2.6, p. 41

2.2 Explain how mental ill health may have an impact on the individual including:
  a. psychological and emotional
  b. practical and financial
  c. the impact of using services
  d. social exclusion
  e. positive impacts
	p. 38	Evidence activity 2.6, p. 41

2.3 Explain how mental ill health may have an impact on those in the individual's familial, social or work network including:
  a. psychological and emotional
  b. practical and financial
  c. the impact of using services
  d. social exclusion
  e. positive impacts
	p. 38	Evidence activity 2.6, p. 41

City & Guilds Level 3 Diploma in Mental Health Care (600/5241/7)		
Understand mental well-being and mental health promotion (F/602/0097)		
Learning Outcome 1 Understand the different views on the nature of mental wellbeing and mental health and the factors that may influence both across the life span		
Assessment Criteria	Page reference	Activity

1.2 Explain the range of factors that may influence mental wellbeing and mental health problems across the life span, including:
  a. biological factors
  b. social factors
  c. psychological factors
	p. 27	Evidence activity 2.1, p. 29

NCFE Level 2 Award in Understanding Working with People with Mental Health Issues (500/9956/5)		
Mental health and mental health issues (M/601/2948)		
Learning Outcome 2 Be aware of the common types of mental health problems and illnesses		
Assessment Criteria	Page reference	Activity
2.1 Define the term mental disorder	p. 96	
2.2 Outline the key features of different models of mental health problems	p. 29	Evidence activity 2.2, p. 32
2.3 Describe the two main means of classifying mental disorder	p. 29	Evidence activity 2.2, p. 32
2.5 Describe other common mental disorders	p. 29	Evidence activity 2.2, p. 32

1 Identify possible causes of mental health problems

When we think about mental illness we will all have different opinions about what it actually is. Every one of us will have experienced some mental health issue in our lives, whether it be slight anxiety about a situation we have found ourselves in, or a period in our life when we were feeling low or even depressed. The point is that our experiences are all different and varied and as such the causes of mental ill health are likely to be equally complex.

If we look at our own lives and backgrounds we can theorise about what caused us to become the people we are today. If we suffered at school at the hands of bullies, or were neglected in some way through poverty or abuse, we might assume that our mental health will have suffered because of these experiences. We could be of the opinion that any mental ill health we have is due to that experience. But is it that simple? Why is it that some people can have traumatic experiences and yet not suffer any form of distress in later life, whereas others who have lived happily in supportive families, been well educated and suffered no traumas suddenly find themselves with mental health conditions which debilitate them?

What, then, are the causes of mental illness? Although research has uncovered a huge amount about mental illness the exact cause of most mental illness remains unknown. What is agreed by many mental health professionals is that many conditions are caused by a combination of biological/physical, environmental/social and psychological factors.

Biological and physical factors

Our genetic makeup may predispose us to the risk of developing mental illness making us more susceptible. Any form of physical trauma, such as a head injury or an infection in the brain, may predispose an individual to the risk of developing changes to their personality which may lead to mental illness.

Recently, links between streptococcal infections of the throat and the development of a condition known as paediatric autoimmune neuropsychiatric disorder (PANDA), which emerges as obsessive compulsive disorders in children, have been found (Swedo, et al., 2012).

Drug and alcohol abuse may also lead to mental illness and research is now showing links between regular marijuana use and depression.

There may also be a chemical link whereby an imbalance in the neurotransmitters in the brain may predispose somebody to mental illness.

In pregnancy, diet and nutrition are important not only to the physical development of the foetus but also to its mental health. For example, a mother who abuses alcohol or drugs or who smokes whilst she is pregnant predisposes the unborn child to mental problems due to changes in chemicals in the brain during development and lack of oxygen, which can also be a risk factor.

Environmental and social factors

As we saw in the first chapter, the things that happen around us have a huge impact on our health, both physical and mental. Where we live and work, the social networks we have surrounding us, such as family and friends, as well as where and when we can relax all have an impact upon our mental health.

Living in poverty or in places where there is a high crime rate or problems with neighbours will lead to pressures and can predispose people to illness.

Being socially isolated, perhaps due to being housebound by physical illness or disability, or due to unemployment, can also be detrimental. So, too, can being in highly stressful jobs where the person feels constantly under too much pressure.

Psychological factors

Coping with past or current traumatic experiences, such as abuse, bereavement or divorce will strongly influence an individual's mental and emotional state which can in turn have an influence on mental health.

There are a number of psychological factors that may contribute to mental illness in adult life, and these may include any form psychological trauma suffered as a child, be it emotional, physical or sexual abuse. The loss of significant people in our lives can also influence our mental and emotional state, whether through bereavement, divorce or a break up of any relationship.

A significant rise in the number of people who are now suffering as a result of traumatic events has seen the recognition of a relatively new diagnosis, that of post traumatic stress disorder.

Stress factors can also trigger mental illness, particularly in susceptible people. Feelings of inadequacy, low self-esteem, anger or loneliness can all come about through upbringing, dysfunctions in the way we think or live, or even through our culture. For example, in Western society celebrity is associated with beauty, wealth and often being thin, and this can lead to dissatisfaction with the way we look and behaviour which seeks to change this. Eating disorders are just one side effect of this culture.

Cultural factors

The DSM-IV TR lists a specific category as 'Culture-Bound Syndromes' recognising that mental illness around the world will present differently depending upon a person's culture. As a care worker it is important to have a knowledge of the different aspects of an individual culture in order to have an understanding about their mental state. For example, in some cultures the belief in ancestral spirits and demonic possession may result in the individual experiencing hallucinations and delusions yet these symptoms may not be considered a problem in such a group. They may simply be viewed as a sign of distress which will correct itself. An understanding of this can make the approach to the individual and subsequent treatment easier to introduce.

We have looked at a number of factors that can cause mental illness, but for many people with mental health problems, it is not one single factor that has led to the development of their problems. It is often a series of events that has occurred that eventually triggers mental illness.

(WebMD, n.d.)

> ### Evidence Activity
>
> **Activity**
>
> Research the causes of mental illness and make notes for your portfolio. Reflect on the potential causes and contributing factors, including cultural factors, for two of your own clients with respect to their mental health issues. Be sure to respect confidentiality and use pseudonyms.

2 Identify examples of mental health problems

When we experience worries and anxiety in our lives the effects on our thinking and subsequently on our quality of life are such that we are suffering mentally. But does this mean that you are suffering from a mental disorder?

Mental health problems can be categorised into the minor worries we all have and more serious long-term conditions.

The main types of mental ill health according to the psychiatric (DSM/ICD) classification system

In defining mental health problems and to enable professionals to refer people for care and treatment, there are two classification systems employed by mental health professionals:

- the Diagnostic and Statistical Manual of Mental Disorders, or DSM-IV -TR (APA, 2000) (a further version, the DSM-V, is promised) (see Figure 2.2.).
- The International Statistical Classification of Diseases and Related Health Problems ICD-10 (WHO, 1992).

Both systems are lists of clinically observable symptoms designed to standardise the practice of diagnosing mental disorder to ensure that there is some form of consistency across the mental health profession.

Figure 2.1 The Diagnostic and Statistical Manual of Mental Disorders and The International Statistical Classification of Diseases and Related Health Problems

The first system, the DSM-IV-TR, is used widely in the USA, Canada, Australia, India and China; whereas the ICD-10, is used in the UK and European countries.

The American Psychiatric Association commented on the revision of the classification in 2000 suggesting that changes that were made to some of the criteria sets to correct errors found in DSM-IV and to change some of the diagnostic codes to reflect updates to the International Classification of Diseases, Ninth Edition. The DSM-V is scheduled for publication in May 2013 (American Psychiatric Association, n.d.).

Diagnostic and Statistical Manual of Mental Disorder (DSM-IV-TR)

The DSM-IV-TR is published by the American Psychiatric Association and explains the signs and symptoms that mark more than 300 types of mental health conditions. It is referred to as a multi-axial system and there are five axes.

Axis 1: *Clinical Disorders and other Conditions that May Be a Focus of Clinical Attention.*

In this category are conditions that are acute and therefore require immediate treatment, which include major depressive episodes, schizophrenic episodes and panic attacks.

Common Axis I disorders include depression, anxiety disorders, bipolar disorder, ADHD, autism spectrum disorders, anorexia nervosa, bulimia nervosa and schizophrenia.

Axis II: *Personality Disorders.*

These disorders are usually life-long problems that first arise in childhood and this category describes personality disorders and intellectual disabilities.

Common Axis II disorders include personality disorders including paranoid personality disorder, schizoid personality disorder, borderline personality disorder, antisocial personality disorder, narcissistic personality disorder, histrionic personality disorder, avoidant personality disorder, dependent personality disorder, obsessive-compulsive personality disorder and intellectual disabilities.

Axis III: *Physical Problems that may be Relevant to Diagnosing and Treating Mental Disorders.*

This category is for medical or neurological conditions that may influence or lead to a psychiatric problem. For example, depression may occur as a result of extreme fatigue from another physical condition, so in this category the mental disorder is secondary to a physical one.

Common Axis III disorders include injury to the brain and other medical/physical disorders which may aggravate existing diseases or present symptoms similar to other disorders.

Axis IV: *Psychosocial and Environmental Problems.*

This category describes recent life experiences and events which may have predisposed a person to mental stress. Fundamentally the physician reports upon life events such as marriage, new job, or loss of a job, and death of a loved one – anything that may affect a patient's mental health diagnosis and treatment. It is usually only stressors from the past 12 months which are taken into account on this axis.

Axis V: *Global Assessment of Functioning Scale.*

The Global Assessment of Functioning (GAF) scale is a reflection of the assessing health professional's judgement of a patient's ability to function in daily life, and the 100 point scale measures psychological, social and occupational functioning. It is designed to be applied over time to monitor progress and not just applied when the patient enters the doctor's office. The GAF takes a practical view of a patient's mental health and rates them over different time frames such as 'current' or 'past week' along with relative ratings such as 'highest level in past year'. Used in this way, the GAF can provide quantifiable information about the patient's state of mental health over time.

The next edition of the DSM is scheduled for publication in May, 2013 and it is believed that it will be more streamlined. In attempts to bring the system into line with the international reporting standards, working groups have recommended that DSM-5 collapse Axes I, II and III into one axis that contains all psychiatric and general medical diagnoses. This change would bring DSM-5 into greater harmony with the single-axis approach used by the international community in the World Health Organization's (WHO) International Classification of Diseases (ICD).

(Adapted from PsyWeb, 2011)

International Statistical Classification of Diseases and Related Health Problems (ICD-10)

The second system, the International Statistical Classification of Diseases and Related Health Problems or ICD-10 (WHO, 1992), constitutes a single list of conditions.

Compiled by the World Health Organization (WHO), the ICD is similar to the DSM, although not quite as widely used, and it identifies a list of conditions similar to that of the DSM-IV-TR.

In both systems, the main categories for mental disorders are as follows:

- Dementia Disorders (Organic Mental Disorders)
- Substance Abuse Disorders
- Schizophrenia and other Psychotic Disorders
- Mood (Affective) Disorders
- Stress Related Somatoform and Anxiety Disorders
- Behavioural Disorders associated with Physiological Disturbances:
  - Eating Disorders
  - Sleep Disorders
  - Sexual and Gender Identity Disorders
- Personality Disorders
- Childhood and Adolescence Psychiatric Disorders
- Learning Disability Disorders
- Attention Deficit and Disruptive Behaviour Disorders.

(Adapted from Singh, 2007)

Alongside the two major systems of classification, you often see the division of mental health disorders into groups such as:

- neurotic
- psychotic.

The 'neurotic' group of symptoms covers those emotions we all experience, such as depression, anxiety or panic, but which sometimes get out of control causing much distress to the individual. Although these were once called 'neuroses' this group is now referred to as 'common mental health problems'.

Psychotic symptoms, on the other hand, are much less common and refer to those signs and symptoms exhibited when an individual has an altered perception of reality. In these types of disorder the person may experience hallucinations such as seeing, hearing, smelling or feeling things that no one else can.

Evidence Activity

 2.2 Activity

Research both classification systems online and look at the various disorders they identify.

Write a definition for each of the following:
- mood disorders
- personality disorders
- anxiety disorders
- psychotic disorders
- substance-related disorders
- eating disorders
- cognitive disorders.

3 Explain the key strengths and limitations of the psychiatric classification system and explain two alternative frameworks for understanding mental distress

The DSM-IV-TR and the ICD-10 provide mental health professionals with a list of clinical signs and symptoms by which a diagnosis may be made and this is one of the strengths of these systems. With only two systems available worldwide, and the wide use of both, this allows there to be a common diagnosis. For example, theoretically, a mental health professional should be able to make the same diagnosis using the signs and symptoms laid down in the DSM or ICD. But is it that simple?

Sobo, in his article 'The strengths and weaknesses of DSM IV: How it clarifies, how it blinds psychiatrists to issues in need of investigation' makes the observation that this may not be the case:

> 'Crucial information and perspectives that don't fit into its diagnostic system get ignored. More importantly, in certain clinical contexts, focusing on a diagnosis may not be the best way to help patients deal with their psychopathology … For the layman and many clinicians, making a diagnosis implies the patient has a distinct illness, in the same way as a patient might have a tumor or an infection. But that may not be true of most psychiatric disorders. DSM IV diagnoses are based on operational definitions, rather than pathogenesis or etiology.'

As individuals we may react to adversity in different ways and this may lead to an incorrect diagnosis being made. For example, different ethnic groups have different rates and experiences of mental health problems, which are reflective of their diverse cultural and socio-economic contexts.

African Caribbean men living in the UK are three to five times more likely than any other group to be diagnosed and admitted to hospital for schizophrenia. Research into this phenomena to test whether there is a genetic predisposition was undertaken and reported, that, despite exhibiting the 'symptoms' of schizophrenia – which can include erratic behaviour and feelings of paranoia – they found this group were disproportionately represented in the data. In comparing the backgrounds of black patients they found that they were no more likely to be drug users than their white counterparts and brain scans revealed that white patients were, in fact, three times more likely to have something wrong with their brain than black patients. The conclusion drawn by the researchers was that it was possible that the assessing mental health professionals were misinterpreting the behaviour of black patients who were not mentally ill, but struggling to cope with social problems. The use of the DSM or ICD in such cases would certainly provide a list of symptoms by which to diagnose the condition but may lead to a misinterpretation of what has been observed.

There is also the view that the classification of mental illness leads to the assumption that the individual is actually suffering and therefore requires some form of treatment. Although this is a somewhat philosophical view it is worth considering. Hoermann writes that people who exhibit signs of mental ill health are viewed as:

> '"sufferers" who need "treatment", although some suggest mental illness is often just another way of living, who's to say they're actually suffering a mental disorder? Laing (1960) suggested that schizophrenia is just another way of living and not a condition.'

> (Hoermann et al., 2011)

To illustrate this, think about the following. In diagnosing a narcissistic personality disorder the clinician would be looking at the signs and symptoms of the disorder, two of which are the display of extreme forms of self-centeredness and grandiosity. As these authors suggest

> 'even ordinary, healthy people will sometimes act in ways that are self-centred and grandiose.'

Figure 2.2 Mental illness can affect anyone

Just judging the patient on a snapshot of their behaviour could lead to a misdiagnosis being made, so there has to be a judgement on the actual extent of this behaviour across time and this requires a more subjective judgement on the part of the health professional. As the authors on this subject go on to say:

> 'Though the dimension of self-centeredness is the same, the difference is in the extremity of expression. People with Narcissistic Personality Disorder behave in a self-centred manner most all the time, while people without this disorder behave this way only some of the time. In this case, it makes sense to talk about a continuum or dimension of self-centeredness, which varies from low to high For instance, just how self-centred do you need to be in order to reach the level of a Narcissistic Personality Disorder?'

Further criticism from the above authors suggests that as no diagnostic system can be perfect, the current DSM diagnostic system for personality disorders is problematic. For example, the suggestion is that individuals present with a variety of symptoms, some of which are described in the DSM in a broad way. This leads to patients being diagnosed with the same disorder despite presenting with a very broad range of symptoms (Hoermann et al., 2011).

Time to reflect

Have a look at the following extract from the DSM-IV-TR and evaluate it in light of what you have read previously. Could this sort of list lead to a misdiagnosis or a missed diagnosis being made? What do you think?

'Anorexia Nervosa

Client will not maintain minimum body weight (e.g. 85% of expected weight for height and age)

Client intensely fears weight gain /obesity

Self-perception of the body is abnormal

Unduly emphasises weight or shape on self evaluation

Denies seriousness of low weight

Has a distorted perception of own body shape or weight

Female client has missed at least three consecutive menstrual cycles.

Binge Eating/Purging Type

Client often purges/vomits, uses laxatives or diuretics) or eats and binges

Restricting Type

No bingeing or purging'

In addition, a perfect diagnosis would take into account underlying factors as well as signs and symptoms, but as we saw in Section 1 the whole concept of what actually causes mental illness is complex and as such diagnosis can often be a flawed process.

In summary, the strengths in the classification systems of mental disorders mean that health professionals on a day-to-day clinical level have a diagnostic tool to help with diagnosis. However, the nature of being an individual and the differences we all experience in our lives may make it difficult to exactly categorise a 'condition'. As Singh writes:

'A perfect clinical diagnosis would usually predict the possible underlying causative factor/s, the patho-physiology, clinical signs and symptoms, response to the treatment and the course of the illness. Such perfect diagnoses are possible in various infectious diseases and to an extent, in surgery. However, in General Medicine and in particular, in psychological medicine, this perfect concept of disease is not possible. This is because of our limited knowledge about the underlying causes of mental disorders and any other objective measurable standard tests.'

(Singh, 2007)

Research and investigate

 Activity

Access either of the two classification systems and look at one of the conditions noted in Activity 2.2. What signs and symptoms are shown in the list?

Reflect on how far they might fit another condition.

4 Explain how mental ill health may be indicated through an individual's emotions, thinking and behaviour

The *Oxford Dictionary* defines behaviour as:

'the way in which one acts or conducts oneself, especially towards others: *he will vouch for her good behaviour; his insulting behaviour towards me*

the way in which an animal or person behaves in response to a particular situation or stimulus: *the feeding behaviour of predators*

the way in which a machine or natural phenomenon works or functions: *the erratic behaviour of the old car'*

In mental illness the signs and symptoms exhibited can result in a marked change in an individual's behaviour and will manifest as effects in emotions and feelings, thoughts and actions/behaviours. There may also be physical changes.

Physical changes affect the body and how it functions, and can include such symptoms as unexplained aches and pains, tiredness and trouble sleeping. In fact, such symptoms may well be the first signs that a mental disturbance is happening.

The emotional and feeling type symptoms may manifest themselves as feeling sad, having excessive fears or worries or even guilt. Feelings of anger or hostility may also be a sign that emotional issues are building up.

Typical examples of a change in thought pattern may be as simple as confused thoughts or an inability to concentrate, or more serious such as when the individual starts to think of suicide, or believes that somebody is going to harm them. Hearing voices or seeing things that others cannot ('hallucinations') may also indicate a change in thought and perception.

Behavioural symptoms show up in the actions of a person who may be suffering from a mental disorder and these relate to what a person is doing. These may include anything from behaving in an aggressive manner, alcohol or drug abuse, major changes in eating habits and a person's sex drive, to attempted suicide.

Put together you can appreciate how they affect all parts of behaviour. When we worry about something (thought complaint) this might make us feel scared (feeling complaint) which makes sleeping a problem (physical complaint) leading to health problems. But is this necessarily a sign of mental illness?

If we are miserable, unable to function in our day-to-day existence and having trouble with coping with stress and other emotions, then perhaps this has become an issue that requires us to seek help. However, some types of mental illness are those that the individual is unaware of and it is a family member who starts to notice that something is amiss. Schizophrenia or bipolar disorder are mental disturbances that some people are unaware of, and it may be a neighbour or family member who seeks help on the individual's behalf.

Case study

2.4 Activity

Read the following case study and complete the task below.

Jane is a 30 year-old married female. She is in her second year as a teacher in a large comprehensive school in London and is finding her job more stressful than she had anticipated. There are high numbers of very demanding pupils and she is constantly spending her days 'controlling the crowd' rather than doing the actual teaching she loves. As a high achiever, graduating with top honours from University, Jane has very high standards for herself and others and is very critical when she does not meet these standards. For the past couple of months Jane has struggled with feelings of worthlessness and shame because of feelings she has about her inability to perform as well in this school as she always has in the past and in other work placements.

Jane is now feeling very tired and is finding it increasingly difficult to concentrate at work. The other teachers have noticed that she is often irritable and withdrawn, and the pupils have commented that she is not quite as friendly or approachable as she once was. She has started to call in sick on several occasions and when she does this she stays in bed all day, watching TV or sleeping.

Jane's husband has noticed a difference and comments upon her lack of interest in sex and her insomnia which is also keeping him awake. Her tearful phone conversations with her closest friend have worried him and yet when he asks if he can do anything to help her she merely tells him that everything is ok. Jane is dissatisfied with her life and although she hasn't ever considered suicide she does have frequent thoughts of wishing she was dead. Her sense of doom is an issue and despite her seemingly happy life she cannot shake the frustration she is feeling.

What is happening here with the thoughts, feelings and actions of Jane and how are they affecting her life physically and emotionally? What might you advise her to do? Do remember that whilst you may have an opinion about what Jane may be suffering from you are in no position to diagnose her condition. Limit your answer to suggestions and advice.

5 List common sources of information on mental health issues and key agencies that can help

There are a number of societies and organisations that can support individuals suffering with mental health issues. In the table below we show some of the main contacts. You may like to add others and display this list on your main noticeboard in your work place.

Table 2.1 Sources of information

Organisation	Work they do	Contact details	Website
Mental Health Helplines Partnership	Independent registered charity that works in partnership with the providers of mental health helplines. They help to improve the quality of services to people suffering from ill health and those caring for or treating them.		http://www.mhhp.org.uk/member-helplines.html

(Continued)

(Continued)

The Mental Health Foundation	A registered charity similar to above.	020 7803 1100	http://www.mentalhealth.org.uk/contact-us/
NHS Direct	Website of the NHS Direct health advice and information service.	0845 46 47 Scotland - 0845 4 24 24 24	http://www.nhsdirect.nhs.uk/ www.nhs24.com
Samaritans	Talk to us anytime you like, in your own way, and off the record, about whatever's getting to you	08457 90 90 90 (uk), 24 hours a day 1850 60 90 90 (ROI)	www.samaritans.org jo@samaritans.org
www.HaveIGotAProblem.com	A free resource about mental health and addiction issues giving advice on issues including depression, anxiety, self-harm, bipolar, eating disorders and coping.		www.HaveIGotAProblem.com
Mind	Offers advice and support to service users; has a network of local associations in England and Wales.	InfoLine 0300 123 3393 info@mind.org.uk	www.mind.org.uk
Rethink Mental Illness	A national advice service which helps everyone affected by severe mental illness, such as schizophrenia and bipolar disorder, recover a better quality of life by providing effective services and supporting campaigns for change.	0300 5000 927 or 020 7840 3188 General enquiries - 0845 456 0455 advice@rethink.org info@rethink.org	www.rethink.org/talk
Sane	SANE services provide practical, emotional and specialist support and information to individuals, families and carers.	0845 767 8000 sanemail@sane.org.uk	www.sane.org.uk/DB
Students Against Depression	Provides information, resources, discussion and real student stories.		www.studentdepression.org
ChildLine	Provides advice, support, topics and games for children.	Helpline 0800 1111	www.childline.org.uk

Figure 2.3 Samaritans

There are organisations that can be contacted for more specific mental health issues and these include: ADD & ADHD, AA, Alcohol concern, Alzheimer's Society, Anxiety UK, beat - Beating Eating Disorders, Bipolar UK, National Self Harm Network and Carers UK.

Evidence Activity

 Activity

Make a list of the sources of information on mental health issues your particular place of work uses. Add to the list in Table 2.1 with other support in your local area.

6 Explain how mental ill health may have an impact on the individual and those in their familial, social or work network and explain how individuals experience discrimination due to misinformation, assumptions and stereotypes about mental ill health

7 Outline how mental health is reported in the media and identify the negative effects media reporting can have on an individual and society

Mental health problems are very common, affecting around one in four people in Britain, yet stigma and discrimination towards such sufferers is rife and there are a lot of myths surrounding mental disorder.

The stigma in mental health is related to three main areas.

- ignorance due to the lack of knowledge about mental health problems
- prejudice due to fear and anxiety
- discrimination or acting upon the negative points and actually causing disadvantage to others.

Stigma can be defined as negative views that affect the way people feel, think and behave towards a certain group and these negative views can lead to the stereotyping of groups. The assumption is made that the stigmatised group have negative qualities and as a result they are treated in a less than favourable way.

The lack of knowledge amongst the general public is manifest in some of the common myths about mental illness. For example Thornicroft et al. (2006) commented upon these and showed beliefs such as the following emerging:

'schizophrenia means split personality, mental illness cannot affect me, there's no hope for people with mental illness, mental illness is the same as learning disability, mental illnesses are brought on by a weakness of character, being treated for a psychiatric disorder means an individual has in some way "failed" or is weak.'

You may even have held some of these views yourself.

In addition to the above, data collected by the Office of National Statistics for the Royal College of Psychiatrists (described in Crisp et al 2000) suggested that most people in the survey sample thought people with schizophrenia were 'dangerous and unpredictable', that 'people with depression, severe depression, schizophrenia and an alcohol or drug addiction were hard to talk to', and that people with schizophrenia feel 'different from the way we feel at all times'.

Time to reflect

Reflect on your own views about mental illness and determine where the gaps in your knowledge lie. Talk to others in your work place and find out what they think about the views mentioned here.

The media has been guilty of publishing negative views about mental ill health and stirring up public fear. In 2003 The Sun newspaper reported on Frank Bruno's admission to a psychiatric hospital using the headline 'Bonkers Bruno Locked Up'. The public outcry about the headline led to a revised version in later editions. In addition, the publication of 'Mind Over Matter: Media Reporting of Mental Health' (2000) reported that media coverage of severe mental illness was still stigmatising, with the media focusing 'on rare incidents of violence linked to people with a mental health problem, feeding exaggerated public fears'. For example, murders committed by mentally ill people represent 5 per cent of the total number of murders and yet whilst this provides us with a much-needed insight into the attitudes held by individuals, these are reported in such a way as to increase the fear of society, leading to negative effects for individuals who suffer mental ill health.

These sorts of beliefs and assumptions unfortunately can lead to discrimination of this group.

Discrimination against someone means we oppress that individual and this impacts negatively upon the way they feel about themselves, damaging their self-esteem and self-concept, their dignity, as well as their opportunities in life. Discrimination can take many forms:

- stereotyping
- marginalising
- invisibilisation
- infantilisation
- medicalisation
- dehumanisation
- trivialisation.

This type of treatment not only isolates the person from mainstream society but makes it very difficult for them to:

- find work
- be in a steady, long-term relationship
- live in decent housing
- be socially included in mainstream society.

(Mental Health Foundation, accessed 11/2012)

The reason for this effect and for the abundance of stereotypes surrounding mental health conditions is widespread fear and ignorance. As noted in the research above, people in society harbour the belief that individuals with mental ill health are subject to violent episodes and so are dangerous. The opposite is more likely to be the case however, as the sufferer is more at risk of being attacked or harming themselves than harming other people.

The stigma and discrimination can lead the mentally ill person into a cycle of illness, see Figure 2.4.

Figure 2.4 Cycle of illness

As we can see from Figure 2.4 the main outcome of discrimination is oppression and this causes harm. The loss of confidence or the undermining of one's self-esteem simply leads to more stress, more anxiety and ultimately depression. This leads to the individual being unable to work and this can spiral them into a cycle of poverty.

With respect to employment, Thornicroft (2006) describes research carried out with 200 Human Resource officers in Britain. In the experiment all the officers were given descriptions of potential employees, but in some cases the employees were described as having either depression or diabetes. The results showed that mention of a mental health problem significantly reduced the likelihood of employment compared to the mention of the diabetic problem. The main reason given for this was that the officers felt that the person with mental health problems was more likely to perform poorly at work. This is worrying since it reinforces the stigma attached to mental illness. People who are depressed and on medication or undergoing therapy can function perfectly well at work whilst still feeling mentally unwell. Somebody with a physical illness, however, may find they cannot do so and have to take time off, and yet the officers in the research above would be more likely to choose the person with diabetes for a post than the individual suffering from a mental health issue.

Another national survey of British employers found that only 4 in 10 employers said they would think about employing someone with mental health problems.

In 2003 the Social Exclusion Unit carried out research which found a link between social exclusion, social inequality and mental health problems.

In their summary paper reference is made to this as follows:

'For some of us, an episode of mental distress will disrupt our lives so that we are pushed out of the society in which we were fully participating. For others, the early onset of distress will mean social exclusion throughout our adult lives, with no prospect of training for a job or hope of a future in meaningful employment. Loneliness and loss of self-worth lead us to believe we are useless, and so we live with this sense of hopelessness, or far too often choose to end our lives. Repeatedly when we become ill we lose our homes, we lose our jobs and we lose our sense of identity … we are perceived as a social burden. We lose sight of our potential, and when we try to move on, discrimination and stigma prevent us getting jobs that use our skills and experience and push us out of housing and education.'

(SEU, 2003)

So the effects are clearly far-reaching. Mental health problems lead to employment issues, social exclusion and discrimination and these things in turn lead to negative feelings/states that can affect mental health and physical health. A vicious circle, as we showed earlier.

One of the ways in which we can help to challenge discrimination is through first-hand contact with people with experience of mental health problems and, as we saw in Section 5, there are a number of national and local organisations who do an enormous amount of work changing public attitudes to mental illness. In addition, by challenging the myths and assumptions people make about mental illness we can also help to educate others. Finally, the Equality Act 2010 makes it illegal to discriminate directly or indirectly against people with mental health problems in public services and functions, access to premises, work, education, associations and transport.

> **Evidence Activity**
>
> **Activity**
>
> Compile a case study of one of your clients and say how their mental health condition has affected their lifestyle and the impact this has had on their family and other social networks. Determine how far they have been discriminated against due to misinformation in the media, assumptions and stereotypes.

Summary

This chapter has shown some of the possible causes of mental ill health including biological/physical factors as well as environmental, social and psychological factors. The two main classification systems, the DSM: IV TR and the ICD-10, together with the key strengths and weaknesses of this type of categorisation have been shown.

The links between social exclusion, social inequality and mental health problems continue to have a major effect on the lives of individuals and others within their network. The discrimination they experience due to misinformation, assumptions and stereotypes continues to cause concern, as the stigma of having a mental illness prevents the individual from accessing jobs that use their skills and experience and pushes them out of housing and education.

Children, adults and the elderly are not immune to these issues, and in the chapters that follow we look at some of the interventions that are being put in place to address this.

References

American Psychiatric Association (2000): *Diagnostic and Statistical Manual of Mental Disorders (4th ed., Text Revision)*. Washington, DC: American Psychiatric Association.

American Psychiatric Association (n.d.) DSM-IV vs. DSM-IV-TR. Available at: http://www .psychiatry.org/practice/dsm/dsm-iv-vs--dsm-iv-tr.

Beecham, J, Knapp, M, Fernández, J-L, Huxley, P, Mangalore, R, McCrone, P, Snell, T, Winter, B and Wittenberg, R (2008): *Age Discrimination in Mental Health Services*. Discussion Paper (May). Canterbury: Personal Social Services Research Unit.

Bewley T (2008) Madness to Mental Illness: A History of the Royal College of Psychiatrists. London: RCPsych Publications.

Crisp, A H, Gelder, M G, Rix, S, Meltzer, H I, & Rowlands, O J (2000): The Stigmatisation of people with mental illness. *The British Journal of Psychiatry* 177, 4–7.

Hoermann, S, Zupanick, C E & Dombeck, M. (2011): Problems with the Current Diagnostic System. Available at: http://www.sevencounties.org/poc/view_doc.php?type=doc&id=41591&cn=8

PsyWeb (2011): Axis V - Global Assessment of Functioning Scale. Available at: http://www.psyweb.com/DSM_IV/jsp/Axis_V.jsp (accessed on 27/9/12).

Rethink Mental Illness (n.d.): What Causes Mental Illness? Available at: http://www.rethink.org/about_mental_illness/what_causes_mental_illness/

WebMD (n.d.): Anxiety & Panic Disorders Health Center. Available at: http://www.webmd.com/anxiety-panic/mental-health-causes-mental-illness (accessed 18/9/12).

World Health Organization (1994): The ICD-10 Classification of Mental and Behavioural Disorders: Classification Descriptions and Diagnostic Guidelines. Available at: http://www.who.int/classifications/icd/en/bluebook.pdf (accessed 27/9/12).

Mental Health Foundation (n.d.): Stigma and Discrimination. Available at: http://www.mentalhealth.org.uk/help-information/mental-health-a-z/S/stigma-discrimination/

Singh, S (2007): Delivery of Psychiatric Services and the Royal College of Psychiatrists, UK. Available at: http://www.clinicaljunior.com/psychdelivery.html

Sobo, S (n.d.): The strengths and weaknesses of DSM IV: How it clarifies, how it blinds psychiatrists to issues in need of investigation. Available at: http://simonsobo.com/the-strengths-and-weaknesses-of-dsm-iv (accessed on 27/9/12).

Social Exclusion Unit (2003): Mental Health and Social Exclusion: Social Exclusion Unit Report Summary. London: Office of the Deputy Prime Minister.

Swedo, S E, Leckman, J F and. Rose, N R (2012) From Research Subgroup to Clinical Syndrome: Modifying the PANDAS Criteria to Describe PANS (Pediatric Acute-onset Neuropsychiatric Syndrome). Paediatrics and Therapeutics 2 (2), 113.

Thornicroft, G, Rose, D, Kassam, A, & Satorius, N (2007) Stigma: ignorance, prejudice or discrimination? British Journal of Psychiatry 190 (3), 192–3.

Mental health interventions

What are you finding out?

In this chapter we look at the diverse needs of people with mental health problems and focus on the key principles for supporting individuals. The main service interventions within mental health are addressed together with a discussion about their strengths and limitations. In addition we will look at the barriers an individual may face in accessing interventions.

The reading and activities in this chapter will help you to:

1. Explain the following key principles for working with an individual to identify their needs:
   a. needs-led not service-led approach
   b. person-centred
   c. promoting self-direction
   d. focusing on strengths, hope and recovery.
2. Describe the range, complexity and inter-related nature of the following needs:
   - physical
   - practical and financial needs
   - social
   - psychological/intellectual and emotional
   - cultural
   - spiritual.
3. Explain how diversity and difference may influence the identification of needs.
4. Describe the strengths and limitations of the main interventions that are used within the mental health system and explain how an individual may access a range of intervention options in their local area:
   a. medication
   b. electro-convulsive therapy
   c. talking and other therapies
   d. psychosocial interventions
   e. complementary
   f. spiritual and religious support
   g. arts therapy
   h. physical activity and diet
   i. self-management approaches and social prescribing
   j. peer support
   k. work, education and volunteering
5. Explain the strengths and limitations of the main service interventions in mental health:
   - in-patient treatment
   - home treatment
   - crisis services
   - assertive outreach.

6. Explain the barriers an individual may face in accessing a range of intervention options in their local area and identify factors that may underpin the choice of intervention from the point of view of service users and mental health practitioners.
7. Explain the importance of the key principles in selecting interventions in relation to:
   - individual needs and wants
   - avoiding unwanted effects
   - equality of opportunity
   - promoting social inclusion
   - a collaborative approach
   - sharing information
   - strengthening networks of support
   - anticipating setbacks and promoting problem solving
   - focusing on recovery.

Assessment criteria covered in this chapter

Reading this unit and completing the activities will provide you with the knowledge, understanding and skills required to meet the assessment criteria listed below.

City & Guilds Level 3 Diploma in Mental Health Care (QCF) (600/5241/7)		
Understand mental health interventions (R/602/0153)		
Learning Outcome 1 Understand the needs of people with mental health problems.		
Assessment Criteria	Page reference	Activity

1.1 Explain the following key principles for working with an individual to identify their needs:
  a. needs-led not service-led approach
  b. person centred
  c. promoting self-direction
  d. focusing on strengths, hope and recovery
	p. 46	Evidence activity 3.1, p. 48

1.2 Explain how a person with mental health problems may have needs in common as well as individual needs	p. 48	Evidence activity 3.2, p. 50

1.3 Describe the range, complexity and inter-related nature of the following needs:
  a. physical needs
  b. practical and financial needs
  c. social needs
  d. psychological needs
  e. cultural needs
  f. spiritual needs
	p. 48	Evidence activity 3.2, p. 50

1.4 Explain how diversity and difference may influence the identification of needs:
  a. gender
  b. age
  c. culture
  d. beliefs
  e. sexual orientation
  f. social class
  g. ability
	p. 50	Evidence activity 3.3, p. 52

(Continued)

(Continued)

Learning Outcome 2 Understand the strengths and limitations of the main interventions in mental health		

2.1 Describe the argument for and against the two main physical interventions that are used within the mental health system:
   a. drug treatment
   b. electro-convulsive therapy
	p. 52	Evidence activity 3.4, p. 58

2.2 Explain the strengths and limitations of other interventions that may be available to people with mental health problems:
   a. complementary/alternative approaches for example acupuncture, reflexology
   b. 'food and mood'
   c. self-management approaches
   d. talking therapies
   e. arts therapies
   f. peer support
   g. social prescribing (eg bibliotherapy, green gyms)
   h. work, education and volunteering
   i. spiritual support
	p. 52	Evidence activity 3.4, p. 58

2.3 Explain the strength and limitations of the main forms of service interventions in mental health:
   a. in-patient treatment
   b. home treatment
   c. crisis services
   d. assertive outreach
	p. 58	Evidence activity 3.5, p. 61

2.4 Explain how an individual may access a range of intervention options in their local area	p. 52	Evidence activity 3.6, p. 61

2.5 Explain the following barriers that an individual may face in accessing a range of intervention options in their local area:
   a. service or professional bias
   b. financial barriers
   c. equalities issues
   d. availability
   e. physical access
	p. 58	Evidence activity 3.6, p. 61

Learning Outcome 3 Know the key principles and factors that underpin the choice of mental health interventions.		

3.1 Identify factors that may underpin the choice of intervention from the point of view of:
   a. service users
   b. mental health practitioners
	p. 60	Evidence activity 3.6, p. 61

3.2 Explain the importance of applying key principles in selecting interventions in relation to:
   a. individuality of experiences, needs and wants
   b. avoiding unwanted effects
   c. equality of opportunity
   d. promoting social inclusion
   e. a collaborative approach
   f. sharing information
   g. strengthening networks of support
   h. anticipating setbacks and promoting problem solving
   i. focusing on recovery
	p. 62	Evidence activity 3.7, p. 62

City & Guilds Level 3 Diploma in Mental Health Care (QCF) (600/5241/7)		
Promote equality and inclusion in health, social care or children's and young people's settings (Y/601/1437)		
Learning Outcome 1 Understand the importance of diversity, equality and inclusion		
Assessment Criteria	Page reference	Activity
1.1 Explain what is meant by • diversity • equality • inclusion	p. 51	Evidence activity 3.3, p. 52

NCFE Level 1 Award in Mental Health Awareness (QCF) (501/0253/9)		
Develop an awareness of mental health (K/600/6596)		
Learning Outcome 3 Be aware of some of the responses to mental health issues		
Assessment Criteria	Page reference	Activity
3.2 Identify possible responses that can be made to support an individual with mental health problems	p. 52	Evidence activity 3.4, p. 58
3.3 Outline factors which can have an impact on whether a response will work	p. 58	Evidence activity 3.5, p. 61
Learning outcome 4 Be aware of cultural diversity in relation to mental health issues		
4.2 Give examples of barriers that may exist for different cultural groups accessing services	p. 60	Evidence activity 3.6, p. 61

1 Explain the key principles for working with an individual to identify their needs

The key principles when working with anybody in care work are to ensure that they maintain their independence and to encourage those individuals with disabling conditions, including those with mental health issues, to maximise their own potential and independence. This means that care workers must have a good understanding of the diverse needs of individuals.

The importance of understanding the value of equality and the respect for diversity and inclusion in all types of care work is paramount.

When an individual with mental health issues first comes into contact with health professionals they are likely to be in a most vulnerable state, and it is at this point that the care professional recognises that person as an individual with their own needs and preferences with respect to the care they require. The way in which the care professional deals with the individual will have a 'direct impact on either increasing equality and nullifying discrimination and disadvantage, or helping to reinforce, perpetuate or even increase inequality, discrimination and disadvantage' (Tilmouth et al., 2011).

A comprehensive assessment of the individual's care needs is therefore crucial and involves taking into account their preferences with respect to their physical and mental support needs, assessing the medications or treatment they require and determining any specialist needs, such as preferred methods of communication and language and the social interests, religious and cultural needs of individuals.

By placing the individual's preferences and best interests at the centre of everything the care worker does, the individual is empowered to take responsibility for communicating their own decisions about their lives.

This way of working with people has led to a number of care assessment approaches.

Needs-led not service-led approach

In recent years the needs-led approach to care has replaced purely service-led provision. A service-led provision refers to looking at the services that are available and then finding the best fit for the service user. The alternative, needs-led, approach is a more user friendly approach and is the preferred method. Needs-led means identifying an individual's needs and planning the best way that they can be met irrespective of what is currently available. So, in assessing an individual with mental health needs, the care plan would be reviewed on the basis of whether or not the service they currently use is the best one to meet their needs.

Although the needs-led approach has certainly improved the delivery of care for service users it is still fraught with difficulties.

One of the problems is that the identification of 'needs' is a highly subjective process. Another, is that 'needs' change over time, and there is no specified point at which the work can be said to have been achieved. Needs also have a tendency to multiply and, once they are identified, others also become apparent and there appears to be no end to the work being done for the client. This means that care work can frequently lack direction and purpose and it becomes almost impossible to measure success or failure.

Person-centred

Person-centred care is another way in which care work has been delivered and, in 2004, the government promoted this approach as 'the essence of high-quality service delivery'. The value of person-centred planning was seen to be a way of moving:

> 'away from mass produced services. Services that too often created a culture of dependency and move towards a future that seeks to develop the potential that is in every single individual.'

> (Ladyman, 2004)

Person-centred care, then, was seen as a way of encouraging the person to become independent and to develop more of a partnership approach to their care. It is a process of life planning in care, based upon the principles of inclusion and the social model of disability. Individuals in the care process are thus seen as the experts in their own lives and care provision is to meet their needs as they see them.

Promoting self-direction

Following on from the person-centred approach, if an individual is to be more independent in their own care they need to become self-directed or guided by their own principles and values. Some of these values may include the ability to make their own choices in their care, and to have more control over the support and assistance they access.

This process became popular in care work and self-directed support was born. The personalisation agenda (2008) came about as a means to empower citizens to become full and active members of their communities. In order to achieve this, the government examined key work force policy issues and explored how these would need to be adapted to enable self-directed support and individual budgets. Self-directed support, therefore, is one way in which an individual can have real power and control over their life and individuals are now able to direct their own care or support in a number of different ways. One of these ways is by means of the allocation of a personal health budget. A personal health budget is an allocation of resources made to a person with an established health need and is used for the purchase of the care that the person or their representative believes they need. It was thought that this sort of support would empower people to shape their own lives according to their own specific needs.

Focusing on strengths, hope and recovery

Solution Focused Therapy (SFT) is a particular model in mental health practice that is based upon the role of strengths in recovery and has been implemented widely in New Zealand, Canada, North America, Japan and the UK. The model is based upon the notion that people with mental health problems have resilience that can be used to enhance their recovery.

Resilience describes an individual's ability to recover from difficult or stressful situations and it appears to be a quality that some people possess in abundance, whilst others lack this ability to bounce back after certain events.

The focus of mental health treatment over the last 100 years has been on the deficits, disorders and the problems an individual is having. This is a somewhat negative assessment of their situation. In this model, it is the strengths and resources that individuals' possess that are the main focus. One of the assumptions is that individuals have strengths, skills and abilities on which recovery can be built; and although the individual may have serious symptoms and distress, the practitioner using this model acknowledges that there is a positive aspect to some behaviour. For example, the following represent how the model finds the strengths underlying a problem area.

Table 3.1 Problem areas (from Scottish Recovery Network: **www.scottishrecovery.net**)

Patient misses appointments	Person attends some appointments
Client mixes with bad peer group	Person has a network of friends
Client is in perpetual crisis	Person continues to exist despite the stress
Client resists agency intervention	Person believes in using own strategies
Client is co-dependant	Person has a close mutually supportive relationship
Patient is paranoid	Person is afraid and the fear may be justified

You can see from the above example that each problem can be viewed in a negative and a positive way just by looking at it from a different perspective.

This type of model focuses upon promoting self-efficacy, aims to give individuals a belief in their own abilities and competencies and can be said to be a truly self-directed, person-centred approach to care. The individual is helped to take control of the goals they wish to achieve to enable them to have the future they want. Even in a vulnerable state an individual will still have some strength in one or other area of their life, and if mental health practitioners take the time to look for these strengths, 'they will find them'.

Evidence Activity

 Activity

Reflect on the four approaches in Section 1 and say which you use the most and why.

How and when might you opt to use an alternative approach?

2 Describe the range, complexity and inter-relatedness of the following needs: physical, practical and financial needs, social, psychological/ intellectual and emotional, cultural and spiritual

In Chapter 1 we very briefly looked at Maslow's Hierarchy of Needs and we shall expand upon the concept here (see Figure 1.1).

In order to stay healthy, individuals need to have a number of basic needs met. In health and social care settings these are often recalled by the mnemonic PIESS: physical, intellectual/psychological, emotional, social, spiritual. Sexual needs are also included in some literature.

We all know we need food, water and shelter to survive, but according to Maslow our basic essentials go far beyond just these needs. In addition we also need to grow as human beings by engaging with others, and through stimulating ourselves intellectually and emotionally.

For Maslow, each need has a specific order of attainment; in other words we need to meet the lower order needs before we progress to the higher needs. In Chapter 1 we showed that this pyramid of needs starts with the basic items of food, water and shelter. These are followed by the need for safety and security, then belonging or love, self-esteem, and finally, self-actualisation or meeting our highest potential. Other writers have contested the hierarchical nature of Maslow's model, however, and say that needs are sought simultaneously. Burton (1990), whilst agreeing in part with Maslow, took the concept further.

His list of human essentials includes:

- **Safety/Security** – the need for structure in our lives, predictability, stability and freedom from fear and anxiety.
- **Belongingness/Love** – the need to be accepted by others and to have strong personal ties with one's family, friends and identity groups. This links in with
- **Identity** – defined by Burton as 'a sense of self in relation to the outside world'. Identity becomes a problem when it is not recognised as legitimate, or is considered inferior or is threatened by others with different identifications. Linked to our identity are:
- **Cultural security** – or the need for recognition of one's language, traditions, religion, cultural values, ideas and concepts. Here we would include spiritual needs.
- **Self-esteem** – This refers to our need to be recognised by others as strong, competent and capable. We also need to appreciate these qualities in ourselves. In addition we need to know that we have some effect on our environment.
- **Personal fulfilment** – the need to reach one's potential in all areas of life.
- **Freedom** – is about having the capacity to exercise choice in all aspects of one's life and having no physical, political or civil restraints.
- **Distributive justice** – is the need for the fair allocation of resources among all members of a community. We might also include here the need for finance and practical support.
- **Participation** – is the need to be able to actively participate in and influence society.

(Adapted from http://www.beyondintractability.org/bi-essay/human-needs [accessed on 1/11/12])

Burton further argues that when these needs are unmet, conflict in the individual arises and this is potentially when physical and mental health suffers.

Let's look at examples of this within mental health.

Case study

John

John, 76, was a widower living in a small rural village. He had a part-time job as a gardener for local people. He ate well, growing most of his own food, and usually slept soundly, although he did not feel particularly rested on waking. Recently he had begun to wake in the early hours and found it difficult to get back to sleep.

He consulted his GP about his feelings of depression and the low moods which were affecting his whole enjoyment of the job he loved and his life in general.

The GP found John to be in good physical shape, but further examination revealed that the thing John seemed to have missing from his life was social contact. His solitary life at home and within his job, which brought him into little contact with people, was affecting his mood. His social needs were unmet. He spent a great deal of time alone and sometimes saw nobody for days on end.

Figure 3.1

This simple example shows that without regular contact with others our mental condition can deteriorate, and this has been demonstrated in the literature with work on social isolation amongst the elderly and those with mental health conditions.

We also need to take care of the physical aspects of our lives. If our diets suffer and we miss out on sleep and exercise, our psychological state can be at risk. Again, there is research to suggest that school children who have poor diets fare less well than those who have good diets (WHO, 2000, Feinstein et al., 2008).

In addition to the above basic needs, as a counsellor I often see people who seem to have all these needs met and are in happy fulfilled lives yet still seek help with mental health issues. The need for purpose in life and meaning is a strong urge without which a person can feel worthless or lacking in direction. The need to have a reason for being, improving on existing skills and expanding horizons, all provide a sense of progress and achievement. Equally we need to feel safe and secure and connected to others.

We can see here that the whole concept of 'needs' is complex, and mental and physical health and wellbeing are maintained only when we are able to meet all these needs in one way or another. Unmet needs may lead to conflict in the individual affecting mental and physical health, but can also leave a person open to discrimination and prejudice. In the next section we look at this in more depth.

Evidence Activity

 Activity

Compile a case study for one of your clients and describe the range of needs they have. Say how they inter-relate and affect the condition they present with and how you are empowering them to meet these needs.

3 Explain how diversity and difference may influence the identification of needs, including references to gender, age, race and culture, sexual orientation, social class, ability

The Equality and Diversity Agenda has been rolled out into almost every part of our lives and requires attention in everything we do. But how do diversity and difference impact upon the identification and the meeting of the needs of an individual with mental health issues?

First, let's be clear about two of the terms. Equality involves fairness and diversity involves valuing difference (Thompson, 2011, p. 9). As Thompson points out, what connects the two is not the level of equality or the fact that something is different, it is the discriminatory response that the inequality or difference provokes in others.

Difference only matters when you are treated less well on the basis of your difference.

Our values, beliefs and attitudes are usually deeply ingrained and they are reinforced by our cultural context which leads us to believe certain things about groups of individuals. It is only when these values and beliefs are challenged, either by new information or different experiences, that the idea that these beliefs may be flawed is demonstrated.

We might be of the opinion that discrimination is often perpetuated unwittingly and that it is unintentional. It may also arise from ignorance, commonly held beliefs or stereotypes that are not challenged. Whatever way you view it, discrimination has no place in care work and your role as a care professional must ensure that anti-discriminatory practice is promoted as a key organisational value.

Time to reflect

Access your own organisation's anti-discriminatory practice policy. How well is it promoted within the work setting?

A prejudice is an attitude or belief that is based on a faulty and inflexible generalisation. We all have them. Many of the prejudices that are held lead to negative emotions and discriminatory actions, although prejudice does not necessarily cause one to discriminate unfairly.

Prejudice can lead to unacceptable behaviours, from harassment and bullying to a substantial abuse of power over others, which leads the perpetrators to violate and infringe others' rights. If this is found to occur there must be penalties for failing to comply with organisational values. However, it is not just individuals and groups that can be prejudiced and discriminatory. As Thompson (2011, p. 32) points out, significant structural barriers exist that discriminate negatively on individuals. For example, women still have discriminatory experiences in health care and the work place and an individual's sexual orientation may also lead to differential treatment by others. In terms of social class, as a society we continue to battle with health differences and a life expectancy which reduces with the type of work we do or the income we have. So how can we ensure that the needs of our mentally ill clients will be met despite their differences?

Overcoming issues with equality and diversity

Examining beliefs and values and questioning why we might hold a particular belief is the first step to breaking down prejudice. In addition, raising awareness about equality, diversity and inclusion, and encouraging debate and devising strategies of care that empower people, are essential.

With respect to needs, we must recognise that individuals are unique beings with different needs and vulnerabilities at different times. If we are to meet these needs effectively, we need to engage with people as individuals, to identify their differences and then address their specific needs. By adopting a 'fair' approach to care work we ensure that individuals receive equally good standards of service and similar consideration and respect.

One method is to adopt an equal opportunities approach which ensures that all individuals have the same opportunities to achieve good outcomes. People with mental health issues often find that they are stigmatised by society and are dealt with in a less than fair way in many areas of their lives. In addition to the mental health issue they may also find that they are treated differently because of other irrelevant criteria such as gender, age, race and culture, sexual orientation, social class or ability.

For example, it would be discriminatory to impose an age limit as the only criterion for qualifying for psychotherapy treatment. This is because age is irrelevant. If the person has the potential to benefit from the treatment, irrespective of their age, they should have the same opportunity to access it; preventing their access would be unfair.

By adhering to an equal opportunity approach practitioners are required to reflect on potential and actual barriers to opportunities and propose and implement active intervention to overcome these barriers.

This approach to managing difference and diversity has had significant success in improving equality and inclusion. Much of this improvement has been brought about by anti-discriminatory legislation such as the Sex Discrimination Act 1975, Equal Pay Act 1970, Race Relations Act 1976, Disability Discrimination Act 1995 and Equality Act 2010.

The law, together with changes to practice, has had a positive impact on many discriminatory practices, and there has been a change in approach to equality which now focuses much more positively on celebrating difference and diversity rather than seeing inequality as a barrier to be overcome. Humans are all unique, which means we all have a personal set of attributes, skills, needs and preferences which comprise our differences.

Raising awareness and challenging attitudes can have a significant impact on breaking down discrimination and prejudice. Prejudice may be a strong, culturally held belief, but it is important that everyone is aware that prejudice leading to discriminatory behaviour cannot be tolerated and that individuals are encouraged, supported and protected to speak out. Creating a culture of discussion and tolerance is important in developing an open-minded community and, until this is done, an individual with mental health issues may find that they are continually ostracised and are at risk of not having their needs met.

> ## Evidence Activity
>
> **Activity**
>
> Using the case study from the previous activity, describe how your client is affected by issues relating to equality, diversity and inclusion. Describe an incident in which the client was dealt with in a less than fair manner and expand upon the outcomes for your client. How would you change the situation?

4 Explain the strengths and limitations of the main interventions that are used within the mental health system and explain how an individual may access a range of intervention options in their local area

In this section we will look at what happens when a person first presents with a mental health issue and go onto discuss the care plan and treatments available to sufferers.

There are so many types of intervention for the treatment of mental illness it is important that an initial assessment is carried out. The first step for anyone who feels they are in need of help or for somebody who is displaying symptoms is to contact the GP or the community mental health team. Occasionally the individual themselves will be unaware of their symptoms and the family may be the first to notice uncharacteristic behaviour. They can also refer to the CMHT or GP. At the initial assessment a diagnosis will be made based on the symptoms the person has. The doctor will then decide on the best treatment for the symptoms and their underlying causes. If the symptoms change, or more information about the person and their illness becomes known, then the treatment can be changed to a more appropriate one.

Access to the mental health service is likely to be through the GP or the local Emergency department and these professionals can make an assessment and prepare a care plan. They may also refer for psychological therapy.

Mental health treatment is largely carried out in the community rather than in hospitals and the care team will comprise:

- **A case manager** who is a health professional who oversees the individual's treatment and ensures they have access to all the services they need (for example, housing and employment support). They also provide help for the family and have an educative role. They bring together a number of different practitioners from a wide range of disciplines to ensure that the care provided is of a holistic nature.
- **Crisis teams** that consist of mental health professionals who assess and support individuals who are seriously affected by mental illness. Hospital admission may be an option in severe cases and this team can arrange this.
- **Support teams** who provide long-term support to the individual in their home. They help to maintain a useful treatment plan and try to reduce the number of admissions to hospital a person may need.

When the individual has been assessed the teams will decide upon the best intervention for the particular symptoms and the person themselves. In the following text we look at some of the interventions available.

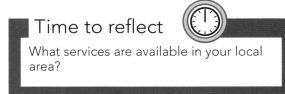

Time to reflect

What services are available in your local area?

Medication

There are a number of different types of medication to treat the numerous types of mental illness:

- Antidepressants help to treat depression and are successful in about 60 to 70 per cent of individuals. They are also used (in combination with psychological therapies) to treat phobias, anxiety disorders, obsessive compulsive disorders and eating disorders.

  There are side effects as with any medication and the prescriber will highlight the main ones to the individual. These may include dry mouth, constipation, a sedative effect which can affect driving or operating machinery, sleep problems, weight gain, headache, nausea, gastrointestinal disturbance/diarrhoea.
- Antipsychotic medications are used to treat psychotic illnesses such as schizophrenia and bipolar disorder. Again, there are general side effects but the newer antipsychotics are more reliable. Some of the older drugs were known to cause stiffening and weakening of the muscles and muscle spasms.
- Mood-stabilising medications are helpful for people who have bipolar disorder (previously known as manic depression). Lithium carbonate can help reduce the incidence of major depression and can help reduce the manic or 'high' episodes.

Electro-convulsive therapy

ECT, despite being a somewhat controversial treatment, is still prescribed for some cases of severe mental illness. It was widely used in the 1950s and 1960s but fell into disrepute due to the damaging physical effects. However, more sophisticated methods for carrying out the treatment have now made it useful in some severe cases of mental illness.

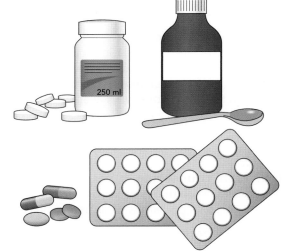

Figure 3.2 Medication

ECT consists of causing a seizure much like an epileptic fit by passing an electrical current through the brain. Research suggests that the treatment effect is due to the fit rather than the electrical current, having observed cases where individuals feel better following seizures.

Some doctors believe that severe depression is caused by problems with certain brain chemicals and subscribe to the notion that a 'fit' causes the release of these chemicals.

The National Institute of Health and Clinical Excellence (NICE) have ruled that the treatment should only be used in severe depression, severe mania or catatonia and in the case of severe depression, only when other treatments have failed.

The limitations of this treatment are mainly due to the fact that as a major procedure it involves the use of a large number of treatments requiring the person to undergo a number of general anaesthetics, in itself a risk. Short term effects of this include:

- headache immediately after ECT
- aching muscles
- feeling muzzy-headed
- nausea
- distress after the treatment causing the individual to be tearful or frightened
- loss of memory
- confusion.

In the longer term the side effects may include memory problems and there is evidence that some people have felt that they have lost skills or that they are no longer the person they were before ECT (Rose et al., 2003).

Talking and other therapies

Psychosocial interventions

As we have seen, some drug therapy can cause side effects and can change an individual's mood by affecting the balance of chemicals. This can often help but the underlying problem is not necessarily being dealt with and withdrawing the drugs may cause the problem to resurface. By talking through an issue with a trained counsellor or psychotherapist really effective results can be seen.

Talking treatments can help an individual to overcome emotional difficulties by reframing the thought process going on behind the issue. They can free the person from self-destructive ways of feeling, thinking and behaving.

The National Institute for Health and Clinical Excellence (NICE) has suggested forms of talking treatment that are brief, cost-effective and supported by clinical evidence. These include the use of CBT or Cognitive Behavioural Therapy which has been the talking treatment of choice for a number of years now. However, research is now showing that other forms of treatment are more effective although these are not always available on the NHS.

There are a variety of talking treatments available from the NHS or in private practice. Some therapies may last for several years, while others take just a few sessions and they are offered in group or individual sessions.

Individual counselling focuses on an individual's current problem, perhaps bereavement or a relationship issue that is causing distress, and the counsellor's ability to listen but not to advise or offer a personal opinion is designed to help an individual to arrive at their own solutions.

Cognitive behavioural therapy (CBT) examines an individual's thought processes and shows how thinking, feeling and behaviour can result in unhelpful patterns. By restructuring how the individual approaches their depression or anxiety new ways of thinking and acting are developed. This sort of therapy usually includes tasks or homework to try outside the therapy sessions.

Group therapy can help an individual to deal with issues relating to and communicating with other people. They are also designed to help the individual become more self aware. With groups of 8 to 12 people this type of therapy can be intimidating, and requires careful handling, but in a group environment, opportunities may arise to hear other points of view about their concerns and to learn how their behaviour affects other people. It provides a safe environment in which the individual can be vulnerable or assertive and can try out new behaviours.

Psychological or psychosocial treatments include therapies such as inter-personal psychotherapy. This sort of therapy addresses the individual's relationships and interactions with others and shows how they are affecting their own thoughts and behaviours. For an individual with a mental illness, stress may be caused by a difficult relationship and improving this part of their life may improve their quality of life overall. This therapy may be useful in the treatment of depression.

Psychotherapy

Similarly to counselling the aim of psychotherapy is to help an individual to understand what lies behind their behaviours and the way they interact with other people and why they feel the way they do. Talking through experiences and releasing painful feelings enables an individual to manage the situation they are in and helps them to understand how they can improve their life. Understanding what has shaped their life can empower an individual to access the reasons behind their self-destructive patterns of behaviour and this can help to overcome specific problems, such as an eating disorder or lack of confidence.

There are many types of therapy that come under the umbrella term 'psychotherapy'. There are therapists who will encourage the person to talk mainly about early childhood, and they may come from a Freudian or Jungian background. They may be interested in the dreams an individual has and will work with these in the sessions. Others, systemic and relational psychotherapists, will be more interested in the relationships the person has and will try to determine how these impact upon the individual's life. An existential psychotherapist adopts a philosophical method of therapy and tries to understand the inner conflict within an individual which they believe is due to confronting certain givens of existence. These givens are the inevitability of death, freedom (fear), responsibility, isolation and meaninglessness within life all causing tension.

Complementary

The Rethink Mental Illness website provides a useful list of complementary therapies that may be useful for helping individuals with mental distress. The website makes the point that complementary therapies adopt a more holistic approach to treating individuals with the focus on physical, psychological and spiritual needs rather than merely looking at the symptoms of the illness. Treatments include massage, aromatherapy, reflexology, acupuncture, shiatsu, exercise, yoga and tai chi.

The more unconventional medicines are homeopathy and herbal medicine, and some newer therapies, such as music therapy, animal-assisted therapy and meditation, are also becoming more popular.

Spiritual and religious support

Some individuals have a deep faith in a higher being and this can help them in times of great distress. There is increasing agreement between health professionals that some aspects of spirituality have real benefits for mental health and as such should form a part of the assessment of an individual.

Spirituality does not necessarily require a link to a religion but involves experiences of:

- a sense of meaning and purpose in life
- a sense of belonging
- a sense of connection of 'the deeply personal with the universal'
- acceptance, integration and a sense of wholeness.

(http://www.rcpsych.ac.uk/mentalhealthinfo/treatments/spirituality.aspx)

These experiences are part of being human and they are clearly present in all of us.

For the person with a mental health problem, there needs to be recognition of the spiritual side of their treatment. This requires the health professional to ensure that the person is able to engage in activities such as those outlined below.

- creative art, work or enjoying nature
- to feel safe and secure
- to be treated with dignity and respect
- to feel that they belong, are valued and trusted
- time to express feelings to members of staff
- the chance to make sense of their life – including illness and loss
- permission/support to develop their relationship with God or the Absolute.

(http://www.rcpsych.ac.uk/mentalhealthinfo/treatments/spirituality.aspx)

For the person who also has a religious belief, the health professional needs to support them by providing a place of privacy in which to pray and worship and reassurance that their beliefs are valued by staff and will not be undermined in any way.

Arts therapy

Art therapy has been used in treating mental illness for almost 100 years and encourages self-expression and self-discovery. Psychotherapists use this therapy to encourage the individual to visualise, and then create, the thoughts they have difficulty talking about. It is the creative process of art making that becomes the therapy and a way to understand the inner worlds of people with mental illness. You may be aware of the Rorschach Inkblot Test and the Holtzman Inkblot Test (HIT) which were used as a diagnostic tool to identify specific types of mental illness. These came about as it was felt that the symbolism of art work was useful in diagnosis.

Figure 3.3a Art therapy   **Figure 3.3b** Rorschach Inkblot Test

Physical activity and diet

Research into the effects of physical activity on depression and other mental illnesses has been carried out for a number of years and the NICE guidelines for the Management of Depression in Primary and Secondary Care support the notion that physical exercise is now a legitimate form of treatment in mental illness and can actually help a great deal (NICE, 2004).

Just as the state of our mind and how we think affects our body so too is the converse true: The mind cannot function unless the body is working properly. If we feel tired or depressed it is likely that we will do even less. This exacerbates the tiredness and makes us feel even worse.

The Royal College of Psychiatrists offers the following advice:

'Broadly speaking, the less you do, the more likely you are to end up with:

- low mood/depression
- tension and worry.

If you keep active, you are:

- less likely to be depressed, anxious or tense
- more likely to feel good about yourself
- more likely to concentrate and focus better
- more likely to sleep better
- more likely to cope with cravings and withdrawal symptoms if you try to give up a habit such as smoking or alcohol
- more likely to be able to keep mobile and independent as you get older
- possibly less likely to have problems with memory and dementia.'

So too with nutrition. A poor diet contributes to poor physical health but can also lead to poor mental health as well. The absence of certain minerals and vitamins and the use of additives can both cause mental illness and hinder recovery. For example, think of the child who is hyperactive because of the food they are given.

By helping an individual with a mental health problem to look critically at their diet and the exercise they partake in and by encouraging some changes the condition can be helped considerably. Simple changes, such as the amount of caffeine or high energy snacks a person has in a day, can help enormously.

Self-management approaches and social prescribing

There are a number of support groups that can help individuals overcome problems and find support from others sharing similar issues. It may be alcohol or drug abuse, depression or being scared to go out of the house and often these groups are led by people who have suffered these issues and overcome them themselves. The format of the meetings involves the opportunity to share experiences, and learn from and encourage each other.

Alongside traditional approaches and self-help groups, non-medical interventions are becoming popular areas of help. Social prescribing or 'community referral' seeks to provide non-medical sources of support including opportunities for creative pursuits as well as physical activity. This is provided in a number of areas by the Green Gym initiative, volunteering, in addition to support with employment, or benefits, and legal advice if needed. The primary care team will usually deliver the prescription and examples include initiatives such as 'exercise on prescription' or 'prescription for learning' – all referral options to help improve mental health and wellbeing.

Bibliotherapy is another area which comes under this umbrella term and refers to directing the individual to appropriate books or other written materials to be read outside of normal sessions to deepen understanding of the particular problem that requires treatment. As an educative tool they help the individual to have a greater understanding about what is happening to them and can be a useful way of encouraging the individual to comply more fully with treatment.

Peer support

This has been defined by the Mental Health Foundation as:

the help and support that people with lived experience of a mental illness or a learning disability are able to give to one another ...'

(The Mental Health Foundation 2012)

Peer support plays an important role. The government is keen to emphasise this and believes that such support can provide 'improved access to timely information, positive role models and greater community resilience and capacity for self-help' which can result in increased prevention and early intervention in many health problems (Department of Health, 2011c, p14).

Peer support can be provided in number of ways:

- from one patient to another in a hospital ward;
- by peer mentors or informal peer groups in the community;
- by peer support workers formally employed by mental health or learning disability services to work alongside individuals.

The report prepared by the Mental Health Foundation entitled 'Peer support in mental health and learning disability' identified some key messages. The benefits of peer support for the individual receiving the support, the person giving it, and for services was seen to be widespread. These benefits include better mental health together with an increased sense of wellbeing and 'confidence, greater social connectedness, and improved recovery and coping skills and fewer hospital admissions.'

Work, education and volunteering

The benefit of this type of intervention is shown in Chapter 1 (see page 3).

There are a large number of interventions available for people with mental health issues and this in itself is a strength. We no longer have to rely on medication as the only way in which to treat mental illness. We now have a vast array of talking therapies and other less conventional or alternative approaches that may appeal to some individuals. Limitations of the interventions on offer often lie with availability and cost in a number of cases. Also the lack of available research as to the efficiency of some of the therapies is likely to lead to resistance by medical practitioners to refer to some of the more alternative types of treatment. In the next section we look again at the limitations with respect to the services that are offered.

> **Evidence Activity**
>
> **Activity**
>
> Referring again to your case study, identify the interventions for this client and say how you think they are having a positive effect. Describe other interventions you think might be useful for this individual and give a rationale for your choice.

5 Explain the strengths and limitations of the main forms of service interventions in mental health

In-patient treatment

As we have seen throughout the book the care and treatment of people with mental health problems has undergone considerable change. As the understanding of the nature of mental illness has grown, together with advances in medical and psychological treatments, the move to community care has been a major advance.

Re-settling individuals from psychiatric hospitals into the community is now the preferred choice but there is still a place for in-patient treatment at times.

In support of in-patient treatment, the DoH in 2002 made the point that

> 'The purpose of an adult acute psychiatric in-patient service is to provide a high standard of humane treatment and care in a safe and therapeutic setting for service users in the most acute and vulnerable stage of their illness. It should be available for the benefit of

those service users whose circumstances or acute care needs are such that they cannot at that time be treated and supported appropriately at home or in an alternative, less restricted residential setting.'

(DoH, 2002)

For those individuals who find they need a safe environment in which to engage with the mental health services and who cannot live solely independently for a period of time, in-patient treatment is the best choice. However, over the last ten years or so changes have had to be made to improve these services. Weaknesses identified by service users were published in the government paper of 2002: Mental Health Policy Implementation Guide; Adult Acute Inpatient Care Provision. They reported:

- Poor physical and psychological environments for care.
- A lack of basic necessities and arrangements for safety, privacy, dignity and comfort.
- Insufficient information on their condition and treatment.
- Lack of involvement and engagement in the planning and reviewing of their own care.
- Inadequate staff contact, particularly one-to-one contact.
- Insufficient attention to the importance of such key factors as ethnicity and gender and protection from harassment/abuse.
- Lack of 'something to do', especially activity that is useful and meaningful to recovery.

(DoH, 2002)

This somewhat negative engagement with in-patient services led to individuals in crisis avoiding contact with mental health services for fear of admission; and this in itself posed a significant risk factor and a weakness in the previous organisation of many services.

The changes put into place led to the amendment of the Mental Health Act and newer government initiatives being put into place to address the above complaints. These are covered in more depth in Chapter 5.

Home treatment and crisis services

One of the key elements in the 1999 National Service Framework for Mental Health; the NHS Plan (2000) made the provision of Crisis Resolution Home Treatment (CRHT) services a national priority. With more individuals with mental health problems receiving treatment in the community from their GP or a Community Mental Health Team these acute services were set up to provide care for those experiencing a severe crisis and requiring emergency treatment. Previously, such treatment would have been provided by admitting the individual to an in-patient ward.

Although the CRHT reduced in-patient admissions, the main aim was to provide individuals with the most appropriate and beneficial treatment possible in the community. The service also ensured that earlier discharge from in-patient wards could be achieved and these were the strengths of this type of service.

Some of the weaknesses of this service have been shown up in the regional variations in the way in which the teams are run.

The National Audit Office in its 2007 publication: Helping People Through Mental Health Crisis: The Role of Crisis Resolution and Home Treatment Services reported that the CRHT staffing is 10 per cent below that required nationally as estimated by the Department of Health, and that

'many teams lack dedicated input from key health and social care professionals, particularly consultant psychiatrists'

restricting their ability to provide comprehensive, multidisciplinary care, which is integrated within local mental health services.

Assertive Outreach

Assertive Outreach was described in the National Service Framework for Mental Health and is aimed at people with severe mental illness who are at risk of recurrent hospitalisation and who experience difficulties with more traditional services.

The teams – usually made up of a range of staff, including psychiatrists, psychologists, community psychiatric nurses (CPNs), social workers, mental health workers and other specialised staff – focus on the delivery of community support, using community resources including family, neighbours, friends, employers, voluntary services and educational establishments. The main aim is to maintain the social inclusion of the individual with the support of professional and paraprofessional staff to ensure that the individual is able to maintain a place in the community without having to constantly refer to other departments or agencies for support.

Assertive Outreach workers then need to work in a flexible way in order to provide a seamless service that enables the individual to carry on with their daily life. This team approach allows closer supportive working by involving relevant people and helping them to understand the individual and develop tolerance and coping strategies. In addition to this the teams work with the individual to help them to take responsibility for their own behaviour in order to control their symptoms. This has been helpful in reducing law breaking and friction within the community.

6 Explain the barriers an individual may face in accessing interventions and identify factors that may underpin the choice of intervention from the point of view of service users and mental health practitioners

In addition to the stigma, prejudice and discrimination that people with mental health issues are subject to (we cover this in Chapter 2) many individuals may also face other barriers, by which we mean the numerous factors which can prevent an individual from getting the care they need or instead receiving inferior health care. In accessing any intervention the service user and the health professional may also have different ideas about what can be offered or is available. The preferences of the service user for a particular intervention must be considered since compliance with a treatment is of paramount importance for it to work. But in addition the health professional must also take into consideration the availability of a service, the budget and resources and staff available to deliver.

These factors underpinning such choice include the following barriers:

- physical
- socio-economic
- cultural and language
- geographical and availability
- service or professional bias
- equality issues.

A physical barrier might be as simple as a mobility problem which causes the person to be unable to walk very far and therefore not be able to get to an appointment. Additionally, the person using a wheelchair may have trouble accessing clinics with steps.

A socio-economic barrier refers to a lack of education or knowledge about the services available, in addition to economic factors which include inability to pay for prescriptions or transport. These may all lead to a person not being able to access health care.

Cultural and language barriers are primarily related to social, linguistic and religious issues. With the increase in the number of immigrants to the UK, cultural difference is a major barrier. The language difference, as well as the other socio-economic factors that these individuals face, may well cause issues with access.

The Rethink Mental Illness group identify black and minority ethnic groups (BME) as facing issues of stigma, acceptance in society and finding work much the same as their white counterparts but with the additional language and cultural differences there are reports of higher rates of mental illness in some communities which they believe are due to the social disadvantage some groups experience. (Rethink.org)

They also make the point that surveys looking at mental illness in the UK rely on western definitions of mental illness which could lead to a greater number of people from BME communities being labelled as having mental illness than white groups due to the way in which symptoms are interpreted.

In addition, Rethink highlight the fact that BME communities are mostly concentrated residentially within inner city areas, where more people are likely to experience higher incidents of mental illness.

(http://www.rethink.org/about_mental_illness/index.html)

Geographical and availability barriers refer predominantly to the impact of the rural-urban divide. Individuals who live in rural areas where facilities and transport are limited may find travel difficult and therefore be disadvantaged. In addition to which the availability of specialist services may be restricted to urban areas and be difficult to get to.

Service or professional bias.

As a barrier to care the views of the health professional in dealing with somebody with a mental health condition are crucial. If professionals hold stereotypical views of groups or they approach individuals with set ideas about the response they are likely to get then bias may creep into their diagnosis. As we saw above with BME groups a lack of understanding about how symptoms are being presented may well lead to inaccurate judgments being made leading to decisions and actions being taken which are not effective. In addition bias may be displayed in the choice of intervention made by the professional. If they favour a particular approach or intervention they may ignore the personal preference of the individual and limit their choice of treatment. We all hold prejudices and from this can develop a biased view of life which can result in unequal treatment and service provision if we are not mindful of this.

Equality issues

Mental health problems lead to employment issues, social exclusion and discrimination and these things in turn lead to negative feelings/states that can affect mental health and physical health. (This is covered more fully in Chapter 2, see page 25).

> ### Evidence Activity
>
>   **Activity**
>
> Referring to the client in your case study, describe the strengths and limitations of the main service interventions for their care and explain the barriers an individual may have faced in accessing interventions.
>
> Reflect on how other interventions may have been more appropriate and comment upon how you as a care worker helped to diminish the barriers to access for them.

7 Explain the importance of applying key principles in selecting interventions in relation to: individual needs and wants, avoiding unwanted effects, equality of opportunity, promoting social inclusion, a collaborative approach, sharing information, strengthening networks of support, anticipating setbacks and promoting problem solving, focusing on recovery

This section constitutes a self-directed activity in which you are expected to engage in a case study to cover the above listed factors.

Underpinning good practice in mental health interventions and promotion are the principles of person-centred care. With respect to the areas identified above, it is the human value of people with mental health issues that is the most important principle in determining how interventions are selected. There are many interventions used today to help mental ill health, and because people are unique it is important to make sure that the correct treatment is given in order to achieve the best possible results for the individual involved. Whilst one treatment may work well for one individual it may transpire that the same treatment could be a source of potential damage to another. Variables such as age, gender and type of mental illness, amongst other factors such as family and community support available, need to be taken into account in order to establish the best treatment to use with the individual.

By ensuring that health professionals respect the individuality of people with mental health problems and by adopting a collaborative approach with families and local communities, the care an individual receives will support them to 'adopt and maintain healthy lifestyles which in turn will create supportive living conditions or environments for health' (WHO, 2004).

Collaboration within the CMHT and the community in which the individual lives requires the sharing of information and developing good support for the whole family.

The key recommendations outlined in the WHO 2004 summary report are worthy of note here:

> 'Mental health is a state of well-being in which the individual realizes his or her own abilities, can cope with the normal stresses of life, can work productively and fruitfully, and is able to make a contribution to his or her community. Promotion of mental health contributes towards overall health and should form an essential component of health promotion.'

Evidence Activity

 3.7 **Activity**

With respect to the client in your case study, explain the importance of the key principles in selecting interventions in relation to:

- Individual needs and wants
- Avoiding unwanted effects
- Equality of opportunity
- Promoting social inclusion
- A collaborative approach
- Sharing information
- Strengthening networks of support
- Anticipating setbacks and promoting problem solving
- Focusing on recovery

Bullet-point each of the points above and say how your clients needs are met within each one.

References

Burton, J (1990) *Conflict Resolution and Prevention.* New York: St. Martins Press.

DoH (2002) Mental Health Policy Implementation Guide; Adult Acute Inpatient Care Provision. London, Crown.

Feinstein, L, Sabats, R, Sorhaindo, A, Rogers, I, Herrick, D, Northstone, K, Emmett, P (2008) Dietary patterns related to attainment in school: the importance of early eating patterns - Research report. *Epidemiol Community Health*; 62: 734–9 doi:10.1136/jech.2007.068213

McCormack, J (2007) Recovery and Strengths Based Practice. SRN Discussion Paper Series. Report No.6. Glasgow, Scottish Recovery Network.

Mental Health Foundation (2012) Peer support in mental health and learning disability. Available at: http://www.mentalhealth.org.uk/content/assets/PDF/publications/need_2_know_peer_support1. pdf?view=Standard

National Archives (2007) Speech by Stephen Ladyman MP, Parliamentary Under-secretary of State for Community, 20 May 2004: Intergrated Care Network National Meeting – Tackling Delays Through Integration and Reimbursement.

National Audit Office (2007) Helping People Through Mental Health Crisis: The Role of Crisis Resolution and Home Treatment Services. London, NAO.

National Institute for Clinical Excellence (NICE) (2004) Management of Depression in Primary and Secondary Care. London, NICE.

Rose, D, Fleischmann, P, Wykes, T, Leese, M, and Bindman, J (2003) Patients' perspectives on electroconvulsive therapy: systematic review. *BMJ*; 326;1363–8.

Thompson, N (2011) *Promoting Equality: Working with Diversity and Difference* (3rd edn). Basingstoke, Palgrave Macmillan.

Tilmouth, T, Davies-Ward, E and Williams, B (2011) *Foundation Degree in Health and Social Care.* London, Hodder Education.

WHO (2004) Promoting Mental Health. CONCEPTS. EMERGING EVIDENCE. PRACTICE. Geneva, World Health Organization.

WHO (2000) Nutrition for Health and Development. Summary Report. Geneva, World Health Organization.

Use effective communication and build relationships in mental health work in all settings

What are you finding out?

In order to develop and sustain positive relationships with service users, carers and colleagues, effective communication skills are essential. This chapter will look at how workers can build relationships and communicate sensitively and effectively with service users. It will show how we can support service users in building and managing their social networks which is a key factor in maintaining mental health.

The reading and activities in this chapter will help you to:

1. Evaluate the role of effective communication in building relationships and promoting recovery of individuals and explain the following key principles that should underpin communication and relationships in mental health work:
   - showing respect and being accepting and genuine
   - reliability
   - clarity of boundaries
   - positive attitude and hopefulness and the importance of relationships for promoting or maintaining wellbeing and mental health
   - self awareness
   - working together as equal partners.
2. Define communication and the reasons why we communicate.
3. Identify different kinds of communication and demonstrate how to establish the communication and language needs, wishes and preferences of individuals.
4. Explain how to build positive relationships using principles from theories about communication.
5. Apply key communication skills to build and sustain relationships in a mental health context:
   - how to initiate communication
   - active listening skills
   - eye contact and body language
   - acknowledging and reflecting feelings and being open to ideas
   - paraphrasing and summarising
   - using questions and sharing information
   - listening to silence
   - ending the communication well.
6. Explain how mental health problems may impact on an individual's ability or wish to communicate and form relationships, and common barriers to communication and relationships between service users, carers/family members and mental health workers and how these may be overcome, including:
   a. conflicting opinions
   b. powerful emotions
   c. past experiences
   d. stereotypes and assumptions

e. environment
f. personality clashes
g. unrealistic expectations
h. issues of power and control
i. cultural differences
j. overload
k. organisational dynamics.
7. Evaluate the potential contribution to communication and relationship building of the following main sources of specialist support and explain how to access extra support or services to enable individuals to communicate effectively:
    a. interpreters and translators
    b. speech therapy
    c. psychologists
    d. advocacy
    e. communication aids and equipment.
8. Ways to maintain confidentiality in day-to-day communication and the potential tension between maintaining confidentiality and disclosing concerns.

Assessment criteria covered in this chapter

Reading this unit and completing the activities will provide you with the knowledge, understanding and skills required to meet the assessment criteria listed below.

City & Guilds Level 3 Diploma in Mental Health Care (QCF) (600/5241/7)		
Promote communication in health, social care or children's and young people's settings (J/601/1434)		
Learning Outcome 1 Understand why effective communication is important in the work setting		
Assessment Criteria	Page reference	Activity
1.1 Identify the different reasons people communicate	p. 72	Evidence activity 4.2, p. 74
1.2 Explain how communication affects relationships in the work setting	p. 77	Evidence activity 4.5 Activities 1–7
Learning Outcome 2 Be able to meet the communication and language needs, wishes and preferences of individuals		
2.1 Demonstrate how to establish the communication and language needs, wishes and preferences of individuals	p. 68	Time to reflect activity, p. 68
2.2 Describe the factors to consider when promoting effective communication	p. 68	Evidence activity 4.1 Activities 1–5
2.3 Demonstrate a range of communication methods and styles to meet individual needs	p. 73	Evidence activity 4.3, p. 74
2.4 Demonstrate how to respond to an individual's reactions when communicating	p. 77	Evidence activity 4.5 Activities 1–7
Learning Outcome 3 Be able to overcome barriers to communication		
3.1 Explain how people from different backgrounds may use and/or interpret communication methods in different ways	p. 82	Evidence activity 4.6, p. 83
3.2 Identify barriers to effective communication	p. 82	Evidence activity 4.6, p. 83
3.3 Demonstrate ways to overcome barriers to communication	p. 82	Evidence activity 4.6, p. 83
3.4 Demonstrate strategies that can be used to clarify misunderstandings	p. 84	Evidence activity 4.7, p. 86
3.5 Explain how to access extra support or services to enable individuals to communicate effectively	p. 84	Evidence activity 4.7, p. 86

(Continued)

(Continued)

Learning Outcome 4 Be able to apply principles and practices relating to confidentiality		
4.1 Explain the meaning of the term confidentiality	p. 86	Evidence activity 4.8, p. 87
4.2 Demonstrate ways to maintain confidentiality in day-to-day communication	p. 86	Evidence activity 4.8, p. 87
4.3 Describe the potential tension between maintaining an individual's confidentiality and disclosing concerns	p. 86	Evidence activity 4.8, p. 87

City & Guilds Level 3 Diploma in Mental Health Care (QCF) (600/5241/7)		
Use effective communication and build relationships in mental health work (R/602/0170)		
Learning Outcome1 Understand key principles for communication and relationships in mental health work		
Assessment Criteria	Page reference	Activity
1.1 Evaluate the role of effective communication in building relationships and promoting recovery of individuals	p. 68	Time to reflect activity, p. 68

1.2 Explain the following key principles that should underpin communication and relationships in mental health work:
  a. reliability
  b. clarity about boundaries
  c. being genuine
  d. positive attitude and hopefulness
  e. open to ideas
  f. non-judgemental
  g. active listening
  h. showing respect
  i. realistic expectations
  j. sharing information
  k. working together as equal partners
	p. 68	Evidence activity 4.1, Activities 1, 2, 3, 4 and 5

1.3 Explain how to build positive relationships using principles from at least one of the following theories about communication:
  a. person-centred
  b. cognitive-behavioural
  c. transactional analysis
  d. motivational interviewing
  e. solution focused
  f. psychodynamic
  g. systemic
	p. 75	Evidence activity 4.4, p. 77

Learning Outcome 2 Apply effective communication skills in building and sustaining relationships in mental health work with individuals and carers		

2.1 Apply key communication skills to build and sustain relationships in a mental health context including:
  a. active listening
  b. empathy and validation
  c. types of questions
  d. checking understanding
  e. summarising
	p. 77	Evidence activity 4.5, Activities 1, 2, 3, 4, 5, 6 and 7

2.2 Explain how mental health problems may impact on an individual's ability or wish to communicate and form relationships	p. 82	Evidence activity 4.6, p. 83

(Continued)

Use effective communication and build relationships in mental health work in all settings

(Continued)

2.3 Explain common barriers to communication and relationships between service users and mental health workers including:
   a. conflicting opinions
   b. powerful emotions
   c. past experiences
   d. stereotypes and assumptions
   e. environment
   f. personality clashes
   g. unrealistic expectations
   h. issues of power and control
   i. cultural differences
   j. overload
   k. organisational dynamics
	p. 82	Evidence activity 4.6, p. 83

2.4 Demonstrate how to overcome at least two common barriers to communication and relationships between service users and mental health workers	p. 82	Evidence activity 4.6, p. 83

2.5 Explain common barriers to communication and relationships between carers/family members and mental health workers and explain how these may be overcome
   a. conflicting opinions
   b. powerful emotions
   c. past experiences
   d. stereotypes and assumptions
   e. environment
   f. personality clashes
   g. unrealistic expectations
   h. issues of power and control
   i. cultural differences
   j. overload
   k. organisational dynamics
	p. 82	Evidence activity 4.6, p. 83

2.6 Identify situations in which a mental health worker may need additional support to communicate and build relationships	p. 84	Evidence activity 4.7, p. 86

2.7 Evaluate the potential contribution to communication and relationship building of the following main sources of specialist support:
   a. interpreters
   b. translators
   c. speech therapy
   d. psychologists
   e. advocacy
   f. equipment
   g. communication aids
	p. 84	Evidence activity 4.7, p. 86

Learning Outcome 3 Understand how to support individuals in their relationships		
3.1 Explain the importance of relationships for promoting or maintaining wellbeing and mental health	p. 68	Time to reflect activities, p. 68
3.2 Describe the factors that can impact on the ability of an individual to develop or maintain a strong social network	p. 77	Evidence activity 4.5 Activities 1–7
3.3 Describe the impact of mental health problems on relationships between individuals and their carers, family and friends	p. 82	Evidence activity 4.6, p. 83

3.4 Describe the support needs of carers, family and friends of individuals at key stages:
   a. when a person first develops mental health problems
   b. if an individual goes into psychiatric care
   c. over the longer term
	p. 82	

(Continued)

3.5 Explain how mental health workers may support an individual in their relationships at different stages in a relationship including: a. initiating b. developing/changing c. maintaining d. ending	p. 82	
3.6 Explain how to enable carers, family and friends of people with mental health problems to access support	p. 84	

1 Evaluate the role of effective communication in building relationships and promoting recovery of individuals and explain key principles that should underpin communication and relationships in mental health work

Showing respect and being accepting and genuine

Your answers to the Time to Reflect activity here might have included some of the following things:

- They listen to what you say and don't interrupt.
- They don't judge you, they accept you as you are.
- They are honest and genuine and don't pretend to be someone they aren't.
- They make you feel valued.

This short list shows what is at the foundation of good communication and good relationships. In order to build a positive relationship with anyone and to contribute to their sense of wellbeing they need to feel respected and valued. Many service users in mental health settings will have experienced people making decisions for them, not consulting them, not listening to what they are saying. In order to build positive relationships with service users we need to have respect for them and accept them in a warm and non-judgemental way. 'The time you spend listening to, and talking with the people in your care can matter and make a difference to them' (Bonham, 2004, p. 21).

Time to reflect

Think of a person who you feel really respects and listens to you. Make a list of all the things he or she does that help you to feel respected and listened to.

Evidence Activity

 4.1 **Activity 1**

Find and read through The Nursing and Midwifery Council's code of conduct entitled The Code: Standards of Conduct, Performance and Ethics for Nurses and Midwives (2008). This can be found at: **www.nmc-uk.org/Publications/Standards**

Reliability

It is not surprising that the people that we trust and feel respected by are the people who are reliable and consistent. It is hard to feel that you can trust someone who lets you down. People who have experienced mental health problems often feel that they have little power to make decisions or implement changes that will benefit them. They might have become mistrustful of friends, family members or professionals who make decisions for them or who don't listen to their concerns. In order to build a positive relationship with someone with poor mental health, reliability is crucial. It is necessary to prove that you can be counted on to do what you say you will do and provide good reasons if you don't.

'Reliability significantly affects people's trust and confidence in you and the service you represent'.

(Koprowska, 2010, p. 32)

It is very important not to make promises or give assurances that can't be kept however much you want to help. It is natural to want to help people in any way that we can but it is important to be aware of appropriate boundaries.

Clarity and boundaries

Boundaries are important in family life, in school, with friendships and in work settings. Boundaries provide security and give people an understanding of what is expected of them. Mental health care settings will have clear guidelines on what workers should and shouldn't do when it comes to working and building relationships with service users. It can be tempting to try to get close to a service user or try to gain their trust by treating them as you would a friend. Being open, honest, relaxed, having a sense of humour, being supportive and helpful are good qualities to have in a friend. It is also true that these qualities are important in building up a good relationship with a service user, but there are important differences and it is the differences that ensure that the relationship is not only positive and trusting but also professional.

Self-disclosure

With friends and family it is natural to talk about yourself and share information. Within a work setting it can be different. One important difference in the building of a relationship whilst maintaining professional boundaries is that in a work setting it is not appropriate to tell the service user personal information about yourself. Telling the service user about your personal life can turn the focus away from the client and their needs towards your issues, which can be distracting. Telling the service user how you feel about a particular situation might add to their anxieties or be used to put you in a difficult situation.

Time to reflect

Discuss with a partner what boundaries are and why they are so important for a worker in a mental health care setting.

Evidence Activity

4.1 **Activity 2**

The NMC Code: Standards of Conduct, Performance and Ethics for Nurses and Midwives (2008) gives the following guidelines on maintaining professional boundaries. Discuss with a partner why they are important and what could happen if these particular boundaries are not kept.

18. You must refuse any gifts, favours or hospitality that might be interpreted as an attempt to gain preferential treatment.
19. You must not ask for or accept loans from anyone in your care or anyone close to them.
20. You must establish and actively maintain clear sexual boundaries at all times with people in your care, their families and carers.

Positive attitude and hopefulness and the importance of relationships for promoting or maintaining wellbeing and mental health

Good mental health means that we are hopeful and positive about life, and we need to be around people who encourage that hope and positivity if we are to maintain that feeling of wellbeing.

Irvin Yalom, a renowned American psychotherapist, (1995) identifies eleven factors that help clients receiving psychotherapy, and one of these is the 'instillation of hope'. The therapist is able to hold on to the belief that the client can improve their situation and resolve problems even when the client can't.

It is likely that many people with mental health problems feel disempowered, unable to change their situations and improve their prospects for a better life. If their illness has been long term it may be that those around them, family and friends, have little hope of things improving. The nature of many mental illnesses, such as depression, means that sufferers have negative thoughts and feel both hopeless and helpless (Donnelly, Parkinson and Williams, 2009). Working with service users who have no hope and whose outlook on life is entirely negative can be draining and the worker might find themselves feeling similarly hopeless. It is hard to be positive when we are surrounded by negativity.

Being positive and hopeful does not mean that we have to try to force people to smile and laugh and think positively. That would be very irritating for them, but more importantly it would communicate that we are not listening and not understanding their concerns. Listening to someone talk about their lives and their problems sensitively and showing them that we are listening and able to empathise with their feelings is essential. In order to build a positive relationship with someone who has very low self-esteem and is negative about anything changing we need to hold within us the attitude and belief that people do have the ability to make changes if they have the right support. Bonham (2004, p. 34) suggests that optimism or hope is not about 'people getting better or cured, it is about them being able to manage a little better, or a little less badly, within their own environment'.

> **Evidence Activity**
>
> **Activity 3**
>
> Discuss with a partner what happens when a teacher or parent tells you:
>
> - You've always been lazy and you'll never amount to anything.
> - That they believe you are capable of doing really well in your exams

Self-awareness

In order to be able to communicate successfully with others we need to know ourselves. We need to be aware of the impact that we might be having on the person we are talking to. There are so many factors that might affect the success of any interaction; our way of speaking; our mood; our clothes; our tone of voice; the level of eye contact we are giving. All these and many more might have an impact on the other person and make them more or less willing to communicate with us.

So often an interaction can be affected by our own personal issues clashing with someone else's. In order to communicate effectively, we need to be able to put aside our own concerns and give our full attention to the person we are listening to.

Imagine this scenario: a care worker in a mental health setting comes into work feeling very stressed about his daughter who has become very withdrawn and has started locking herself away in her room. He is concerned about her self-harming as she has been covering her arms in spite of the hot weather. He is doing an assessment of a new in-patient who has a long history of self-harm and has just attempted suicide. How might this affect the way that he communicates with this new patient? He might lose his non-judgemental and empathetic stance because he imagines his daughter in the same situation. He might not be listening carefully enough to the service user because he is thinking about his daughter.

If we are able to put aside our own concerns and separate out our issues and current problems from those of others, we are more able to be fully present for them. We will be able to give them our full attention without distractions, enabling them to feel valued and heard.

Sometimes a mental health worker will feel completely exhausted, physically or emotionally and often both. It is very important that we recognise times when we find it hard to communicate effectively because of emotional 'overload'. We can feel 'full up' and unable to give the space and time to service users that they need. We might make mistakes, speak rudely or not listen carefully enough. At times like this we need to be honest with ourselves and our colleagues and make sure that we have some time to recharge our batteries. A good line manager or supervisor will be alert to the times when the staff in their care are reaching this point and make sure that there are times when the worker can take some time out or be able to talk about the difficulties they are experiencing.

It is also important to know our limitations and not expect to be able to sort everything out and help everyone. A patient in a hospital who has attempted suicide might come to a worker and want to talk about very difficult issues or make a disclosure about their life. If we feel out of our depth or know that the patient should be talking to another professional we need to have the confidence to ask for help.

Evidence Activity

 4.1 **Activity 4**

Do a SWOB analysis in which you identify your Strengths and Weaknesses, Opportunities and Barriers.

Strengths

- What are you good at?
- What about yourself are you happy with?
- How do you get on with other people?
- What approaches do you take to life?
- What have you achieved in your life so far? What does this tell you about your strengths?
- What experiences have you had that provide a foundation for your course/work placement?

Weaknesses

- What would I like to change about myself?
- What things have not been successful?
- What things have I not achieved that I wanted to by now?
- What disappointments have I had that affect the ways I think about the future?

Opportunities

- What is available within the course/work placement to help me?
- Who can help me?
- What support do I have that will help me?

Barriers

- What actual obstacles are there to me achieving what I want? E.g. time limitations, travel, family commitments, financial concerns.
- What perceived obstacles are there to me achieving what I want? E.g. Ideas you have about yourself like 'I'm bad at writing essays'.

Jasper M (2003).

Working together as equal partners

The government's white paper entitled No Health Without Mental Health emphasises the importance of 'putting the person at the centre and sharing decision making'. It states that the principle 'No decision about me without me' should be a governing principle in service design and delivery (HM Government, 2011, p. 32). It is essential that service users feel that they are equal partners with the mental health worker when it comes to making decisions about their lives. A positive relationship is built on trust and the service user needs to know that you have their best interests at heart. However, it would be unrealistic to imagine that all service users are free to do exactly as they wish, especially those in institutional settings. There are always restrictions and health professionals might have strong ideas about what kinds of treatment are necessary for a service user. Nonetheless, the principle that the service user is a 'member of their own care team' should never be swept aside (Bonham, 2004, p. 54). It is important to try to give the service user choice, even when choices are limited. They need to know that they have the power to make some decisions, even if that is just about what activity they are going to do or what meal they are going to have that lunch time. It is important to try to involve the service user in their care as much as possible. The knowledge that their opinions and likes and dislikes are valued and taken notice of is hugely important especially when they often feel disempowered and isolated.

It is true that some people with mental health problems might find it extremely challenging to make a decision or be involved in their own care. They might find choice stressful and actively want others to make decisions for them. In situations like this it is important to quietly and gently encourage their involvement by offering only two choices and reassuring the service user that they can change their mind.

Evidence Activity

 4.1 Activity 5

Download a copy of No Health Without Mental Health from the Department of Health's website. Read page 32 entitled 'Principles of High Quality Care'.

2 Define communication and the reasons why we communicate

- Communication is an active process that requires reciprocity by both communication partners and involves the passing of verbal and non-verbal messages (Cooper et al., 2005, cited in Donnelly and Neville, 2008).
- Communication is a process in which individuals interact with and through symbols to create and interpret meaning (Wood, 2004).
- Communication is any interaction that takes place between people (Donnelly and Neville, 2008).

It is clear from these definitions that communication is not solely reliant on speech but on a complex interplay of language, gesture and facial expression. It is further influenced by the context of both the environment and the culture of the people involved in the interaction. It is important to be able to distinguish between the different kinds of communication and to understand how each will affect the interaction between two or more people.

Evidence Activity

 4.2 Activity

Write a list of the different ways in which you communicate with others in your daily life.

3 Identify different kinds of communication

There are three main kinds of communication to consider:

- Inter-personal communication: that which takes place between people.
- Environmental communication: that which takes place within our environment.
- Intra-personal communication: that which takes place within ourselves.

(Donnelly and Neville, 2008)

Inter-personal communication

There are three main kinds of inter-personal communication which come together to create a particular kind of interaction:

1. verbal
2. non-verbal
3. paralinguistic.

Verbal

It is true that we do not need words to communicate and many people either cannot use words or choose not to. However, for most of us, language is central to our existence as human beings. So language, whether it be spoken or signed, is the vehicle for allowing us to express who we are and how we relate to those around us.

The way that we use language, our verbal communication, can be complex. When considering the importance of verbal communication with people with mental health issues we need to be aware of the impact of our choice of language on them. Words and phrases can have an explicit or surface meaning, and an implicit or hidden meaning. The relationships that you will have with people in the work setting will be dependent on how well you can relate to them and so it is essential to remember that the context of the words spoken can depend on so many different things:

- the way they are said
- where they are said
- who says them
- and who hears them.

Language is subjective and people may attach different meanings to the same message depending on their experience, environment, age, gender, culture, even what might have happened to them five minutes ago (Adler et al., 2007).

Paralinguistic

Paralinguistic communication refers to the different ways we might moderate our speech according to the situation. The pitch, tone, volume, rhythm and timing as well as grunts, ahs, and ums can greatly affect how verbal communication might be perceived. Hargie (2011, p. 81) says 'How information is delivered paralinguistically has important consequences for how much of the message is understood, recalled and acted on'. Awareness of what message our tone is communicating can help us to avoid difficult situations, and being aware of the mismatch between word and tone is very important (Culley and Bond, 2006).

Non verbal

Non-verbal communication is visual rather than linguistic and can often be more effective than words alone. 'Nonverbal communication contributes a great deal to shaping perceptions'

(Adler et al., 2007, p. 147). In building positive relationships we have to be aware of what message our non-verbal communication is conveying. Eye contact, body language, facial expressions, gestures, inter-personal space, touch and smell are all important ways of communicating meaning and can completely change the impact of words if two are at odds with one another. It is essential to be aware of the non-verbal communication of people we work with as it often gives us more information than the words they use, particularly when the person is in distress and is unable to find the words to express themselves or, in some cases, fearful of using words.

Environmental communication

It is extremely important to consider the environment in which we communicate and how it might affect an interaction. Someone working in a health setting might have to see people in quite clinical surroundings and this can make some people feel uncomfortable.

Figure 4.1 A health setting may not be the best place for counselling

Time to reflect

Think about how the following environments communicate with the people in them: How might they help or hinder effective communication?

- A police station
- A doctor's surgery
- A head teacher's office

Intra-personal communication

On a simple level, intra-personal communication might be the argument we have with ourselves when we know we should go to the gym.

'I'm exhausted, I can't be bothered today.'

'I haven't been for two weeks – I should go.'

On a deeper level, it is more complicated than that. The internal workings of our minds are complex and much of the time we can be completely unaware of the inner discourse that goes on when we are interacting with others. We all come to every relationship with our own thoughts, feelings, beliefs, values and experiences and every interaction we have will be determined by what is going on for us internally. It is essential to be aware of how our internal world might be influencing our interactions with others and, in turn, be aware of how their internal world is affecting how they are interacting with us. A person with mental health problems might have distorted thoughts which will further influence what is going on for them internally and how they might respond to you.

Evidence Activity

 Activity

Over the next week, keep a diary of the different interactions you have with different people and write a short description of how the interaction made you feel.

For example: 'Spoke to my tutor about being late for lessons – I was quite nervous and then upset because he didn't look at me while he spoke – he was going through papers and cut me off, saying he didn't care why I was late – that I would fail the module if I missed any more time.'

In addition to this, it is important to establish the needs of the individual with respect to how they wish to communicate. An investigation into the preferences of the person needs to be undertaken and specialist services contacted if necessary. We deal with this later on in the chapter.

4 Explain how to build positive relationships using principles from theories about communication

The person-centred approach

This approach was developed by Carl Rogers, a psychologist and therapist working in America in the latter half of the twentieth century (Casemore, 2006). It is an approach which is used in one form or another in a variety of settings and certainly the fundamental principles form the foundations of most therapeutic approaches. Rogers believed passionately in the importance of listening to clients' experiences and developing a trusting relationship with them which would enable them to grow and cope with their difficulties and function more effectively.

Rogers (1951) suggests that that there are three core conditions required in a therapeutic relationship:

Unconditional positive regard: the helper accepts and values the client with warmth and without judgement. The feeling of being judged is very strong in many people, particularly those with mental health problems. It is natural to put up barriers when we feel we are judged and to hide our feelings or deny them altogether. The experience of talking to someone who doesn't judge us can be very powerful and can enable us, in time, to allow ourselves to feel difficult, uncomfortable and sometimes frightening feelings which we keep hidden. Rogers (1967) says that unconditional positive regard 'involves an acceptance of and caring for the client as a "separate" person, with permission for him to have his own feelings and experiences, and to find his own meanings in them'.

Empathy: an empathetic understanding of the client's internal reference. To have empathy for someone is the willingness to understand what it might be like to live in their shoes. To walk alongside someone and have a strong sense of how they experience life. It is not sympathy and it is not saying that you know what they are going through because you've been through it too. It is a willingness to understand their own unique experiences and feelings and to be able to reflect that understanding back to them so that they feel understood.

Congruence: the helper is genuine, honest and true. To be congruent with someone is to be completely honest and without pretence. It is important when listening to someone who is full of difficult feelings; who is confused and has learnt to defend themselves against painful feelings, that as a helper we should be as open as possible. We need to be able to respond to the people in our care in an honest and real way.

Transactional analysis

Transactional analysis (TA) was created and developed by Eric Berne in the 1950s and it became very popular in the 1960s. Transactional analysis is a theory of how personality is structured in the ego state model which helps us understand and analyse communication and interactions between people. Transactional analysis is a way of looking at what goes on between people – inter-personal communication, and what goes on inside people – intra-personal communication. It is a way of studying and making sense of intra-personal and inter-personal relationships.

Personality structure

When people communicate with each other they do so from three ego states called parent, adult and child.

The *parent* ego state is divided into nurturing parent and controlling parent (Stewart and Joines, 1987).

The *adult* ego state is logical and able to solve problems. When we are in our adult ego state we are thinking and feeling in an appropriate way for the situation we are in and the child and parent ego states do not interfere with the process. The adult ego state is not divided.

In the *child* ego state we act like we did when we were children. The child ego state is divided into free child and adapted child (Stewart and Joines, 1987). When we are in child ego state we are creative, spontaneous and also naughty.

Throughout the day we can make many shifts from one ego state to another, often depending on the ego state that other people are in (Berne, 1961).

An understanding of TA can be useful for the mental health worker in that it helps us to understand why some interactions are more successful than others and it reminds us to stay within the adult ego state when working with service users who might be talking to us from their parent or child ego state.

The cognitive behavioural approach

This is an approach developed by Aaron Beck in the early 1960s and is the most widely used approach in mental health settings. There is a wealth of evidence-based research suggesting that it is an effective way of helping people to understand and control their behaviour (Bonham, 2004). This approach encourages service users to become more aware of how their thinking affects their feelings and behaviour and shows them how to identify unhelpful, irrational and distorted thoughts and replace them with more flexible, accurate and evidence-based ones (Neenan and Dryden, 2006).

Motivational interviewing

This approach was created by William Miller in 1983 and came from his work with people with substance misuse disorders. It uses principles from both person-centred and behavioural approaches in that it encourages behavioural changes in people whilst respecting their personal values and beliefs and their willingness to change. Motivational interviewing focuses on the service user's ambivalent feelings around changing their behaviour. Together, service user and therapist work at identifying and examining cause of the ambivalence, then work together at the service user's own pace to resolve the issues around the ambivalence.

The psychodynamic approach

There are numerous ways that psychodynamic approaches are practised and the majority have their foundations in the writings of Sigmund Freud who practised in the latter half of the nineteenth century (Howard, 2006). At the core of any psychodynamic approach is an interest in the unconscious processes of the mind. Therapists working in a psychodynamic way are concerned with our inner world which is made up of feelings, memories, beliefs and fantasies. One of the aims of the therapist is to make more of our minds available to us so that we can understand more about what motivates us and therefore have more freedom to make choices about how we act (Howard, 2006).

Solution-focused brief therapy

This approach was developed in the 1980s by Steve de Shazer and Insoo Kim Berg and aims at bringing about change through finding a preferred future rather than focusing on problems. The therapist works with the service user and helps them to look for what they do have rather than what they don't have. They encourage them to look for the possibilities in their life and on identifying a preferred future. They then help them to see what is already contributing to the future they want. The relationship is important and the therapist doesn't deny the problems in the service user's life, they simply see the person and resources they have more than they see the problem (Nelson-Jones, 2011).

The systemic approach

This approach, closely linked to family therapy, is very different from all the above in that it focuses not on the intra-personal processes of an individual but on the inter-personal processes. This approach sees the service user as part of a wider system, usually the family, and emphasises family relationships as an important part of psychological health. The Milan Team, a group of Italian psychotherapists working in the 1980s, developed Family Systems Therapy and worked with the identified patient together with their family. The therapy is carried out by a team of therapists and aims to help bring about change by highlighting the role of the family or other members of the client's system in problem resolution (Hedges, 2009).

> **Evidence Activity**
>
> **Activity**
>
> Find out which approaches to therapy are used by your local mental health service.

5 Apply key communication skills to build and sustain relationships in a mental health context

How to initiate communication

Initiating conversation can be difficult. We all have our comfort zones; some are happy to strike up a conversation with a stranger, others will avoid making eye contact, let alone start talking.

Initiating conversation is an important first stage in building up a relationship. Sometimes this will be straightforward if the service user is happy to chat or initiates conversation themselves. However, there will be times when the service user is reluctant to talk. Someone who is depressed and withdrawn might not want any interaction and someone who is very anxious might find it extremely hard to talk to someone they don't know.

If you are approaching a service user that you don't know, it is important to say who you are and what your role is and to ask if it's ok for you to join them for a bit. If they do not react, or say no, it is a good idea to withdraw a bit but to stay near and get on with something like reading a paper, book or magazine. This indicates that you are available if they do want to talk but that you are not invading their space. If they still don't want to talk you could get up and leave, saying 'See you later ...' which leaves an opening for you to return later on (Bonham, 2004).

> **Evidence Activity**
>
> **Activity 1**
>
> With a partner, role-play a situation where one of you approaches the other and initiates conversation. Discuss how each of you felt and try a different approach if it felt awkward. Write some tips for a new worker on how to initiate communication.

Active listening skills

We have all experienced times in our lives when it seems as if our problems will overwhelm us and we need to talk to someone who we hope will help or at least listen and empathise. There are also times when we are really happy or proud about something and really want to talk about it. If we turn to someone who hasn't got the time to listen to us or who starts to talk about their own problems or achievements, sweeping ours away, it can really affect our mood and ability or willingness to talk any more. Not being listened to can leave us feeling unimportant, invisible, angry and worthless. Listening is absolutely essential if we are going to communicate effectively with the people in our care. If we can show someone that we are really listening to them rather than simply hearing them, we are already communicating effectively. In order to show that we are really listening and that we are empathetic, non-judgemental and genuine, we need to use active listening skills (Culley and Bond, 2006). The following skills are particularly important:

- eye contact and body language
- acknowledging and reflecting feelings
- summarising
- questioning
- using silence.

Eye contact and body language

Eye contact and body language are key non verbal indicators that someone is listening to you and paying attention to what you are saying. When talking to someone it is important that you keep eye contact with them to show that they have your full attention. It is not a good idea to stare at them intensely as this can make them feel uncomfortable. Your eyes will naturally break contact with theirs every couple of seconds as it does with a conversation you have with a friend.

There are times when some service users will find it very hard to maintain eye contact with you, especially if they are very anxious or uncomfortable. Sometimes a person's low self-esteem can make it feel almost impossible to maintain eye contact. Their feelings of worthlessness make it hard for them to accept that another person is taking an interest in them. It is important not to increase their discomfort by constant eye contact but to settle on what is comfortable whilst still letting them know that you are listening closely.

Body language is very important and can tell us a lot. If we approach someone and they are curled up, covering their face, we may assume that they are closing themselves off to contact. It is equally important for us to be aware of our own body language and think of what messages it is sending. It is important to maintain an open posture (Culley and Bond, 2006). Crossed arms and legs can suggest that you are closed off to the person you are talking to. If talking to someone who is sitting, it is important for you to be sitting too. You need to look relaxed, and your body should be angled towards the person, giving them enough personal space but being close enough to show you are listening to them attentively. If you are sitting, your chairs should be angled towards each other rather than squarely opposite as that could feel like an interrogation. It is sometimes best with eye contact and body language to try to mirror the person you are talking to whilst encouraging openness. If they are sitting almost horizontally in the chair, head back, needing to relax and think, it is more appropriate to relax back in your chair too.

Acknowledging and reflecting feelings and being open to ideas

There may be times when a service user wants to talk to about experiences or situations that are very important to them. It is important to validate what they are saying by showing that you have really heard what they have said and that you empathise with them when they feel strongly about what they are telling you. Equally, being open to new ideas or new information they give you will help to build rapport and trust. They may express strong feelings or they may keep those feelings hidden. In any situation, it is important to show them that you empathise with those feelings by acknowledging and reflecting them back. If they have just told you about an argument they have had with a family member you could say something like 'It sounds like it was really difficult to get your point over, that must have been frustrating'.

The most obvious way of acknowledging feelings is to ask directly. Sometimes they will simply tell you and you can go on to explore that. Often, they may shrug their shoulders and say 'I dunno'. They might say that they don't care or they might give a very watered down version of their real feelings. They might say what they think you want to hear. In situations like these it is important not to tell the service user how you think they are feeling, but it is possible to tentatively offer an idea of how they might be feeling. For example:

'I'm wondering if you're feeling angry about what happened this morning?'

'It sounds like you're feeling sad about what happened with your wife.'

'I'm guessing it would have been pretty frightening when you heard your parents talking about you like that.'

The service user has to be given the opportunity to accept or reject those feelings. They might reply 'No, I'm not sad, I'm more angry than sad' and so through the process of exploring those feelings you are enabling then to understand them more clearly.

Evidence Activity

4.5 **Activity 4**

Think of five words which you could use instead of the following feeling words:

- Angry
- Sad
- Happy
- Afraid

Paraphrasing and summarising

Paraphrasing is the skill of rephrasing the important parts of what you have heard someone say. It is a way of showing that you understand their point of view. In using this skill you will:

- check your understanding of what they have said
- communicate the core qualities of acceptance and empathetic understanding
- gain information about how they see themselves and their concerns
- build a trusting relationship (Culley and Bond, 2006).

You need to be accurate when paraphrasing and sometimes you might get it wrong, so if you are not sure, you can offer the paraphrase tentatively using phrases like 'It sounds like ...' or 'It seems that ...' or 'I'm wondering if I've got that right'.

An example of paraphrasing would be:

Service user: 'I get so angry whenever I talk to my partner, it's like he doesn't listen to me at all. Then I go to work and everyone gets on my nerves. I lose my temper, I take it out on them and they start to ignore me.'

Helper: 'It sounds like it's hard to contain your anger and that ends up with you being ignored by your partner and your colleagues.'

Summaries are longer paraphrases and enable you to bring together the important aspects of what the service user has said in an organised way (Culley and Bond, 2006). Quite often a service user might want to talk about many things that are causing them distress. They might talk in quite a chaotic way, jumping from one subject to another, digressing and changing their tone of voice. This can make it quite difficult to follow but it's often a reflection of the chaos in their lives and their swiftly changing moods. Summarising is useful when the conversation is coming to an end or when they've talked for quite a long time as it can help you and the service user clarify what is going on for them. It can also serve to organise and prioritise what the problems and issues are.

Here is an example of a summary that a helper uses after talking to a service user who is distressed about numerous relationships:

> 'So it sounds like your problems are overwhelming you. You boyfriend has finished with you. Your friends are really unsupportive and seem to be siding with him. Work is piling on the pressure and you feel like they aren't going to continue supporting you through this difficult time, and on top of that you aren't sure that your doctor has got your medication right. I'm wondering which of these feels like it's taking up the most space in your head at the moment?'

Culley and Bond (2006) offer the following guidelines for paraphrasing and summarising:

- Be tentative and offer your perception of what the client has said.
- Avoid telling, informing or defining the client.
- Be respectful, do not judge, dismiss or use sarcasm.
- Use your own words; repeating verbatim may seem like mimicry.
- Listen to the depth of feeling expressed and match the level in your response.
- Do not add to what the client says, evaluate it or offer interpretations.
- Be congruent and don't pretend you understand.
- Be brief and direct.
- Keep your voice tone level. Paraphrasing in a shocked or disbelieving tone is unlikely to communicate either acceptance or empathy.

> **Evidence Activity**
>
>  **Activity 5**
>
> Write out a conversation between a service user with anxiety and a mental health worker in which the skills of paraphrasing and summarising are used.

Using questions and sharing information

There are so many different kinds of questions which elicit so many different responses that it can be difficult to know what to ask and what impact the questioning might have on a service user who might be confused and distressed. In my first year of training as a counsellor I was discouraged from asking any questions at all because it is so important for a client to be able to talk about their problems without being led or directed by questions. It is surprising how much one can learn by simply using reflection and paraphrasing. However, when working in mental health care settings it is inevitable that we will ask the service user questions. It is important that thought goes into what kind of question are asked. They should not be too challenging, they should be tentative and invite the service user to talk as fully as possible about what is going on for them (Bonham, 2004).

There are two main kinds of questions: open and closed (Culley and Bond, 2006).

Open questions – these are often questions which beginning with 'what', 'where', 'how' and 'who'. These are the most useful kinds of questions as they involve the service user more and encourage exploration and thoughtfulness. Try to avoid 'why' questions as they put pressure on the service user to justify their position.

Closed questions – these invite the service user to answer 'yes' or 'no', they are non-exploratory and tend to shut the conversation down.

In general it is better to use open questions, but with people who find it difficult to express themselves or who are shy or reluctant it is advisable to use closed questions at the beginning because they are much less threatening and complex and they can enable you to at least get a sense of what is going on for them. As they feel more comfortable it is likely that they will give fuller, more detailed answers and at this point you are able to share more information with the client. As they become more comfortable with the process a dialogue can be established which leads to a more two-way process of eliciting and imparting information.

Evidence Activity

4.5 Activity 6

Write down three open questions which invite further exploration and three closed questions which close conversation down.

Listening to silence

Silence can be awkward or threatening and uncomfortable but we can learn a lot from what people do not say as well as from do what they do say (Culley and Bond, 2006). It is important to allow silences when we are listening to someone. It is natural in normal conversation to try to fill silences, but in a therapeutic relationship it is essential to allow space for the person to process their thoughts. Imagine a conversation with someone with suicidal thoughts who has started to explore their feelings with you. It is important not to jump in as soon as they have paused for breath but to wait for a few seconds as they may have something to add to what they have just said. It might be the case that whatever they have added has great significance and invites further exploration (Bonham, 2004).

It's possible that they will come to you obviously in distress but saying very little. When this happens it might well be enough for them to have a safe place to think, in the presence of someone who is trusted and undemanding. We can show that we are emotionally available to them by our non-verbal communication, our open and relaxed body language, our attentiveness through eye contact and the occasional encouragment like a smile or a nod. It might be that they never open up but that they still seek you out – it's important to trust that they are benefitting from being with you even when you are not actually communicating verbally.

Ending the communication well

Ending a conversation well is as important as initiating it. If a conversation is ended abruptly or insensitively it can leave the person you are talking with the feeling that they have not been heard properly or that what they have said has not been valued.

As a mental health worker you will inevitably be busy and have to use your time carefully. You might not have an unlimited amount of time to talk to service users, but it is important to be respectful and sensitive when you know that you have to move on to another task. Here are some tips to help you to do this:

- Try to set the time boundaries at the beginning of the conversation. 'I really want to hear about that – I need to go to a meeting in 10 minutes but can you tell me about it and if we run out of time, I'll come back after the meeting.'
- Find an appropriate pause in the conversation to remind the service user that you'll have to go.
- If you do run out of time, reassure the service user that you will return to finish the conversation and give them an approximate time.
- When you are about to go, try to summarise what the service user has said so that they know that you have been listening.
- Go over any important points in the conversation, especially if you or they have said that you are going to do something before you next see each other.

Being non-judgemental and maintaining realistic expectations

We meet all sorts of people in mental health work and may deal with some individuals who engage in behaviour we may find difficult to understand. In some cases we feel disbelief at the actions of a person or simply saddened at their plight. In these circumstances it is important to maintain a non-judgemental stance and be realistic about the outcomes we and the individual can expect.

Often the individual already feels that society has judged them and they present for treatment because they have carried the hidden trauma of such judgements. We all have biases and judgments but can overcome these by applying more self-reflection and working on your own feelings about situations. Humans seek acceptance and understanding and also lead very complex lives. We are not so very different form the people we meet; we are just more fortunate to be able to handle the traumas thrown our way. In developing our relationships and helping the individual in our care we need to adopt a compassionate stance and be realistic about the outcomes they can expect from the interaction they have with us.

> **Evidence Activity**
>
> **Activity 7**
>
> Discuss with a partner why it might be important for a support worker in a hospital to sit quietly with a patient who is crying and obviously distressed but who hasn't told you why. How might you then leave that patient in a sensitive way?

6 Explain how mental health problems may impact on an individual's ability or wish to communicate and form relationships, and common barriers to communication and relationships between service users, carers/family members and mental health workers and how these may be overcome

Sometimes it is really difficult to establish a good rapport with someone or it might feel as if you have been listening but haven't really heard them. There are many ways in which communication can be blocked and it is important to be aware of the blocks and barriers to good communication.

Some blocks might be external ones like:

- tiredness
- hunger
- feeling ill
- noise
- inappropriate environment
- personal hygiene.

In overcoming such barriers and with most physical and environmental blocks it is usually enough to be aware and responsive to them. Being open and honest is important – pretending that you are listening or that you have heard someone can be damaging to the relationship. Simply saying to a service user that you are finding it really hard to listen because of background noise and suggesting you go somewhere else or that you do a different activity is so much better than struggling on and risking them feeling that their concerns weren't being heard.

Other blocks and barriers might be internal and often more complex to negotiate:

- conflicting opinions
- powerful emotions
- personality clashes
- your past experiences
- unrealistic expectations
- issues of power and control
- overload
- getting upset about what the service user is saying
- trying to find solutions
- feelings of inadequacy
- difficulties in your life
- feeling unsafe
- differences in culture
- stereotyping, assumptions and prejudice.

This is where your own self-awareness is so important. It is essential to be aware of how events in your own life are affecting you so that you can avoid responding to the service user or a colleague from your own frame of reference. Equally we should always try to be aware of their frame of reference. This is particularly relevant when working with people with abnormal perceptions like schizophrenia. Communication with people with schizophrenia can be difficult as it is important to not to dismiss their delusional beliefs but equally not to reinforce or collude with them (Bonham, 2004).

Sometimes the service user might be abusive or have views that are abhorrent to you. It is hard not to react to someone's prejudiced views but it's important to be non-judgemental and not be drawn into conflict. Remember that we can show empathy without having to agree with or like what the service user is saying.

There may be times when someone is telling you things that upset you or cause you to worry about how to respond to them. They might well be asking you to sort their problems out for them. Perhaps you feel overwhelmed by what they are saying and feel you can't respond. In these situations you have to remember to use active listening skills. A carer's role is not to fix their problems, it is to listen and help people to find their own solutions.

We live in a multi-cultural society and will inevitably have to consider the cultural and ethnic background of the service users just as they will be treated by and cared for by workers from different cultural and ethnic backgrounds. Different cultures might view mental illness in different ways. You might be caring for someone with no English and find communication very difficult. It is important to remember that although they may not understand your verbal communication, they still understand and respond to the non-verbal communication of respect and warmth. There might be a temptation or a tendency to stereotype certain people because of their race, culture or gender. Whatever someone's background, ethnicity, culture, age, gender or sexual orientation, it is essential to remember that they are individuals and should be listened to and responded to without prejudice.

Evidence Activity

 Activity

Think of a time when you found it very difficult to communicate with someone.

- Describe what the situation was and why you found it difficult.
- Describe your feelings and thoughts while the interaction took place.
- Describe what you and they said and did.
- How else might you have handled that situation?

7 Evaluate the potential contribution to communication and relationship building of the following main sources of specialist support and explain how to access extra support or services to enable individuals to communicate effectively

Interpreters or translators

An interpreter is someone who works with spoken language and a translator is someone who works with written language. It is more likely that workers in mental health settings will need the help of an interpreter.

A carer's inability to communicate effectively might be due more to the service user not speaking English or not being able to use spoken English because of a disability. One of the main features of therapeutic communication is the relationship between the service user and the carer and the rapport and trust that is built up between them. Most good relationships are reliant on good interpersonal communication and this is immediately hindered by language barriers. Sometimes it will be necessary to use an interpreter with a service user who does not speak English. Interpreting is essential if non-English speakers are to gain access to mental health services and not offering this service could be seen as discriminatory (Smith, 2008). The same is true of deaf service users who are reliant on signing. The job of the interpreter is complex as they need to know two languages well and be able to interpret both the spoken word and the tone and pace of the worker and service user. They act as interpreters, not only of language, but also of cultural information. It is very hard to find interpreters who can work therapeutically alongside the worker and sometimes it will be necessary to use family members or friends or people with little knowledge of mental health issues, and so breakdown in communication still occurs.

Speech therapy

Communication can also be hindered if the service user is unable to use spoken language because of a disability and they are reliant on communication aids or equipment. It might be necessary to gain the help of a speech and language therapist who will work with the service user to help them to express themselves and help other carers to communicate more effectively with them. Service users with dementia often suffer from language deficit, such as difficulties with understanding, reasoning, talking and memory. With other forms of mental illness such as bipolar disorder there may be no change to language skills but a reduction in non-verbal communication and changes in social interaction can occur.

The Association of Speech and Language Therapists states that speech therapists in mental health settings will perform a number of services to help support mental health professionals and patients. They might carry out communication assessments and give guidance to mental health professionals. They might run group therapy focusing on social skills for patients, encouraging their non-verbal skills, their assertiveness and problem-solving skills. They might run groups for older patients targeting communications skills through reminiscence and validation therapy. (http://www.helpwithtalking.com/speech-issues/mental-health)

Psychologists

The role of the psychologist should not be confused with the role of a psychiatrist. A psychiatrist is qualified as a medical doctor and is able to prescribe medicines. A psychologist works in mental health settings, both in hospitals and within a community mental health team. The psychologist sees patients who have been referred by GPs or by a mental health team and will assess the mental health needs of a patient and carry out appropriate psychological therapies with that patient and sometimes their families. The psychologist can support the mental health worker by suggesting particular approaches to building and sustaining relationships. For example, the psychologist might be using cognitive behavioural therapy with a service user who has severe anxiety and finds it very difficult to communicate with anyone outside their family.

Advocacy

Advocacy in mental health settings is particularly important in that it ensures that people within the mental health system are able to speak out and express themselves. Unfortunately it is sometimes the case that people with mental health problems are overlooked and their ideas and opinions are ignored or not taken seriously. An advocate would work with a service user supporting and enabling them to:

- express their views and concerns
- access information and services
- defend and promote their rights and services
- explore choices and options.

An advocate might attend meetings or appointments with the service user and help them to express their ideas, needs and concerns in an unbiased way. Sometimes friends or family members might have particular ideas about the care of their relative or might not agree with or approve of their actions or attitudes towards certain things. The advocate is there to express the wishes of the service user without judging them or expressing their own personal opinion.

An example of where advocacy might be used is in a hospital where a person with psychosis is being treated without understanding what the treatment plan is. The advocate might help to explain the treatment or they might ensure that the service user is being cared for in a way that is appropriate to their religious or cultural background.

Communication aids and equipment

Communication is a basic human right (Jones, 2002) but people with learning disabilities often have communication difficulties and are dependent on professional intervention to help them to communicate. If this is not available it can lead to frustration, anger, feelings of isolation, depression and challenging behaviour. Often speech and language therapists will be involved in assessing a service user's communications needs and will suggest appropriate communication methods and aids. These might include the following:

- High-tech Augmentative and Alternative Communication (AAC), including Voice Output Communication Aids (VOCAs).

  These are electronic devices that generate spoken language through eye or head pointing. Some are single message devices onto which a spoken message is recorded and then played back.
- Objects of reference.

  These are used to communicate to the person with a learning disability what is about to happen or to offer choices. On a basic level showing the service user a certain cup will signal that they are being offered a drink. A more abstract object might be a remote control to symbolise the offer to watch television.
- PECS Picture Exchange Communication System.

  This was originally designed for children with autism but has become more widely used. PECS encourages the use of pictures to communicate what a person wants.
- Communication passports.

  Quite often a person with profound learning disabilities will have their own way of communicating through gesture or voice which is understood by family members or very familiar people. A communication passport is put together to enable those people who are new to working with the person with communication needs to understand more about them and how they might be communicating (Goldbart and Caton, 2010).

Figure 4.2 Picture exchange communication system

8 Ways to maintain confidentiality in day-to-day communication and the potential tension between maintaining confidentiality and disclosing concerns

Confidentiality is the ethical principle of holding 'secret all information relating to a patient, unless the patient gives consent permitting disclosure' (http://medical-dictionary.thefreedictionary.com/confidentiality).

The relationship between the care worker and the client is always one of trust and staff are expected to maintain confidences obtained in their work. The clients in our care have a right for us to keep their personal information confidential and not pass information to third parties without their consent. It is imperative then that any information we have is kept in secure files or in computer records that are only accessible to those who are involved in the clients care.

The law underpinning the requirements for confidentiality is the Data Protection Act. This act gives individuals the right to access personal information that is kept about them. For carers, the act does not give automatic rights to access all personal information about the person you are caring for. This is only on a need to know basis.

For individuals who lack the mental capacity to make their own decisions it may be necessary to see information held about them and it is then up to the authority who holds such information to consider the issues involved. Although they have a duty of confidentiality to the person who lacks the mental capacity, if disclosing that information to the carer or relative is in the individual's best interests they may need to do so. It is in these circumstances when tensions arise and it may be necessary to break confidentiality.

Breaching confidentiality is usually only appropriate in extreme circumstances such as:

- to report or prevent a crime
- to report malpractice
- to report suspected child abuse
- to prevent suicide
- to report professional misconduct
- to prevent terrorism.

A breach of confidentiality outside of these instances can be met by disciplinary action by an employer and/or legal action by clients for damages.

In daily communication with clients and other members of staff an important consideration is to ensure that discussions do not breach confidentiality. The case of the nurse who divulged information about the royal client in her care to a radio presenter in 2012 had a major impact on all who were touched by the devastating outcomes.

As a care worker you need to be very clear about the confidentiality policy you work within and not open yourself up to confidentiality breaches by discussing clients openly in public areas.

Evidence Activity

 Activity

Get a copy of the confidentiality policy for your workplace and make some reflective notes on how to safeguard yourself against breaching confidentiality.

References

Adler, R, Rosenfeld, L, Proctor, R (2007) *Interplay – The Process of Interpersonal Communication.* Oxford: OUP.

Bannerjee, R (2205) *Cultural Differences in the Experience and Expression of Emotion. Social and Emotional Aspects of Learning: Guidance.* London: DfES.

Berne, E (1961) *Transactional Analysis in Psychotherapy.* New York: Grove Press.

Bond T, Culley, S (2004) *Integrative Counselling Skills in Action.* London: Sage Publications.

Bonham, P. (2004). *Communicating as a Mental Health Carer.* Cheltenham: Nelson Thornes.

British Association for Counselling and Psychotherapy (BACP) (2007) *Ethical Framework for Good Practice in Counselling and Psychotherapy.* Lutterworth: BACP.

Casemore, R (2006) *Person Centred Counselling in a Nutshell.* London: Sage.

Davies-Ward, E, Tilmouth, T, Williams, B (2011) *Foundation Degree in Health and Social Care.* London: Hodder Education.

DoH (2011) No Health Without Mental Health. Available at: http://www.dh.gov.uk/en/Publicationsandstatistics/Publications/PublicationsPolicyAndGuidance/DH_123766

Donnelly, E and Neville, L (2008) *Communication and Interpersonal Skills.* Devon, Reflect Press.

Donnelly, E, Parkinson, T, and Williams, B (2009) *Understanding and Helping People in Crisis.* Devon: Reflect Press.

Geldard K, and Geldard, D (2010) *Counselling Adolescents: The Proactive Approach for Young People.* London: Sage.

Goldbart, J and Caton, S (2010) *Communication and People with the Most Complex Needs and What Works.* London: MENCAP.

Hargie, O (2011) *Skilled Interpersonal Communication – Research Theory and Practice.* 5th edn. London: Routledge.

Hedges, F (2005) *An Introduction to Systemic Therapy with Individuals.* London: Sage.

Howard, S (2006) *Psychiatric Counselling in a Nutshell.* London: Sage.

Jasper, M (2003). *Beginning Reflective Practice.* Cheltenham: Nelson Thornes.

Jones, J (2002) *Factsheet Communication.* British Institute of Learning Difficulties: Worcestershire.

Koprowska, J (2010) *Communication and Interpersonal Skills in Social Work*. 3rd edn. Exeter: Learning Matters.

McLeod, J (2003) *An Introduction to Counselling*. 3rd edn. Berkshire: Open University Press.

National Autistic Society (2012) What is Autism? Available at: www.autism.org.uk.

Neenan, M, and Dryden, W (2006) *Cognitive Therapy in a Nutshell*. London: Sage.

Nelson-Jones, R (2011) *Theory and Practice in Counselling and Psychotherapy*. London: Sage.

Nursing and Midwifery Council (2008) *The Code: Standards of Conduct, Performance and Ethics for Nurses and Midwives*. London: NMC.

Rogers, C (1951) The necessary and sufficient conditions for therapeutic change. *Journal of Consulting Psychology*, 21: 95–103.

Rogers, C (1967) *On Becoming a Person: A Therapist's View of Psychotherapy*. London: Constable.

Smith, H C (2008) Bridging the gap: therapy through interpreters. *Therapy Today*, 19 (6), p. 21. Lutterworth, BACP.

Stewart, I and Joines, V (1987) *TA Today: A New Introduction to Transactional Analysis*. Melton Mowbray, Lifespace Publishing.

Wood, J. (2004). *Communication Theories in Action: An Introduction*. Belmont: Wadsworth/Thomson Learning.

Yalom, I (1995) *Theory and Practice of Group Psychotherapy*. New York: Basic Books.

The legal policy and service framework in relation to promoting wellbeing and mental health

5

What are you finding out?

In this chapter we will look closely at the framework within which mental health services are delivered, focusing on the systems, roles and responsibilities within the current legal and policy context.

In addition we focus on the rights of service users and informal carers and the role of advocacy in promoting rights.

The key points of mental health legislation within the UK and relevance of other legislation including legislation relevant to some of the following will also be addressed:

a. Mental capacity
b. Disability rights
c. Human rights
d. Eligibility for services
e. Safeguarding vulnerable adults
f. Health and safety
g. Data protection

The reading and activities in this chapter will help you to:

1. Describe the current national policy initiatives that are relevant to mental health and explain how these are intended to change or improve service provision.
2. Identify the key points of legislation relating to carers of people with mental health problems, with reference to:
   a. mental capacity
   b. disability rights
   c. human rights
   d. eligibility for services
   e. safeguarding vulnerable adults
   f. health and safety
   g. data protection.
3. Describe the framework of national mental health service provision.
4. Describe the role and responsibilities of the key statutory, voluntary or private agencies involved in mental healthcare.
5. Describe the role and responsibilities of the main professionals and workers within mental healthcare namely:
   a. mental health nurses
   b. support workers
   c. general practitioners
   d. psychiatrists
   e. occupational therapists

f. psychologists
g. social workers/care managers
h. independent advocates.
6. Describe the contribution of carers and those who give informal support to people with mental health problems and explain why and how carers/informal supporters should be involved in service delivery.
7. Identify the rights and responsibilities of people with mental health problems and the need to challenge discrimination.
8. Explain the role of independent advocacy in promoting the rights of people with mental health problems and their carers and those giving informal support.
9. Describe the framework of national service provision and how the different sectors relate to each other:
   a. education
   b. employment and benefits
   c. health and social care
   d. housing
   e. justice.

Assessment criteria covered in this chapter

Reading this unit and completing the activities will provide you with the knowledge, understanding and skills required to meet the assessment criteria listed below.

City & Guilds Level 3 Diploma in Mental Health Care (QCF) (600/5241/7)		
Understand the legal, policy and service framework in mental health (J/602/0165)		
Learning Outcome 1 Know the legal and current policy framework for mental health		
Assessment Criteria	Page reference	Activity
1.1 Explain the key points of mental health legislation within their own country	p. 92	Evidence activity 5.1, p. 95
1.2 Explain the relevance of other legislation within their own country to working with a person with mental health problems including legislation relevant to at least four of the following: a. mental capacity b. disability rights c. human rights d. eligibility for services e. safeguarding vulnerable adults f. health and safety g. data protection	p. 92	Evidence activity 5.1, p. 95
1.3 Describe two current national policy initiatives that are relevant to mental health in their own country	p. 92	Evidence activity 5.1, p. 95
1.4 Explain how both of the current national policy initiatives that are relevant to mental health are intended to change or improve service provision	p. 92	Evidence activity 5.1, p. 95
1.5 Identify the key points of legislation relating to carers of people with mental health problems within their own country	p. 96	Evidence activity 5.2, p. 103

(Continued)

(Continued)

Learning Outcome 2 Know the service framework for mental health		
2.1. Describe the framework of national mental health service provision within their own country	p. 103	Evidence activity 5.3, p. 104
2.2. Describe the role and responsibilities of the key statutory, voluntary or private agencies involved in mental health care in their own country	p. 105	Evidence activity 5.4, p. 109

2.3. Describe the role and responsibilities of the main professionals and workers within mental health care in their own country:
  a. mental health nurses
  b. support workers
  c. general practitioners
  d. psychiatrists
  e. occupational therapists
  f. psychologists
  g. social workers/care managers
  h. independent advocates
	p. 109	Evidence activity 5.5, p. 115

2.4. Describe the contribution of carers and those who give informal support to people with mental health problems	p. 115	Evidence activity 5.6, p. 116
2.5. Explain why and how carers/informal supporters should be involved in service delivery	p. 115	Evidence activity 5.6, p. 116
Learning Outcome 3 Understand the rights of individuals using services and of those who give informal support		
3.1. Identify the rights and responsibilities of people with mental health problems	p. 116	Evidence activity 5.7, p. 118

3.2. Explain why workers should promote the rights of and challenge discrimination against people with mental health problems in relation to the following:
  a. legal basis within their own country
  b. moral/human rights
  c. promote mental health and wellbeing
  d. codes of conduct/professional ethics
  e. policy and charters
	p. 116	Evidence activity 5.7, p. 118

3.3. Explain how to promote the rights of people with mental health problems within their own practice context	p. 116	Evidence activity 5.7, p. 118
3.4. Explain how to challenge discrimination against people with mental health problems within their own practice context	p. 116	Evidence activity 5.7, p. 118
3.5. Explain the role of independent advocacy in promoting the rights of people with mental health problems	p. 109	Evidence activity 5.5, p. 115
3.6. Explain the role of independent advocacy in promoting the rights of carers and those giving informal support	p. 109	Evidence activity 5.5, p. 115

NCFE Level 1 Award in Mental Health Awareness (QCF) (501/0253/9)		
Develop an awareness of mental health (K/600/6596)		
Learning Outcome 3 Be aware of some of the responses to mental health issues		
Assessment Criteria	Page reference	Activity
3.1 Identify the rights of people experiencing mental ill health	p. 116	Evidence activity 5.7, p. 118

NCFE Level 2 Award in Understanding Working with People with Mental Health Issues (QCF) (500/9956/5)		
Mental health and mental health issues (M/601/2948)		
2.1 Define the term mental disorder	p. 96	
Learning Outcome 3 Be aware of the legislation and guidance that applies to those with mental health issues		
Assessment Criteria	Page reference	Activity
3.1 Identify the key legislation and guidance that relates to people with mental health	p. 92	Evidence activity 5.1, p. 95
3.2 Explain the need to challenge discrimination against people with mental health problems	p. 116	Evidence activity 5.7, p. 118

NCFE Level 2 Award in Understanding Working with People with Mental Health Issues (QCF) (500/9956/5)		
Approaches to care and management in mental health (K/601/2950)		
Learning Outcome 2 Understand aspects of good practice in the care planning process		
Assessment Criteria	Page reference	Activity
2.6 Outline the role of key agencies involved in the care process	p. 105	Evidence activity 5.4, p. 109

Promote equality and inclusion in health, social care or children's and young people's settings (Y/601/1437)		
Learning Outcome 1 Understand the key features of the care planning process		
Assessment Criteria	Page reference	Activity
1.1 Identify local and national standards on care	p. 92	Evidence activity 5.1, p. 95
Learning Outcome 2 Be able to work in an inclusive way		
2.1 Explain how legislation and codes of practice relating to equality, diversity and discrimination apply to own work role	p. 96	Evidence activity 5.2, p. 103

1 Describe the current national policy initiatives that are relevant to mental health and how these are intended to change or improve service provision

The statistics demonstrating the extent of mental health problems in the UK have moved recent governments to address their policies with respect to updating the mental health services offered. Indeed, many of the changes over the last 30 years to legislation and policy initiatives have demonstrated a commitment to a growing problem which affects not only the mental health of society but also the physical health and wellbeing of individuals.

With at least one in four people destined to experience a mental health problem at some point in their life, and current statistics showing that one in six adults has a mental health problem at any one time, wider recognition of the problem of mental health has elicited a huge response in terms of policy change. Further statistics inform us that almost half of all adults will experience at least one episode of depression during their lifetime and that one in ten children aged between 5 and 16 years who already has a mental health problem will continue to have mental health problems into adulthood (HMG/DH, (2011).

These sorts of statistics have not only led to changes in the way mental health is viewed in society but have also forced government to give wider recognition to the problems associated with this type of ill health.

Historically, mental illness was seen as something to be feared and care often focused upon the perceived dangers and threats to others that such an illness posed (see Chapter 2). This led to a less than sympathetic service being developed and one in which compulsory detention and incarceration of mentally ill people became the norm. Mental illness became stigmatised and something to be hidden.

Figure 5.1 Historic attitudes to mental illness

The contents of the box below provide a brief overview of how mental health legislation and various bills by government have tried to address mental health needs over the last 50 years or so. It shows a slow move towards a more sympathetic view of the problems individual may experience and how the mental health service has tried to improve the services available.

1961 Enoch Powell addressed the annual conference of the National Association for Mental Health with a speech about his forthcoming hospital plan and its effect on psychiatric services.

1971 DHSS publishes Better Services for the Mentally Handicapped Cmnd 4683 (DHSS) HMSO.

1975 Government announces their intention to review the 1959 Mental Health Act.

1975 DHSS Better Services for the Mentally Ill Cmnd 6233 HMSO. A paper emphasising the provision of a comprehensive range of local services in place of asylums.

1978: DHSS Review of the Mental Health Act 1959 Department of Health and Social Security HMSO. Cmnd 7320.

1981 DHSS Care in the Community. A Consultative Document on Moving Resources for Care in England.

This document was a green paper that suggested ways of moving money and care from the National Health Service to local councils for services for mentally handicapped, mentally ill and elderly patients.

1981 HMSO Reform of Mental Health Legislation Department of Health and Social Security HMSO Cmnd 8405 November 1981.

1983 Royal Assent given for the 1983 Mental Health Act.

1985 DHSS Community Care with Special Reference to Adult Mentally Ill and Mentally Handicapped People. Second Report from the Social Services Committee, 1984–1985 session. HMSO 1985.

1989 DoH Working for Patients. Department of Health. London: HMSO.

1990 Griffiths report and the white paper Caring for People became part of the National Health Service and Community Care Act of 1990.

1990 DoH National Health and Community Care Act: Social Services Departments had to set up 'arms length' inspection units and to prepare a Community Care Plan which would entitle users to a Community Care Assessment of needs.

1998 DoH Modernising Mental Health Services: Safe, Sound and Supportive. Department of Health.

1999 DoH National Service Framework for Mental Health. Modern Standards and Service Models. Executive Summary. Department of Health.

2007 The Mental Capacity Act.

January 2011 Amendments to Mental Capacity Act via Health and Social Care Bill.

(Adapted from http://studymore.org.uk/7.htm)

The most recent mental health strategy was that published in 2011, the government's No Health Without Mental Health policy document. This strategy combines adult and child mental health and gives equal priority to physical and mental health, recognising the links between the two. It supersedes the previous government's initiative New Horizons: A Shared Vision for Mental Health document published in 2009. This initiative set out to target the root causes of mental illness and support a more personalised quality service at a local level. To achieve this aim the document explored how the prevention of mental illness and earlier intervention could be more effective, and it looked at how services could be encouraged to work together in a more effective way.

In particular, the main objective was to examine how government, services and communities could work together to ensure that everyone would be involved in improving mental wellbeing and make it easier for people to get the right help when they need it. The promotion of equality and a fairer society, and one in which the stigma attached to the mental health was reduced, was also high on this agenda.

With a change in government the No Health Without Mental Health strategy took the mental health agenda further forward, commenting that:

> 'Mental health is everyone's business – individuals, families, employers, educators and communities all need to play their part. Good mental health and resilience are fundamental to our physical health, our relationships, our education, our training, our work and to achieving our potential … good mental health and wellbeing also bring wider social and economic benefits. But to realise these benefits, we all need to take action and be supported by the Government to do so. We all need to take responsibility for caring for our own mental health and that of others, and to challenge the blight of stigma and discrimination. Our objectives for employment, for education, for training, for safety and crime reduction, for reducing drug and alcohol dependence and homelessness cannot be achieved without improvements in mental health.'

Recognising the centrality of mental health to success in education, employment and the building of a stable society, as well as showing the links between poor mental health and poverty, homelessness and violence and abuse was somewhat of a breakthrough in terms of the way in which mental health is viewed.

Research has shown that mentally ill individuals and those who are prone to such problems often have fewer qualifications, and find it harder to get into employment and to stay there. They also have lower incomes, are more likely to be homeless, and suffer from poor physical health. In addition, many live in areas of high social deprivation.

The legal policy and service framework in relation to promoting wellbeing and mental health

The concept of promoting good mental health rather than just treating ill health when it occurs, together with intervening early – particularly in the childhood and teenage years – shows a huge commitment to the way in which society is changing with respect to how mental ill health is viewed. There seems to be an adoption of a social justice perspective, recognising the needs of certain groups who are more at risk of experiencing mental health problems, including those from black and minority ethnic groups and those from lower socio-economic groups.

Whilst cost is an issue to every government, and with mental ill health costing an estimated £105bn a year, the strategy showed that mental health problems represent 23 per cent of the total burden of ill health in the UK and are the largest single cause of disability. In promoting the strategy the government pointed out that:

> 'this strategy is not just about statistics and economics: It is not just about saving money, but about quality of life and, especially for children, giving them a good experience of childhood which will enable them to go on to become good parents themselves and so avoid another generation with mental health problems. The strategy addresses both prevention and treatment of mental health problems.'

(DoH, 2011a)

To summarise, the strategy sets out six key objectives:

- Objective One: More people will have good mental health.
- Objective Two: More people with mental health problems will recover.
- Objective Three: More people with mental health problems will have good physical health.
- Objective Four: More people will have a positive experience of care and support.
- Objective Five: Fewer people will suffer avoidable harm.
- Objective Six: Fewer people will experience stigma and discrimination.

Supporting the No Health Without Mental Health strategy is the Improving Access to Psychological Therapies (IAPT) programme, and in 2011 the publication of Talking Therapies: a four-year plan of action, set out how the programme would be rolled out over the next four years. It states that;

> 'In the four years to April 2015: the nationwide roll-out of psychological therapy services for adults will be completed, a stand-alone programme for children and young people will be initiated, and models of care for people with long-term physical conditions, medically unexplained symptoms and severe mental illness will be developed.'

The new guidelines show how the government's commitment to expanding access to psychological therapies will be achieved over the four years from April 2011, and how talking therapies are to be more readily available for the treatment of depression and anxiety disorders.

The IAPT programme was first targeted at people of working age, but in 2010 was opened to adults of all ages. It guaranteed a 'realistic and routine first-line treatment, combined where appropriate with medication'.

Evidence Activity

 5.1 Activity

1. Download a copy of the No Health Without Mental Health strategy and read the executive summary. Make notes on how your service provision is changing as a result of the initiatives set out.
2. Comment on how the IAPT programme is working in your local area.

2 Explain the key points of legislation relating to carers of people with mental health problems with reference to: mental capacity; disability rights; human rights; eligibility for services; safeguarding vulnerable adults; health and safety; data protection

Although this section is mainly concerned with those who care for individuals with mental health problems, a discussion about the more general legislation applied to care work is undertaken here. It is important for mental health professionals to understand the key points within the law in addition to the main changes that have been made to the Mental Health Act of 1983 in 2007. This act also made amendments to the Mental Capacity Act 2005 and the Domestic Violence, Crime and Victims Act 2004.

The Mental Capacity Act 2005 was a legislative move to address concerns about the rights of adults who may 'lack capacity' in decisions about their care and treatment. It was felt at this time that some individuals in long-term care and those who required treatment due to acute problems may lack the ability to make informed decisions about their own care. This made them particularly vulnerable, therefore, to the process set down in the Mental Health Act which often meant the individual was detained for safety reasons. Let's look more closely at this.

The Mental Health Act of 1983 was mainly concerned with the detainment of individuals with mental health problems. Its main purpose was to ensure the health and wellbeing of an individual and the safety of the public and it set out to ensure that those with serious mental disorders did not pose threats to this safety. If a person was believed to be at risk in some way, either to themselves or others, this act made it possible for the police, courts and health professionals to detain and treat that person.

To this end, the act set out the processes to be followed together with safeguards for patients, in order to ensure that they were not inappropriately detained or treated without their consent.

This act was an important piece of legislation setting out the legal framework for compulsory powers, and in 2007 the Act was amended rather than replaced. Along with the 1983 Act, a Code of Practice giving guidance on how the Act should be applied in both England and Wales was supplied and this has now been rewritten to reflect the changes in the 2007 Act. In Wales The Mental Health Act Code of Practice for Wales came into force in 2008.

The Mental Health Act 2007 (MHA) has amended the following areas that were initially addressed in the 1983 Act.

Definition of mental disorder

The 1983 Act's four categories of mental illness have now been simplified and a single definition of mental disorder now refers to 'any disorder or disability of the mind'. In addition, individuals with learning disabilities are not considered to be suffering from a mental disorder, unless there is evidence of 'abnormally aggressive or seriously irresponsible conduct'. Drug or alcohol dependency is no longer classed in the amended act as a mental disorder.

Criteria for detention

The former manner in which long-term powers of detention enabled people to be detained due to the so-called 'treatability test' is now replaced by an 'appropriate treatment' test. Professionals now have to guarantee the availability of medical treatment, including psychological intervention, which is appropriate to each case and an individual cannot be detained unless this is done.

Roles of care professionals

Anyone with experience in supporting people with mental health problems, such as nurses, occupational therapists and psychologists are now referred to in the amended act as 'approved mental health practitioners' and this is a change to the 1983 Act's 'approved social worker' role. Also, there is now a responsible clinician role, and this role may be undertaken by social workers or any of the other professions listed above. Previously this was undertaken by medical practitioners. If, however, the individual is required to be detained under sections 2 and 3 of the 1983 Act, two 'registered medical practitioners' are still required to make this recommendation. (See the next section for the Ten Essential Shared Capabilities.)

Roles of relatives

The changes here are that individuals have the right to apply for the removal of their nominated nearest relative if they believe that person to be unsuitable. Eligible relatives now include civil partners giving them the same status as husband and wife.

Community treatment orders

In the 1983 Act a 'supervised discharge' allowed individuals to live at home under supervision, ensuring that they continued with the medical treatment that they needed. 'Community treatment orders' now replace this and where certain criteria are met, patients who are discharged from hospital will be allowed to live at home. Individuals may be recalled to hospital if they do not comply with conditions such as making him or herself available for examination.

Tribunals

Mental Health Review Tribunals (MHRT) determine whether community patients or those individuals detained in hospital can be formally discharged.

Services for under-18 year olds

In the 2005 amendments, individuals under the age of 18 who are admitted to hospital for mental disorder must be accommodated in an environment that is suitable for their age.

Electro-convulsive therapy

The application of this treatment is now subject to full consent from the individual except in an emergency or when the individual lacks capacity to consent. In such cases the treatment can only be given if this is deemed appropriate and does not conflict with the safeguards set out in the 2005 Mental Capacity Act, which we deal with later in the section.

Advocacy and Safeguarding Vulnerable Groups Act 2006

An individual may require the services of an independent mental health advocate. The appropriate national authority, that is the UK government in England and the Welsh Assembly in Wales, is responsible for providing this service.

The 2007 MHA was also used to introduce deprivation of liberty safeguards through amending the 2005 Mental Capacity Act. The introduction of the Mental Health and Mental Capacity (Advocacy) Amendment Regulations in 2009 put into place the government's intention to commence the barring provisions of the Safeguarding Vulnerable Groups Act 2006 and the new provisions in Part V of the

Police Act. The effect of the amendments was that an enhanced criminal record certificate with adult suitability information is now required in order to assess whether a person satisfies the requirement of integrity and good character in connection with their appointment as an Independent Mental Capacity Advocate (IMCA) or an Independent Mental Health Advocate (IMHA) (see next section).

The term 'safeguarding practices' is most commonly applied to children and young people under the age of 18 and is further differentiated in some texts where 'children' refers to those under the age of 18 who are still in full-time education, and 'young people' as those under the age of 18 who have left full-time education. With respect to adults, key aspects of legislation include similar standards of protection to 'vulnerable adults'.

A vulnerable adult is defined as an individual aged 18 or over who depends upon others for assistance with respect to the performance of basic functions or who has a severe impairment in their ability to communicate and therefore a reduced ability to protect themselves from assault, abuse or neglect. But there is a debate about the difference in definitions which seem to raise issues with this subject.

The Department of Health's definition of vulnerable adults refer to persons who

> 'may be in need of community care services by reason of mental or other disability, age or illness; and who is or may be unable to care of him or herself, or unable to protect him or herself against significant harm or exploitation'.

> (DoH 2000:8–9)

This definition seems to identify groups of people such as the elderly as being vulnerable and we may find this unacceptable. It is, after all, the situation in which the person finds themselves that makes them vulnerable. The CSCI in their 2008 document Raising Voices: Views on Safeguarding Adults added to the debate, going as far as commenting that such a lack of clarity with respect to the terms used also led to confusion over the roles and responsibilities of care workers responding to concerns (McKibbin et al., 2008).

The following laws provide guidance as to the rights and requirements for service provision but there was limited mention of protection per se until the Care Standards Act was published in 2000. This Act set out the Protection of Vulnerable Adults (POVA) scheme which was then implemented on a phased basis from 26 July 2004.

- National Assistance Act 1948
- Mental Health Act 1983
- Mental Health Bill 2004
- Mental Capacity Act 2005
- Chronically Sick and Disabled Persons Act 1986
- Disability Discrimination Act 1995
- NHS Community Care Act 1990
- Safeguarding Vulnerable Groups Act 2006
- Adult Support and Protection Act (Scotland) 2007

These laws have developed over a number of years and have occasionally come about as a response to cases of concern being highlighted in the media. This has led to an alarming number of changes to law over time as a result of investigations into abuse in institutions and towards individuals. Clearly things had to change and the response of the government was to address the protection of adults through guidelines and policy documents. The year 2000 and a couple of years leading up to this date saw several publications from the government all seeking to address the issue of adult abuse.

The **Human Rights Act** of 1998 aimed to protect adults from abuse, and if we have a role in the public sector we also have responsibility to comply with this act.

The government's white paper, Modernising Social Services, published at the end of 1998, sought to provide better protection for individuals needing care and support, but it was with the express intention of addressing the need for greater protection for victims and witnesses of abuse that the government actively implemented the measures proposed in Speaking Up for Justice, a report on the treatment of vulnerable or intimidated witnesses in the criminal justice system. Recognising the difficulties in dealing with expressions of concern about abuse and the consequences of reporting abuse crime against vulnerable adults in care settings, it was agreed that local multi-agency codes of practice would be the best way forward.

The No Secrets 2000 government publication came about as a response to the ever increasing media coverage of adult abuse. The guidance ensured that local authorities were responsible for coordinating the development of policy to protect the vulnerable individual through multi-agency working and the setting up of Safeguarding Adults Boards and Vulnerable Adults Safeguarding policies and procedures. In addition the Care Standards Act of the same year set out the Protection of Vulnerable Adults (POVA) scheme to be rolled out on a phased basis – being fully implemented by 2004. The Welsh Assembly also published their guidance In Safe Hands, Implementing Adult Protection procedures in Wales (July 2000) as a response to the Welsh white paper Building for the Future (1999) which identified the protection and promotion of the welfare of vulnerable adults as a priority and reinforced the Welsh Assembly's respect for human rights and the provisions of the Human Rights Act 1998.

Disability rights

The white paper Valuing People: A New Strategy for Learning Disability in the 21st Century – published in 2001 – was a landmark paper for people with learning disabilities and set out ways in which services would be improved, highlighting four main principles: civil rights, independence, choice and inclusion. Quality of care for vulnerable adults was set to improve in a marked way because of these new initiatives, not least because of the changes to staff training, quality controls and the response by professional bodies to addressing codes of practice to bring them into line with National Minimum Standards.

It was the POVA scheme set out in the Care Standards Act 2000 and implemented in 2004 that went further to protect those in care from abuse by care providers. Central to the POVA scheme is the POVA list of care workers who have harmed vulnerable adults in their care. It became a legal requirement from July 2004 to undertake checks through the Standard or Enhanced Disclosure application process from the Criminal Records Bureau (CRB) when employing people in care roles.

Changes to the reporting system by way of the Vetting and Barring Scheme ('the Scheme') came about following the publication of the Bichard Inquiry (2004) which recommended a new scheme under which everyone working with children or vulnerable adults should be checked and registered. The Bichard inquiry was commissioned following the murders of Holly Wells and Jessica Chapman and revelations that certain checks had been missed. Recognising the need for a single agency to vet and register individuals who want to work or volunteer with vulnerable people the Independent Safeguarding Authority (ISA) was set up and the Criminal Records Bureau was made responsible for managing the system and processing the applications for ISA registration.

The inquiry led to The Safeguarding Vulnerable Groups Act 2006 ('the Act') and the Safeguarding Vulnerable Groups Order (Northern Ireland) 2007 ('the Order') which set up the scheme.

The Mental Capacity Act 2005

This important piece of legislation protects the rights of people to plan for their future in the event of becoming incapacitated, and additionally clarifies and strengthens the rights of those who already lack capacity to make decisions about their care.

The Act states:

> 'A person must be assumed to have capacity unless it is established that he lacks capacity.
>
> A person is not to be treated as unable to make a decision unless all practicable steps to help him to do so have been taken without success.
>
> A person is not to be treated as unable to make a decision merely because he makes an unwise decision.
>
> An act done, or decision made, under this Act for, or on behalf of, a person who lacks capacity must be done, or made, in his best interests. Before the act is done, or the decision is made, regard must be had to whether the purpose for which it is needed can be as effectively achieved in a way that is less restrictive of the person's rights and freedom of action.'

(MCA, 2005)

The Act also provides guidance for people who are acting on behalf of someone who cannot make decisions for themselves and includes a 'best interests' checklist of the person's wishes, feelings, beliefs and values.

With respect to lasting powers of attorney, individuals are able to appoint an attorney to act on their behalf, which is like the current Enduring Power of Attorney. Although this role covers financial decision making, under the MCA the role includes health and welfare decisions. There is also a provision for Court-appointed deputies to make decisions on behalf of an individual, replacing the system of receivership which covered financial decision making and extending it to include health and welfare.

In defining 'lack of capacity' the act refers to the inability of an individual to make a decision in relation to specific matters and recognises that whilst an individual may lack capacity for a particular decision they may not necessarily lack capacity to make other decisions. It makes the distinction between the ability to make day-to-day and care-related decisions, whilst being unable to make more complex decisions in areas such as finance. A single clear test for assessing whether a person lacks capacity to take a particular decision at a particular time is therefore applied and it is for the person making the assertion of incapacity to prove that the patient lacks capacity.

Other provisions made within this act are for an advocate to support and represent people lacking capacity who have no one else to speak for them and the recognition of advance decisions to refuse treatment or 'living wills'. These directives enable individuals to set out in advance how they wish to be treated should they lose capacity, and these are legally binding under common law.

For older people with long-term mental health problems and their carers there are a number of key features of the Mental Capacity Act 2005 that are likely to be of benefit. The focus on 'decision specific' assessment of capacity and the principle that no one should be labelled 'incapable' as a result of a particular medical condition is an important consideration. As we age we are increasingly at risk of having things 'done to us' without being involved much in the decision. Elderly people may be forgetful at times or even confused and therefore can have a fluctuating ability to make decisions, but whilst more major decisions can be left to third parties to make, the day-to-day decisions as to treatment and care can still be made by the individual.

The Mental Health Act of 2007 also makes a number of amendments to the Mental Capacity Act 2005 (MCA) and these came about as a response to a judgment made in 2004 at the European Court of Human Rights. In the case of an autistic man who was kept at Bournewood Hospital by doctors against the wishes of his carers, the European Court of Human Rights ruled that admission to and detention in hospital under the common law of necessity amounted to a breach of Article 5(1) ECHR (deprivation of liberty) and of Article 5(4) (right to have lawfulness of detention reviewed by a court). This ruling led to the introduction of the MCA Deprivation of Liberty Safeguards and led to procedures being set up to authorise the deprivation of liberty of a person in a hospital or care home who lacks capacity to consent to being there. This means that in supporting a person to make a decision the MCA principles require acting at all times in the person's best interests and in the least restrictive manner.

The Domestic Violence, Crime and Victims Act 2004

The changes to the Domestic Violence, Crime and Victims Act 2004 introduced new rights for victims of mentally disordered offenders who have been detained in hospital without being made subject to special restrictions. In 2005 these rights applied to victims of offenders who were detained in hospital under Part 3 of the Mental Health Act 1983 and who were subject to special restrictions (restricted patients), but from 2008, these rights were extended to victims of offenders detained in hospital under Part 3 of the 1983 Act who were not subject to special restrictions (unrestricted patients).

New statutory duties to enable the victims to exercise those rights now apply and it is up to probation services to identify eligible victims and, with their consent, to pass on their details to hospital managers. In discharging unrestricted patients, consideration of the victims' representations when deciding what conditions to include in the community treatment order of an unrestricted patient must be made.

The changes to the 1983 Mental Health Act have resulted in a new era of mental health policy ensuring that the rights of individuals who suffer from mental health problems are at the forefront of treatment. As a result of these changes to law, the emphasis now is on developing a mental health service which stresses the importance of initiatives to assist people with mental health conditions to be able to maintain their own decision-making capacity and to provide guidance for those charged with caring for mentally ill individuals.

The Mental Health Act of 1983 was concerned with detaining those individuals who were deemed to pose threats to society or themselves and this resulted in a number of human rights infringements. The subsequent changes to this act now reflect a fairer system which ensures that inappropriate detention or treatment can be challenged.

In addition to the above acts there are others you need to have knowledge of as a worker in mental health care. In Table 5.1 we have summarised them in terms of their purpose and your responsibility with respect to each.

Table 5.1 Legislation and your responsibilities

Legislation	Purpose	Your responsibility
The Health and Safety at Work Act 1974 (HASAWA)	Anyone affected by work activity must be kept safe.	To ensure all staff are aware of their part in Health and Safety and to regularly check the policies in place meet all needs. Ensure that written policies are in place.
Health and Safety (First Aid) Regulations 1981	To ensure that everybody has access to immediate first aid care in the work place.	To maintain first aid training of designated first aiders and to supply resources for first aid.
Mental Health Act 1983	This act allows compulsory action to be taken, where necessary, to ensure that people with mental disorders get the care and treatment they need for their own health or safety, or for the protection of other people.	Ensure staff are aware of the reason for the act.

(Continued)

(Continued)

Legislation	Purpose	Your responsibility
Electricity at Work Regulations 1989	To minimise the risk due to electricity in the work place.	To maintain the upkeep and ensure regular safety checks are made.
Food Safety Act 1990 and the Food Hygiene Regulations 2006 Manual Handling Operations Regulations 1992 (MHOR)	To minimise the risk due to food handling in the work place. To minimise the risk due to moving and handling.	Ensure good personal hygiene procedures are upheld. Ensure any hazards are identified and controlled. Ensure staff are trained in moving and handling protocols.
Workplace (Health, Safety and Welfare) Regulations 1992	To minimise the risk due to working conditions in the work place.	Ensure that standards for heating, lighting, sanitation and building upkeep are maintained.
Personal Protective Equipment at Work Regulations 1992 (PPE)	To minimise the risk due to cross infection in the work place.	To ensure staff are aware of infection control procedures and are trained in dealing with potential cross-infection. To supply work wear and PPE.
Reporting on Injuries, Diseases, and Dangerous Occurrences Regulations 1995 (RIDDOR)	Ensure that procedures are in place for the reporting of injury and illness to HSE or local authority where appropriate.	Maintain the policy in the work place and ensure that accident forms and reports are in place.
Disability Discrimination Act 1995 (DDA)	Ensure that access and exits to the work place are safe for those with disabilities in the event of the need to evacuate the premises.	Update premises and ensure policy is known to staff and visitors.
Provision and Use of Work Equipment Regulations 1998 (PUWER)	Risks due to the use of equipment must be minimised.	Train staff in use of equipment and ensure upkeep of equipment is maintained and safe to use.
Data Protection Act 1998 Management of Health and Safety at Work Regulations 1999 (MHSWR)	Ensure that personal information is kept private and safely and carry out risk assessments to minimise any risks to safety.	Check policy on confidentiality and arrange to undertake regular risk assessments.
Control of Substances Hazardous to Health Regulations 2002 (COSHH)	Minimise the risk from the use of substances that may be hazardous to health.	Carry out risk assessments and ensure staff are trained in use of hazardous substances.

(Continued)

The legal policy and service framework in relation to promoting wellbeing and mental health

(Continued)

Legislation	Purpose	Your responsibility
Regulatory Reform (Fire Safety) 2005	Minimise fire hazards.	Regular checks of fire safety in the work place.
Corporate Manslaughter and Homicide Act 2007	If the death of somebody occurs in suspicious circumstances then an organisation may be convicted of negligence.	Ensure staff are aware of duty of care and are following policy.
Family Law Reform Act 1969	Reduced the age of majority from 21 to 18 and provided for the maintenance for children under guardianship to continue to the age of 21. Also allowed consent by persons over 16 to surgical, medical and dental treatment.	Ensure staff are aware of duty of care and are following policy.
Children Act 1989 and Children Act 2004	The Act set boundaries and gave help for local authorities to regulate official intervention in the interests of children. It also made changes to laws that pertain to children.	Ensure staff are aware of duty of care and are following policy.
Mental Capacity Act 2005	It provided a legal framework for acting and making decisions on behalf of adults who lack capacity to make particular decisions for themselves.	Ensure staff are aware of duty of care and are following policy.
Health and Social Care Act 2008	It highlighted significant measures to modernise and integrate health and social care.	Ensure staff are aware of duty of care and are following policy.

Tilmouth and Quallington (2011).

All the laws above will be enshrined in the policies and procedures which you are required to follow in your work place. Policies set out the arrangements for complying with the law and procedures identify the activity surrounding practice in order to implement the policy.

Evidence Activity

 Activity

Prepare a handout for staff and carers in your work placement which shows the key changes to the Mental Health Act of 1983 and safeguarding arrangements for adults

How have the changes been of benefit to the clients in your care?

In addition state your responsibilities and those of the manager with respect to the health and safety of your client in the work place.

3 Describe the framework of national mental health service provision

Mental health care has undergone enormous change not just because of changes in law but also because of the development of policies which address the ways in which the service is delivered and mental health is viewed.

In 1999 the government published The National Service Framework for Mental Health (NSF MH) (1999) a ten-year plan for improving mental healthcare in England. From 2010, this was replaced by New Horizons: A Shared Vision for Mental Health (see Section 1) a policy intended to improve the quality and accessibility of services in mental health.

No Health Without Mental Health, launched in 2011, was the Coalition Government's strategy for mental health (Section 1) and this policy set out six objectives to improve the mental health and wellbeing of the nation. In addition it sought to improve the outcomes for people with mental health problems through the delivery of high-quality care services. To address the stigma surrounding mental health problems and to improve the experience of those with such problems one of the objectives set out to ensure that:

'more people will have a positive experience of care and support'.

Surveys carried out on an annual basis by the NHS aim to monitor changes in public attitudes towards mental illness over time, the findings of which assess the progress we have made as a society in improving the experience of healthcare for people with a mental illness.

Subsequent policy statements and guidance have been published, including NICE guidelines, and these have supplemented the mental health framework.

The Department for Work and Pensions commissioned an independent review entitled Realising Ambitions: Better Employment Support for People with a Mental Health Condition. This paper described how employment, health and wider state support could be strengthened to help people with mental conditions who are out of work, and a further document, Work Recovery and Inclusion sets out a series of commitments to support people in contact with secondary mental health services into work.

Working our Way to Better Mental Health; A Framework for Action (2009) describes how action by government, employers, healthcare professionals and the third sector can help people with mental health conditions prepare for work, find work and stay in work.

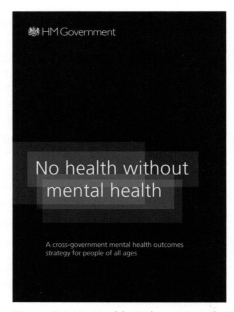

Figure 5.2 No Health Without Mental Health

In discussing how the mental health service is delivered in an efficient manner we should address the change that is going to be implemented with the Health and Social Care Act (2012) and how this will affect the Mental Health Framework. The way in which NHS services are commissioned in England is going to undergo change with the responsibility for commissioning all health services being passed to new 'clinical commissioning groups' led by GPs and including other health professionals with different areas of expertise. These groups will decide which specialist health services the local population need, and then pay NHS trusts, voluntary or private organisations to provide those services. The emphasis will be on 'joint commissioning' with local authorities to provide integrated services, offering both health and social care expertise. How this will affect the delivery of mental health service is covered in the next section.

Evidence Activity

 Activity

Prepare a Powerpoint presentation for staff showing all the policy documents and legal aspects of mental health care described in Sections 1–3 of this chapter. Highlight the main areas of each.

4 Describe the role and responsibilities of the key statutory, voluntary or private agencies involved in mental healthcare

In this section we shall look at how mental health services are structured and delivered through various statutory organisations and teams. In Chapter 3 you can access information on some of the voluntary and charitable organisations.

The changes to the way in which NHS services are commissioned in England were set out in the Health and Social Care Act (2012).

Plans for new 'health and wellbeing boards' to help plan local health and social care services are in progress and these boards bring together representatives from clinical commissioning groups, local authorities and public health experts. They will replace the primary care trusts (PCTs) which previously had this remit. Here we look at the various organisations and teams that are particularly concerned with the delivery of mental health services.

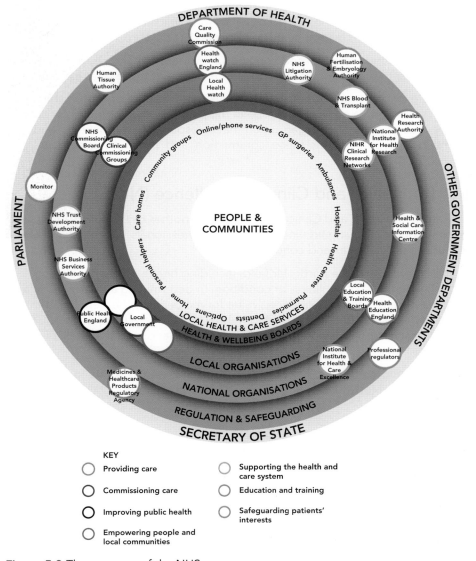

KEY

○ Providing care

○ Commissioning care

○ Improving public health

○ Empowering people and local communities

○ Supporting the health and care system

○ Education and training

○ Safeguarding patients' interests

Figure 5.3 The structure of the NHS

The NHS

The NHS provides healthcare for all UK citizens based on individual need and funded by taxes. Led by a Secretary of State for Health, this minister is responsible for the work of the Department of Health and reports to the Prime Minister.

The NHS has undergone an enormous amount of restructuring since its inception in 1948 and will now undergo a further restructuring. With the passing of the Health and Social Care Act 2012, changes in the NHS have led to a number of new initiatives with respect to the services offered and the ways in which they are delivered.

One of the newer changes has been the new GP-led clinical commissioning groups which have been set up to manage local NHS budgets. At the time of writing, the PCTs remain as statutory organisations and will still be accountable for the NHS budget until they officially hand over commissioning duties in 2013. From 2013 an NHS Commissioning Board will oversee the new clinical commissioning groups and allocate their budgets.

With respect to the mental health service, these are run by specialist NHS mental health trusts as well as charities, voluntary organisations and private organisations. The term 'integrated' services refers to the mental health services which are run jointly by an NHS organisation and a local authority social services department. Those NHS organisations which work closely with local authorities through 'care trusts' run both mental health services and social care services.

Mental health services are largely community-based and specialist treatment and support is given by different teams of mental health professionals. We look more closely at these roles in Section 5.

The services that are available in local areas depend on how the commissioning group wishes to spend its budget and this has been a contentious issue in the past with the cutting of services that are deemed too expensive. It is the NHS organisation that is responsible for planning and organising services for the local population and these 'commission' and 'purchase' specialist mental health services.

National Institute for Health and Clinical Excellence (NICE)

NICE or the National Institute for Health and Clinical Excellence is another key statutory body set up by the government to produce 'clinical guidelines' for health professionals, which describe the treatment and services for specific illnesses and conditions.

The guidance is produced by experts in the particular field, including health professionals and people who have personal experience of an illness or condition. In determining a treatment or a drug's effectiveness, all the relevant research evidence, 'value for money' and the benefits of the treatment or service are taken into account. In the field of mental health there is separate NICE guidance for the treatment of schizophrenia and the treatment of bipolar disorder as well as other guidance for other conditions.

In other parts of the United Kingdom there are links to NICE guidelines and in Scotland the Scottish intercollegiate Guidelines Network develops evidence-based clinical practice guidelines for the NHS.

Care Quality Commission (CQC)

In order to check the quality of the health and social services available in England a regulatory body – the Care Quality Commission – has been set up. As an independent regulator of health and social care, it checks and inspects at various intervals the quality of health and adult social care services that are provided by the NHS, local authorities, private companies and voluntary organisations. Another very important role is the protection of the rights of those individuals who are detained under the Mental Health Act and the CQC is responsible for this too.

Foundation trusts

The status of 'foundation trust' gives the NHS more power over how it spends its budget and how it plans to runs its services. The Health and Social Care Act wants all NHS trusts to work towards having foundation trust status by 2014.

An independent organisation called 'Monitor' processes NHS organisations' applications to become foundation trusts, and regulates already established NHS foundation trusts.

Care Programme Approach (CPA)

The Care Programme Approach is an initiative whereby individuals with a number of mental health needs are offered a package of mental health services. The needs of the individual are assessed and a 'care plan' is then produced, which gives details of all the services that individual is to be offered. The care plan also includes information about what to do in a crisis.

In addition to a care plan the individual also has access to a care coordinator who is a mental health professional responsible for making sure the services in the care plan are provided. The care coordinator will be a member of the community mental health team and will ensure that the care plan is reviewed at least once a year to make sure the services are still appropriate and available. The individual should have a copy of the plan but family members are only able to see a copy with the permission of the individual themselves.

Community mental health teams (CMHTs)

Your local CMHT will be made up of a group of professionals including psychiatrists, psychologists, community psychiatric nurses, mental health social workers and occupational therapists and these teams have worked together for a long time. Since the movement of mental health services to the community they have become an important part of mental health care. They operate according to local policy and therefore in different parts of the country there may be slightly different ways in which the service is delivered. It is not unusual to see the service divided in to 'assessment' and 'treatment' teams or groups of professionals who focus on particular conditions.

Crisis resolution teams (also called home treatment teams)

These teams are in place to treat individuals with serious mental illness either at home or at a day centre. The aim of this sort of intervention is to avoid admission to hospital and deal with the crisis until it is over.

Assertive outreach teams (AOTS)

These teams are set up to stay in touch with individuals who have a history of mental health problems but who may be finding it difficult to keep in contact with mental health services. The health professionals involved in these teams make flexible home visits or to a location of the individual's choice, to give support and treatment.

Early intervention in psychosis teams

It is very frightening to experience an episode of psychosis for the first time and these specialist teams work with individuals aged between 18 to 35 who have been unwell for less than three years and may experience periods of psychosis at various times or for the first time. Early intervention teams such as these are a major resource for families and individuals.

Early intervention services became a political priority in the United Kingdom when the NHS Plan stated that 50 early intervention teams would be put into place by 2004. These services were to work with individuals between the ages of 14 and 35, who were at risk of or were experiencing a first episode of psychosis.

Made up of professional staff including psychiatrists, psychologists, community psychiatric nurses, social workers and support workers, the teams were set up as a result of research which showed that the longer mental illness – in particular psychosis – went untreated the poorer the outlook for the individual. In addition a reduction in hospital stays and reduced suicide rates were also a driver for the development of the early intervention team.

Singh, et al. (2005) in their study supported the notion that:

> 'Early intervention in psychosis services produce better clinical outcomes than generic teams and are also cost-effective.'

The study provided evidence from two large trials in the UK and Denmark (Peterson et al., 2005; Craig et al., 2004) which showed that specialised early intervention services reduced hospital stays and the risk of a second relapse, as well as being highly valued by service users and their carers.

Other research has shown that when compared to standard mental health services, early intervention results in:

● shorter periods of untreated psychosis
● lower hospital bed use (McGorry, 2010)
● decreased relapse rates (Warner, 2005)
● better recovery, better engagement with services
● increased service user/carer satisfaction
● lower suicide rates.

The development of the early intervention service means it is now available across England (and in many other European countries, and Australia and America) providing treatment to support young people who are having symptoms of psychosis for the first time. Frequently these teams also work with young people who are showing warning signs which might lead to the development of psychosis.

In order to access the early intervention team, the individual will need to be referred by the GP. Once referred they will be able to talk to the team about their experiences, signs and symptoms and this will lead to a plan of support, help and treatment.

The team aims to give individuals and their families the help they need to understand what's happening to them and to provide information about medication and talking therapies.

Acute day hospitals/outpatient clinics/psychiatric hospitals

In cases where community care is not sufficient, individuals with mental health needs can access various hospital settings.

Acute psychiatric day hospitals are for those individuals who require treatment without being admitted to a traditional psychiatric hospital ward. For those who are detained under the Mental Health Act however, admission to a psychiatric hospital is the best option particularly if it is in the interests of their safety, or the safety of other people.

Specialist outpatient clinics run by NHS mental health trusts, are also available for individuals to visit if this is their preferred option for treatment.

Children and young people (CAMHS)

For children and young people aged up to 18, mental health services are provided by Child and Adolescent Mental Health Services, known as CAMHS.

The health professionals working in CAMHS are employed by a range of organisations, including NHS trusts and local social services and education departments, and all specialise in working with children and young people.

The teams include psychiatrists, psychologists, psychotherapists, social workers, psychiatric nurses, occupational therapists and family therapists.

CAMHS teams are organised into four 'tiers' of services.

- **Tier 1** services are provided by professionals who are not necessarily mental health specialists and these refer the young person to the relevant service. These include: GPs, health visitors, school nurses, teachers, social workers, youth justice workers and voluntary agencies.
- **Tier 2** services are provided by mental health specialists who work in the community and include GP practices, paediatric clinics or schools.
- **Tier 3** services are for children and young people with more serious mental health problems and are provided by specialist teams of different mental health professionals.
- **Tier 4** services are provided in day units, and highly specialised outpatient clinics or in-patient units and are for children and young people with serious mental health problems.

Forensic mental health services

Forensic mental health services are specialist services for individuals with mental health problems who have been arrested, or who have been to court and been found guilty of a crime.

They provide an alternative to prison offering specialist treatment and care. As 'secure' units, the individual is not at liberty to leave the service and they are detained under mental health legislation.

A referral to a forensic unit can be made following an assessment of an individual's needs or at the production of a psychiatric report and an individual may be referred when they are under police custody or detained whilst awaiting trial.

> **Evidence Activity**
>
> **Activity**
>
> Where does your own work environment fit into the structures shown above? Write a reflective account of how your service fits into the others organisations we have described in the section.

5 Examine the role and responsibilities of the main professionals and workers within mental health care

The amended Mental Health Act 2007 makes considerable changes to the way in which the care for individuals suffering from mental ill health is delivered and by whom. A major change has been to allow a broader range of professionals to carry out care and the new professional roles of Approved Mental Health Professional, Approved Clinician and the Responsible Clinician have been developed. This has largely come about as a result of the changes in the way care is delivered, higher caseloads of staff and increased needs of individuals suffering with mental ill health. The NIMHE National Workforce Programme in partnership with professional bodies and employers and under the banner heading 'New Ways of Working' responded to the need to address the working practices of professional staff from all disciplines and have been instrumental in bringing about changes. The new role of Approved Mental Health Professional is being opened up to occupational therapists, nurses and psychologists and the role of the Approved Clinician to psychologists, nurses, occupational therapists and social workers, in a major move to help address recruitment problems as well as support certain services to run more smoothly. With the changes to staffing and a more modern work force it is anticipated that continuity of care for the service user will be vastly improved.

We now look at the roles of individual staff within the CMHT.

Mental health nurses

The role of the mental health nurse (Registered Mental Health Nurse or RMN) is to work with individuals suffering from mental health conditions and their family and carers. It is a complex and demanding area of nursing since in some cases the individual being worked with maybe in crisis and will require careful handling. This sort of nursing demands a high level of communication skill, and as stigma remains attached to this sort of illness, empathy and skills of advocacy are required.

Mental health nurses come under specialist teams and may undertake further training in work with children or older people, or with people who suffer from specific conditions such as eating disorders.

The type of work the nurse carries out depends entirely upon the setting but the main responsibilities of the role include:

- assessing and talking to individuals about their problems and planning and delivering care;
- building relationships with individuals;
- ensuring the correct treatment is given;
- responding to distressed individuals and attempting to understand the source of distress in a non-threatening way;
- applying techniques to help people manage their emotions;
- undertaking group and/or one-to-one therapy sessions, both individually and with other health professionals;
- encouraging patients to take part in art, drama or occupational therapy where appropriate and organising social events;
- preparing and maintaining patient records;
- producing care plans and risk assessments for individuals;
- ensuring that the legal requirements are observed;
- working with individuals families and carers, helping to educate them and the patient about their mental health problems;
- promoting a 'recovery'-based approach to care.

The role of the community mental health nurse is to:

- coordinate the care of individuals;
- visit individuals in their home to monitor progress;
- assess individuals' behaviour and psychological needs;
- identify whether and when individuals are at risk of harming themselves or others.

(adapted from: http://www.nhscareers.nhs.uk/explore-by-career/nursing/careers-in-nursing/mental-health-nursing)

In 2006 the publication of the Best Practice Competencies and Capabilities for Pre-registration Mental Health Nurses in England identified the

> 'core competencies and capabilities, including knowledge and performance criteria, essential for mental health nurses (MHNs) at the point of registration in England.'

The need to build these competencies through programmes of professional development to enable mental health nursing students to develop and promote positive attitudes towards individuals with mental health problems was outlined.

The document referred to several other frameworks which have been instrumental in informing the outcomes of mental health education and training. These include:

- The Ten Essential Shared Capabilities (ESC) for Mental Health Practice
- The Standards of Proficiency for Pre-registration Nursing Education: First level Nurses – nursing standards of education to achieve the NMC standards of proficiency (Standard 7) (NMC)

- National Occupational Standards and National Workforce Competencies
- The Knowledge and Skills Framework (KSF).

Ten Essential Shared Capabilities (ESC)

The ESC set out the minimum requirements or capabilities that all staff working in mental health services across all sectors must have. In this way the ESC forms part of the

> 'basic building blocks for all mental health staff whether they are professionally qualified or not and whether they work in the NHS or social care field or the statutory and private and voluntary sector.'

Standards of Proficiency for Pre-registration Nursing Education (NMC)

In order to enter the register for mental health nursing, proficiency in the competencies and outcomes as stated within these standards has to be achieved. The Standards set out the minimum mandatory requirements for entry to the programme, together with the nature and assessment of learning.

National Occupational Standards and National Workforce Competencies

Skills for Health (SfH) have outlined the National Occupational Standards and National Workforce Competencies to provide performance measures in the health service. The NOS provide detailed descriptions of the competencies required in terms of the knowledge, understanding and skills required to perform a task, or to provide an intervention.

There are a number of standards that apply to mental health professionals. These include frameworks for:

- Mental Health, Allied Health Professions
- Clinical Health Skills
- Managing Work Related Violence
- General Health Care
- Healthcare Science
- Health and Social Care
- Older People
- Public Health Practice
- Drug and Alcohol National Occupational Standards (DANOS).

The Skills for Health work force tools enable users to map competencies within a role profile or job description against the NHS Knowledge and Skills Framework.

The Knowledge and Skills Framework (KSF)

The KSF is a further competency framework developed as part of the NHS Agenda for Change initiative. It applies specifically to career progression and pay for NHS staff, establishing pay levels and salary increments.

See the box below for the competencies as outlined in the 'Best Practice' document.

The Best Practice Competencies and Capabilities for Pre-Registration MHNS in England

1. Putting values into practice

Values

Promote a culture that values and respects the diversity of individuals, and enables their recovery.

2. Improving outcomes for service users

Communication

Use a range of communication skills to establish, maintain and manage relationships with individuals who have mental health problems, their carers and key people involved in their care.

Physical care

Promote physical health and wellbeing for people with mental health problems.

Psychosocial care

Promote mental health and wellbeing, enabling people to recover from debilitating mental health experiences and/or achieve their full potential, supporting them to develop and maintain social networks and relationships.

Risk and risk management

Work with individuals with mental health needs in order to maintain health, safety and wellbeing.

3. A positive, modern profession

Multidisciplinary and multi-agency working

Work collaboratively with other disciplines and agencies to support individuals to develop and maintain social networks and relationships.

Personal and professional development

Demonstrate a commitment to the need for continuing professional development and personal supervision activities, in order to enhance knowledge, skills, values and attitudes needed for safe and effective nursing practice.

Support workers

In all areas of the NHS and social care the support worker has a considerable role. It is likely that you yourself are such a worker. In the Mental Health Service this role has been an important one. This role also carries it with it other titles such as Community Support Workers, Home Care Support Workers or Mental Health Workers.

In 2003 the Department of Health suggested that by 2006, 3000 support time recovery workers would be in post across England (DoH, 2003) to aid the mental health teams' frontline staff. It was envisaged that this new worker would help in the recovery and independent living processes (DoH, 2003), hence the job title 'support time recovery worker'.

The role continues to evolve and change with each new government policy. Essentially support workers need specialist skills and experience to enable individuals with mental health problems to become more independent and confident in their own communities. The role can be a varied one depending upon the type of difficulty being worked with. For example, the support worker of an individual with autism or attention deficit disorder (ADD) will require a range of skills which may differ from those working with individuals who have obsessive compulsive disorder (OCD) or depression.

Support workers are based in a range of settings and their responsibility is to care for the individuals needs, including physical needs if necessary, together with household chores and tasks, or spending time with the individual and offering a friendly chat.

With the development of the role of the care coordinator, the support worker has an additional role of support for this person in the team of mental health workers. Both roles support carers and provide information and support.

General practitioners

The first person an individual with mental health needs is likely to come into contact with is their own GP.

Many mental health problems are dealt with by GPs without referral elsewhere but if more specialised treatment is needed a referral to secondary mental health services, such as in-patient hospital care or community mental health services, is made.

Generally a GP provides acute care for those in their own locality and offers preventative information and education for all ages and both sexes. They need to be skilled in treating people with multiple health issues.

Psychiatrists

Psychiatrists are specialist physicians with specific training in the assessment, diagnosis, treatment and prevention of mental illnesses. Based within the CMHT and in hospitals they are health professionals who have undergone further training following their basic medical school training.

Figure 5.4 Many mental health problems are dealt with by GPs

Occupational therapists

The role of the occupational therapist (OT) in mental health is to help individuals to build up the confidence and skills needed for personal, social, domestic, leisure and work activities.

Working in either hospitals, day centres or the community they are skilled in teaching specific skills and techniques, including arts, crafts, drama, dance, writing, and group work. In addition they often take part in individual counselling and training activities in daily living as well as helping individuals to overcome anxiety.

Psychologists

Psychologists differ from psychiatrists in the training they have undertaken. There are a number of specialties within this particular field of work, and training can be undertaken to work in clinical settings, educational roles as well as counselling and therapeutic settings.

Psychologists seek to understand the role of mental functions and behaviour in individuals and explore concepts such as why people behave in certain ways, how they are motivated, and what underlies their thinking and cognitive functions and behaviours.

Most psychologists are involved in some kind of therapeutic or research role and may work in university psychology departments or teach in other academic settings. Others may work in industrial settings.

Social workers/care managers

A social worker is a member of the health team who is able to form relationships with people and assist them to find solutions to their problems. This sort of work involves engaging with individuals themselves as well as their families and friends. They also work closely with the police, local authority departments, schools and the probation service.

As part of the Improving Access to Psychological Therapies (IAPT) service social workers may undertake further training to work as high intensity therapists, to better assist those with mental health issues.

Social workers who work with adults may specialise in working with people with mental health problems or learning difficulties and may be located in residential care, or help offenders in the community by supporting them to find work. They generally assist people to access healthcare, housing or benefits. When working with children or young people the social worker's role attempts to keep families together by providing advice and assistance, as well as managing adoption and foster care procedures. They also provide support to younger people leaving care or who are at risk or in trouble with the law. Children who are having difficulties at school or in their own homes are also helped by the social work service.

Independent advocates promoting the rights of people with mental health problems and their carers and those providing informal support

An advocate is someone who speaks on behalf of somebody else and represents their interests.

Under the revised framework for mental healthcare the role of the Independent Mental Health Advocacy (IMHA) is now a legal requirement and this new arrangement means that individuals who have been detained under the Mental Health Act are called 'qualifying patients' and are now entitled to the support of an advocate to provide information about their rights and care or treatment.

Mental health professionals must inform detained patients of their entitlement to an IMHA service and make relevant parts of their records available to the advocate. They may also find that the patient wants an advocate to represent them at decision-making meetings.

This role requires the person in it to have undergone training and it is up to the attending health professional to check that they meet regulated appointment requirements such as:

- having the appropriate training or experience or a combination of both;
- that they are a person of integrity and good character who is able to act independently of any person who requests an advocate to visit and interview the patient;
- that they are able to act independently of any person who is professionally concerned with a patient's medical treatment.

For individuals caring for people with mental issues a carers' advocate can be approached for help. Staff in the CMHT team can put carers in touch with support groups as well as individuals who have been trained in this role.

Carers' advocates act in much the same way as for the patient and will provide support throughout all processes.

Other workers in the CMHT

A more recent role is that of the primary care graduate mental health worker, sometimes known as PCGMHWs, or graduate mental health workers (GMHWs). This role has been developed to improve the management of common mental health problems by providing another worker in the primary care setting.

The key roles in this type of work include:

- Face-to-face client work with the delivery of brief interventions such as cognitive behavioural approaches for individuals with common mental disorders.
- Promoting positive mental health.
- Supplying information for individuals about mental health.
- Strengthening the knowledge about the network of community resources available for individuals with mental health problems.
- Wider community networking and liaison.

Primary care graduate mental health workers are different from primary care mental health workers who are professionally qualified workers – such as nurses, social workers or psychologists and those who work mainly in the Child and Adolescent Mental Health Services (CAMHS).

PCGMHWs are graduates usually with a relevant subject degree such as psychology, with work experience in a health and/or social care setting.

Evidence Activity

 5.5 **Activity**

Interview one of the above members of the mental health care team and describe in more detail how their role complements others in the team.

Explain what you understand by the independent advocacy role.

6 Understand the contribution of carers and those who give informal support to people with mental health problems and describe how carers/informal supporters should be involved in service delivery

Informal carers are those people who provide help and support to a family member or friend without payment. Carers can be anyone: spouses caring for loved ones, adults caring for neighbours, or even parents caring for ill or disabled children. There are also young people aged under 18 who care for a family member, perhaps a parent or sibling. Research, however, suggests that many carers continue to face barriers and feel that that their own particular health and social care needs are overlooked (Arskey et al., 2003).

They often feel marginalised and believe that some professionals fail to recognise the value of their contribution and that they are often at the mercy of inflexible hospital and appointment systems. Lack of transport, additional funds and respite care together with information breakdown all add to the burden of caring for an individual with mental health needs.

For those carers of individuals with mental health problems the need for greater access to information on issues such as medication and specific mental health problems has not been forthcoming and has proved very difficult to achieve.

The paper 'Valuing carers – calculating the value of carers' support' (2011) by Buckner and Yeandle updates the 2007 'Valuing carers', paper and highlights the role of over 6 million carers who deliver unpaid care. It recognises that:

> 'Without it, society would collapse.'

When we understand that the economic value of the contribution made by carers in the UK is £119 billion per year we can start to appreciate just how much these informal carers mean to the mental health service.

Carers UK is a charity which has been set up to help the millions of people who care for family or friends. They provide much needed advice and guidance for such people and also campaign to improve the carers' lives and to and influence policy makers, employers and service providers. With carers contributing so much by looking after the people they love we need to recognise that the isolation and lack of support many feel leaves them feeling devalued and helpless.

As a result of the work of this charity and with support from the government and research bodies there has been a call for action. As the section above shows, there has been improvement in a number of areas such as new rights to flexible working for carers, protection from discrimination in equality legislation and new pension rights.

Although the NHS still has a long way to go before it recognises its duty of care to carers and not just to those with mental health needs, healthcare professionals can start to change their own practice with respect to them. By involving the carer in the care assessment process and by actively seeking to engage them in the delivery of care we can at least show how their contribution is valued. In addition the recognition that they also require care themselves and respite from their duties, much the same as you need a break from work, can go a long way to helping them to feel valued in their role.

> **Evidence Activity**
>
> **Activity**
>
> Write a case study of one of your clients who has an informal carer. What are the needs of the carer in this particular case and what information might you be able to supply them to help them in their role?

7 Identify the rights and responsibilities of people with mental health problems and explain why workers should promote the rights of and challenge discrimination against people with mental health problems

The WHO Mental Health Declaration for Europe, the WHO Mental Health Action Plan for Europe and the European Pact for Mental Health and Wellbeing, acknowledge that action to address discrimination, stigma and social exclusion related to mental health problems is both a priority and a challenge since it can occur in all areas of life.

The WHO makes the point that to improve the quality of life of individuals with mental health problems we need to focus on involving people in their own treatment, recovery and tackling of stigma and discrimination.

Human rights

Discrimination around mental health is a human rights issue. According to the United Nations human rights are rights and freedoms that everybody should have and 'All persons with a mental illness ... shall be treated with humanity and respect for the inherent dignity of the human person.'

We all have the right to live without discrimination of any kind whether this is due to mental ill health or otherwise. Yet despite the laws in place to protect us, discrimination still occurs and individuals suffering from mental ill health are still denied their basic human rights, due to the fear and prejudice which accompanies mental illness.

But what exactly is discrimination and how can we challenge it?

Two types of discrimination are shown in the literature; direct and indirect:

- **direct discrimination** refers to the less favourable treatment some people get simply because of their age, race, sexual preference, disability or belief;
- **indirect discrimination** is the applying of practices that might favour one group over another, or applying conditions that a particular group are less likely to be able to comply with.

With respect to mental health issues, the discrimination and stigma sufferers are subjected to leads to social exclusion and poor quality of life. There are a number of factors that lead to discrimination including fear, inaccurate beliefs and blame.

- **Fear:** fear of violence and being attacked by somebody with a mental health problem is something the media has been guilty of reinforcing. Also, fear of the condition itself may affect our mind and behaviour.
- **Inaccurate beliefs:** such as the belief that people will always be ill and won't recover or that they cannot participate in their communities.
- **Blame:** individuals may be blamed for the conditions they have or may simply be labelled as being weak. Think about the person with depression who may be labelled as being unable to cope and may therefore not be given opportunities as a result.

Discrimination of those with mental health issues can prevent them from accessing basic things that most of us take for granted. For example they may be unable to find work or risk not getting a promotion. In addition they may not fit into the local community and may be made to feel unproductive and useless. Even simply attending school can be a major challenge.

Legal basis

Although the Disability Discrimination Act (1995 and 2005) prohibits discrimination against disabled people, those experiencing mental health problems have been continually disadvantaged in terms of accessing work, welfare benefits, housing, education and employment.

The Equality Act (2010) brings together the Disability Discrimination Act (DDA), the Race Relations Act, and the Sex Discrimination Act under one act to try to challenge and deal with discrimination.

For those with mental health problems, if the condition has a serious impact on the individual's daily life over a long period then it might be considered a disability under this law.

This act applies to all employers in the UK and provides protection for those with mental illness in a number of areas. It is now unlawful to treat a disabled (and we can include mental ill health within this definition if it affects daily life) person less favourably than another and reasonable adjustments to work practice must now be made to accommodate ill health. When being recruited to a post, pre-employment questionnaires are no longer used to ask about your heath prior to employment.

Policy and charters

Acts of parliament are in place and demonstrate moves towards a more egalitarian society; one in which individuals with mental health issues can expect to have their human rights met. But how can we, as care professionals, help to make a difference in terms of challenging discrimination? Research by the Institute of Psychiatry has shown that personal contact with individuals suffering from mental health problems is an effective way to reduce discrimination and prejudice, and that social marketing campaigns can make a real difference.

This research has helped inform the development of Time to Change, the biggest ever anti-stigma campaign in England. The move to tackle stigma in mental health was first addressed in 1996 following a report prepared by MIND 'Not Just Sticks and Stones'. The years following this report saw major funding input and a name change to 'Time to Change' in September 2008 led by the mental health charities MIND and Rethink Mental Illness. The Institute of Psychiatry is its evaluating the success.

The Time to Change programme includes 35 national, regional and community level projects to build an evidence base of effective strategies for reducing stigma and discrimination against people with mental health problems. The evaluation group led by the Institute of Psychiatry will assess three elements of stigma: knowledge, attitudes and behaviour, using the annual National Public Attitudes to Mental Illness survey (see Chapter 2). This survey has been conducted by the Department of Health since 1993.

Since the Time to Change project has been up and running some changes have been implemented. In February 2011, the government, in the No Health Without Mental Health document committed to 'support and work actively with Time to Change and other partners on reducing stigma for people of all ages and backgrounds'. In October of the same year £16 million was committed to Time to Change over the next four years. With £4 million also coming from Comic Relief the £20 million funding means that this campaign can continue its work until March 2015. Time to Change Wales was launched in February 2012, with three years' worth of funding from the Big Lottery Fund, Comic Relief and the Welsh government.

But is there any evidence to suggest that anti-stigma campaigns work? The surveys being carried out by the government and evaluated by the Institute of Psychiatry (IoP) have shown a gradual improvement in attitudes towards those with mental health issues. Overall a 4 per cent reduction in discrimination was reported between 2008 and 2009. People who were interviewed in 2009 reported less discrimination from family members (46 per cent in 2009 compared with 53 per cent in 2008) and less discrimination from friends (39 per cent in 2009 compared with 53 per cent in 2008). Unfortunately, in both years, about one third of those interviewed said they had experienced discrimination from health professionals. So clearly awareness still needs to be raised amongst health professionals as well as the general public.

In other countries around the world there have also been anti-stigma campaigns like Time to Change. In New Zealand the Like Minds, Like Mine campaign included a programme of adverts featuring celebrities speaking about their experiences of mental ill health which has led to a gradual improvement in attitudes in New Zealand. The Scottish campaign, See Me, launched in 2002 with a national publicity programme has worked with the media to encourage responsible reporting.

In addition to the above, the Mental Health (Discrimination) Bill aims to reduce the stigma and negative perceptions associated with mental illness by repealing legislative provisions that can prevent people with mental health conditions from serving as Members of Parliament, members of the devolved legislatures, jurors or company directors. More recently, the Labour Party leader has brought the whole issue of taboo and stigma in mental health to his party's campaign for re-election. His promise in October 2012 to address this issue has brought the subject back into the political arena.

How to challenge discrimination in practice

Evidence Activity

 Activity

The results of the 2011 government survey 'Attitudes to mental illness' are available online. See http://www.hscic.gov.uk/pubs/attitudestomi11

Have a look at this now and comment upon the progress of the anti-stigma campaigns to date.

Write a reflective account for your portfolio on how you promote the rights of individuals within your own care setting.

It appears that there is much being accomplished to reduce discrimination towards individuals with mental disorders and as care professionals we need to be aware of how we might also contribute to the changing of such attitudes. We can do this by speaking up when we see discrimination or become aware of a law or policy that unfairly excludes people, by adopting people-centred language like, 'A person living with …' and by thinking about how we can personally support and treat people around us who are living with a mental health problem.

8 Describe the framework of national service provision and how the different sectors relate to each other: education; employment and benefits; health and social care; housing; justice

The government's No Health Without Mental Health strategy clearly sets out to tackle the wider underlying causes of mental ill health and recognises that 'a life course approach' needs to be taken to change attitudes and experiences with mental health.

In achieving this, it is imperative that there is a cross-agency approach with education, justice, housing, health and employment departments all working together. The strategy puts forward six shared high-level mental health objectives which describe a shared vision for mental health and, as the government points out.

> 'for the first time ... there is a set of shared objectives and priorities for mental health that cover better mental wellbeing in the population, better mental health care and support and better physical health for those with mental health problems, across the life course.'

Education

The role of schools and colleges is upheld as being 'essential contributors' in ensuring that children who need professional health support are able to access services, and within the strategy several objectives have been outlined including the following:

- **A whole-school approach to supporting all pupils' wellbeing and resilience** which includes approaches and services for children and young people with, or at risk of, behavioural difficulties or emotional problems. Interventions to improve wellbeing include behavioural support, school-based counselling and parenting interventions.
- **Addressing bullying.**
- **Ensuring staff are aware of how mental health relates to their work.** Mental health awareness training to help staff recognise signs of mental ill health and understand the link between mental health and behaviour, attendance and attainment.
- **Accessing the e-learning packages for non-health professionals, being developed as part of the Children and Young People's IAPT programme.**
- **Knowing what specialist mental health support is available.** Schools and colleges can ensure they are aware of the services offered by local CAMHS and by the independent and voluntary sector, and of how children, young people and their families can access them.
- **Knowing when to intervene early to tackle mental health problems.** Schools and colleges should have a proactive approach to identify children and young people with the risk factors for, or the early signs of, behavioural problems. To achieve this, school leaders need to create a whole-school culture and ethos which supports good outcomes. A focus on high-quality teaching and learning, enriching extra-curricular activities and good pastoral care would promote this outcome.
- **Challenging mental health stigma** by ensuring students and staff know about mental health, how and when to seek help, and how to improve their own mental health and wellbeing. The Time to Change programme is currently piloting approaches to tackling mental health stigma and discrimination amongst young people.

Employment and benefits

The importance of work and its positive impact upon a person's mental health is widely recognised. Section 4 of the 'No Health' document states:

'Employment can also be an important part of many people's recovery from mental health problems. People with mental health problems can and do work – and supporting them to do so can save employers significant costs relating to staff turnover, under-performance and untapped potential.'

In addition the Department for Work and Pensions is undertaking a reform of the Welfare to Work programme, to ensure that work always pays and to try to tackle the benefit-dependant culture some people currently find themselves in. This will be achieved by replacing existing means-tested working-age benefits with a single universal credit.

A new integrated Work Programme to provide help for people to move into work will be developed and additional support for those who require more help, such as those currently receiving incapacity benefit, will be forthcoming.

In encouraging people to get back into work the government is targeting employers to raise their awareness of mental health issues. The support that individuals need will be provided by organisations such as Jobcentre Plus or other employment providers in conjunction with the health services.

Health and social care

The NHS white paper Equity and Excellence: Liberating the NHS, together with the public health white paper Healthy Lives, Healthy People and A Vision for Adult Social Care: Capable Communities and Active Citizens have all re-shaped the way in which the NHS delivers care.

The changes have recognised the link between the physical and mental health of individuals and the impact this may have on a person's general wellbeing.

Three outcome frameworks have been developed: for the NHS, public health and adult social care, all of which provide a comprehensive approach to tracking national progress against critical outcomes which apply equally to mental and physical health. An example of this is from Domain 2 in the NHS Outcomes Framework:

'Enhancing quality of life for people with long-term conditions'

In meeting this outcome two improvement areas of specific relevance to mental health are addressed and these are:

- enhancing the quality of life for people with mental illness – employment of people with mental illness; and
- enhancing the quality of life for carers – health-related quality of life for carers.

In another outcome for public health – 'Tackling the wider determinants of ill health' – all the proposed indicators measure determinants of mental ill health. In turn, reducing mental ill health will contribute to the improvement of overall health and wellbeing.

Housing

When individuals with mental health issues are discharged from long-term care it is imperative that they are discharged to accommodation, but this has not always been the case. For many people poor mental health is linked to insecure, poor-quality and overcrowded housing and homelessness.

The housing service and providers therefore have a key role in improving mental health outcomes by providing both settled housing and the services people need to maintain their homes as independently as possible.

In addition, with homeless people 40–50 times more likely to have higher rates of mental ill health, a commitment to address this issue is laid down in the No Health Without Mental Health strategy. The government is investing in the Places of Change programme to help improve the quality of hostel accommodation, and is committed to helping providers deliver more appropriate services to rough sleepers to help them to make the transition into a settled home, training or employment.

In outlining the changes that housing associations can make the following are proposed:

- **To link housing and health needs assessments**. Housing organisations have been charged with improving the evidence of housing needs of people with mental health problems, and using it to inform local needs assessments and commissioning plans. They also need to provide reviews of how housing waiting lists take account of mental health needs as well as physical needs to ensure 'parity of esteem' with physical health.
- **To identify tenants with risk factors for mental ill health, and deliver appropriate prevention and early intervention services**. Such services might be parenting or intensive family support, floating support to single tenants, and pre-tenancy and signposting services.
- **To work with NHS organisations to provide integrated support for people with mental health problems** in order to improve outcomes and to reduce overall costs and enable people to access the services they need.
- **Ensure staff and contractors receive mental health awareness training.** Training to be offered, and tailored to the organisations' specific needs. In addition, there will be training for landlords to improve their awareness of mental health issues in order to support them to let accommodation to people living with mental health problems.
- **Ensure debt and rent arrears collection processes are sensitive to people with a range of needs**. This includes offering reasonable adjustments for repayment.

(Adapted from No Health Without Mental Health.)

Justice

The publication of Lord Bradley's report on improving mental health and learning disability in 2009 presented evidence that there are now more people with mental health problems in prison than ever before. In efforts to maintain public protection from offenders with violent tendencies, custodial sentences have been commonly sought, but there is now a growing consensus that prison is not always the right environment for those with severe mental illness. Being in prison may result in an exacerbation of mental ill health increasing the risk of self-harm and suicide (Bradley Report, 2009).

With approximately 70 per cent of prisoners suffering from one or more mental health issues and with growing concerns about certain groups, such as women and people from black and minority ethnic communities as well as young offenders, the government is now acknowledging the need to improve mental health care for prisoners.

The Department of Health, the Ministry of Justice and the Home Office are working with the NHS, which has funding and commissioning responsibility for diversion services to identify a number of diversion pathfinders from existing services that will help to shape best practice. Further work will support the development of a mainstream service capacity to treat those referred by diversion services in order to ensure that offenders have the same access to mental health services as the rest of the population. In addition to this, Lord Bradley's report proposed rolling out a national liaison and diversion service, which was agreed by the government for implementation by 2014.

Evidence Activity

 Activity

Show how your own work setting links in with these different sectors and how you relate to each one.

a. Education
b. Employment and benefits
c. Health and social care
d. Housing
e. Justice

Demonstrate by providing evidence of each link within your portfolio.

Summary

The extent of mental health problems in the UK has moved recent governments to address their policies with respect to updating the mental health services offered as well as changing the roles and responsibilities of the staff delivering those services. Much of the change over the last 30 years has demonstrated a commitment to this growing problem which affects not only the mental health of society but also the physical health and wellbeing of individuals.

The Mental Health Act of 1983, the Mental Capacity Act 2005 and the Domestic Violence, Crime and Victims Act 2004 have all undergone amendments and change to make the decision-making process in dealing with individual with mental health issues a fairer one.

In addition, this chapter has also addressed the government's health strategies designed to supplement the laws.

The main policy, No Health Without Mental Health, launched in 2011, is the Coalition Government's strategy for mental health, and sets out six objectives to improve the mental health and wellbeing of the nation and the outcomes for people with mental health problems.

In delivering the strategy, changes to the roles of the people in the CMHT are reviewed and the role of informal carers has been more formally recognised.

Finally the chapter looked at how the wider welfare sectors such as education and healthcare all work together to ensure that a seamless service is provided.

References

ADSS (2005) 'Safeguarding Adults' A National Framework of Standards for good practice and outcomes in adult protection work. Available at www.adss.org.uk/publications/guidance (accessed on 5/9/11).

Arskey, H, Jackson, K, Wallace, A, Baldwin, S, Golder, S, Newbronner, E & Hare, P (2003) Access to Health Care for Carers: Barriers and Interventions. Report for the National Co-ordinating Centre for NHS Service Delivery and Organisation R&D. Available at www.sdo.lshtm.ac.uk/pdf/access_arksey_report.pdf

Buckner, L and Yeandle, S (2011) *Valuing Carers 2011: Calculating the value of Carers Support*. Universits of Leeds and Carers UK.

Craig T K, Garety P, Power P, Rahaman N, Colbert S, Fornells-Ambrojo M, et al. The Lambeth Early Onset (LEO) Team: randomised controlled trial of the effectiveness of specialised care for early psychosis. BMJ 2004; 329: 1067.

CSCI (2008) 'Raising voices: views on safeguarding adults'. London:CSCI.

CSCI (2005) Safeguarding Children The second joint Chief Inspectors' Report on Arrangements to Safeguard Children: A Summary. London CSC.

Department for Work and Pensions and the Department of Health (2009) Working our way to better mental health: a framework for action. London: HMSO.

DHSS (1975) Better Services for the Mentally Ill. Cmnd 6233. London: HMSO.

DoH (1999) Building For The Future: A White Paper for Wales. London: HMSO.

DoH (1999) *National Service Framework for Mental Health*. London: Department of Health.

DoH (1999) *National Service Framework for Mental Health: Modern Standards and Service Models*. Available at www.dh.gov.uk/en/Publicationsandstatistics/Publications/PublicationsPolicyAndGuidance/DH_4009598

DoH and the Home Office (2000) No Secrets: Guidance on developing and implementing multi-agency policies and procedures to protect vulnerable adults from abuse. Available at www.dh.gov.uk; www.gscc.org.uk (accessed on 30/8/11)

DoH (2001) Valuing People: A New Strategy for Learning Disability in the 21st Century' London: HMSO.

DoH (2003) *Inside Outside: Improving Mental Health Services for Black and Minority Ethnic Communities in England.* London: Department of Health.

DoH (2003) *Mainstreaming Gender and Women.* London: Department of Health.

DoH (2003) *Personality Disorder: No Longer a Diagnosis of Exclusion* London: Department of Health.

DoH (2006) Best practice competencies and capabilities for pre-registration mental health nurses in England. The Chief Nursing Officer's review of mental health nursing. London: DoH.

DoH (2006) The White Paper Our Health, Our Care, our Say: a new direction for community services: A brief guide. London: HMSO.

DoH (2007) Putting people first: a shared vision and commitment to the transformation of adult social care. London: HMSO.

DoH (2009) Lord Bradley's review of people with mental health problems or learning disabilities in the criminal justice system. London: DoH.

DoH (2009) New Horizons: towards a shared vision for mental health consultation. London. Department of Health.

DoH (2011a) No Health without Mental Health. London: The Stationary Office.

DoH (2011b) Talking therapies: A four-year plan of action: A cross-government mental health outcomes strategy for people of all ages. London: Department of Health.

Griffiths, R (1988) Community Care: an Agenda/or Action. London: HMSO.

Henderson C, Thornicroft G (2009) Stigma and discrimination in mental illness: Time to Change. Lancet; 373(9679):1928–30

HMG/DH (2011) No Health Without Mental Health: cross-government mental health outcomes strategy for people of all ages.

Home Office (1999) Action for justice (implementing the Speaking Up For Justice report on vulnerable or intimidated witnesses in the criminal justice system in England and Wales). London: HO Communication Directorate.

The Home Office (1989 and 2004) The Children Act 1989. London: Crown.

House of Commons (2005) Elder Abuse: Second Report of Session 2003–04. Available at http://www.dh.gov.uk/en/Publicationsandstatistics/Publications/PublicationsPolicyAndGuidance/DH_123766

http://www.centreformentalhealth.org.uk/criminal_justice/a_better_way.aspx (accessed on 30/10/12)

http://www.dh.gov.uk/en/Publicationsandstatistics/Publications/PublicationsPolicyAndGuidance/DH_123766

McKibbin, J, Walton, A, Mason, L (2008) *Leadership and Management in Health and Social Care for NVQ/SVQ Level 4.* London: Heinemann.

McGorry, P, Johanessen, J O, Lewis, S, Birchwood, M, Malla, A, Nordentoft, M, et al. (2010) Early intervention in psychosis: keeping faith with evidence-based health care. Psychol Med 40: 399– 404.

Petersen, L, Jeppesen, P, Thorup, A, Abel, M B, Ohlenschlaeger, J, Christensen, T O, et al. (2005) A randomised multicentre trial of integrated versus standard treatment for patients with a first episode of psychotic illness. BMJ; 331: 602.

Tilmouth, T and Quallington, J (2011) Diploma in Leadership for Heath and Social Care and Children and Young People's Services. London: Hodder Education.

Warner, R (2005) Problems with early and very early intervention in psychosis. British Journal of Psychiatry; 187 (suppl 48): s104–107

WHO (2005) European Ministerial Conference on Mental Health: Facing The Challenges, Building Solutions. Helsinki, Finland. 14 January.

Enabling mental health service users and carers to manage change

What are you finding out?

Dealing with the changes that we all encounter from time to time often brings a certain amount of stress. Whether it is change we have expected or something which has taken us by surprise it can lead to all sorts of alterations to our lives that impact upon our mental wellbeing. In this chapter we will look at the different ways in which change may impact on individuals and how we as health professionals can help to support service users and carers through the change process, including changes an individual wants to make and those which are due to circumstances.

The reading and activities in this chapter will help you to:

1. Understand the different ways in which individuals react to change and the contribution of others in facilitating change.
2. Explain the positive and negative changes that may be experienced by people with mental health problems and carers, family, friends and others in the individual's network and describe how to support individuals to become more independent.
3. Explain how change may impact on mental health workers.
4. Explain how a theory about the impact of change may help us understand the different ways in which people respond to change.
5. Apply an active approach in supporting service users or carers to manage change and explain how mental health problems may affect an individual's ability to cope with and manage change.
6. Explain how to help service users take each of the following active approaches to managing change:
   a. encouraging openness
   b. exploring options
   c. identifying losses and gains
   d. exploring obstacles
   e. problem solving
   f. goal planning
   g. identifying sources of support
   h. finding ways of keeping motivated
   i. maintaining hopefulness
   j. acknowledging and anticipating setbacks
   k. reinforcing achievements.

Assessment criteria covered in this chapter

Reading this unit and completing the activities will provide you with the knowledge, understanding and skills required to meet the assessment criteria listed below.

City & Guilds Level 3 Diploma in Mental Health Care (QCF) (600/5241/7)

Enable mental health service users and carers to manage change (Y/602/0171)

Learning Outcome 1 Understand the different ways in which individuals may react to change

Assessment Criteria	Page reference	Activity
1.1 Explain the positive and negative changes that may be experienced by people with mental health problems	p. 130	Evidence activity 6.2, p. 131
1.2 Explain the positive and negative changes that may be experienced by carers, family, friends and others in the individual's network	p. 130	Evidence activity 6.2, p. 131
1.3 Explain how change may impact on mental health workers	p. 131	Evidence activity 6.3, p. 132
1.4 Explain how a theory about the impact of change may help us understand the different ways in which people respond to change	p. 132	Evidence activity 6.4, p. 134
Learning Outcome 2 Apply an active approach in supporting service users or carers to manage change		
2.1 Explain how mental health problems may affect an individual's ability to cope with and manage change	p. 134	Evidence activity 6.5, p. 136
2.2 Explain how to help service users and carers take each of the following active approaches to managing change: a. encouraging openness b. exploring options c. identifying losses and gains d. exploring obstacles e. problem solving f. goal planning g. identifying sources of support h. finding ways of keeping motivated i. maintaining hopefulness j. acknowledging and anticipating setbacks k. reinforcing achievements	p. 136	Evidence activity 6.6, p. 137
2.3 Apply an active approach to enable service users or carers to manage change	p. 134	Evidence activity 6.5, p. 136

NCFE Level 2 Award in Understanding Working with People with Mental Health Issues (QCF) (500/9956/5)

Change and support in relation to mental health (T/601/2952)

Learning Outcome 1 Be aware of how mental health change occurs

Assessment Criteria	Page reference	Activity
1.2 Identify what needs to be in place for mental health change to occur	p. 127	Time to reflect activity 6.1, p. 129
1.3 Outline key areas of support in making change	p. 130	Evidence activity 6.2, p. 131
1.4 Outline the role of the support worker in fostering change	p. 130	Evidence activity 6.2, p. 131
1.5 Explain how to support people during mental health change	p. 130	Evidence activity 6.2, p. 131
1.6 Describe how to support individuals to become more independent	p. 130	Evidence activity 6.2, p. 131
Learning Outcome 2 Understand the role of others in the individual's mental health change		
2.1 Explain the component parts of the support workers relationship with service users	p. 136	Evidence activity 6.6, p. 137

1 Understand the different ways in which individuals react to change

Change happens and is inevitable. Those two facts are irrefutable. However, despite the fact that at some point in our lives we will all be subject to change, our reaction to both positive and negative change can have a huge impact upon our mental wellbeing.

Increasingly, in both our professional and personal lives, change seems to occur at an alarming rate. Scientific and technological change is happening so quickly in today's society that we are bombarded with new products all the time. The mobile phone is one such advance. Twenty years ago these phones required carrying cases and had large batteries making their mobility a little difficult at times. Now we have phones which can fit into our palm and can do so much more than merely make a call! We find with such change that we need to constantly revise our skills in order to keep up with the changing technology and this can have a marked effect on our wellbeing.

In addition, society changes at a rapid pace. No sooner do we get used to one situation we find that we are thrust into the path of yet another.

It is no wonder that this can cause us to feel overwhelmed and out of control and in some instances this leads to stress. Toffler (1970) researched the acceleration of change and its psychological effects. His findings suggested that it could lead to a set of physical and mental disturbances which he termed 'future shock' syndrome. He found that individuals who were being exposed to rapid changes responded with stress and feelings of helplessness and inadequacy.

So what is it about change that makes us feel uncomfortable and stressed? Think about how you might feel when you are learning something new. I meet a lot of students who react to the work they are engaging in at university and college in vastly different ways. Some feel self-conscious as they try to make changes to the way in which they previously did something and this brings about feelings of inadequacy. Others prefer not to engage with the work at all and complain about everything being too difficult. Both situations cause them to feel stressed. This then tends to lead to the adoption of coping behaviours.

Our instinctive behaviour in stressful situations such as this is to fight, or resort to flight or fright. You may have heard of this before. Physiologically, we are in a state of arousal due to the adrenaline release getting us ready to fight or run away. Some people like the adrenaline rush and therefore may

Figure 6.1 Fight, fright and flight

greet the change positively. They find the whole situation exciting. Others find the change a negative event and respond with confusion and concern.

If we respond with a fight reaction we may exhibit anger or aggression, or elation if it is positive to us. We cannot sustain this for too long, however, because our bodies become physically exhausted, so we may then resort to the flight and fright responses. With these responses we may display anxiety or helplessness and despair. If the stress continues for a long time the person is likely to be in a chronic state of anxiety and depression may result if this continues.

In mental ill health our clients are often stressed in some way, whether as a consequence of the condition itself or the situation they find themselves in. It may be necessary for the client to make certain changes to the way they do things or their lifestyle as a result of their condition and this in itself can lead to even more stress and the exhibition of the reactions shown above. This reaction may be because the person is focusing on what they are giving up or just cannot take on any more change.

In the case of the student, they are moving out of the comfort zone of a previous course and finding that the work at a higher level is becoming more difficult. This requires a new response and a more concerted effort on their part. The client, on the other hand, may fail to acknowledge that the change is likely to have a positive result as there is still a sense of loss regarding old habits, and however irrational this may appear this can lead to frustration and resistance.

Too much change at one time can also have negative effects on a person's wellbeing. When introducing change to a client's care or lifestyle the care worker needs to include the client in the decision making and by asking them simply 'How would you feel if …' you get a good idea about their reaction before you start the change process. This is a more supportive way of facilitating change and can be a useful approach to adopt

Knowing that individuals interpret change in a variety of ways is important for health professionals to enable them to anticipate and respond to clients' concerns and feelings. In situations where a client has undergone a major change in their lives, whether it be a physical or a mental change or a change in their living circumstances, the health professional can try to identify the kinds of reactions and questions that the client may have and prepare their responses. It is imperative that, in order to achieve this, the client case file includes a detailed reaction analysis based upon a good knowledge of the client and their emotional health status. This can be obtained by engaging with the client and identifying how they view change at the assessment stage. By helping the individual to have a certain amount of control over an event you can eliminate the threat to a certain extent and empower the person to grow stronger mentally.

Researchers have found a positive correlation between change and physical illness. The way change affects our physical state is evident through its effects on our mental state. You may be aware of the 'Life Change Scale' by Holmes and Rahe (1967), which is a psychological tool developed that measures the amount of change experienced by a person over a given time interval (Holmes and Rahe, 1967).

As you can see from the extract shown in Figure 6.2, the questionnaire scores responses to changes that individuals undergo. These changes are things such as moving house, changing jobs, getting married or divorced, the birth of a child, or the death of a family member. Each life change has a score and the total score for the individual is calculated as the sum of all changes that the person has experienced, multiplied by the score. So, for example, the death of a loved one will carry a high score as it is a significant change event.

When we use this scale we can see that individuals with a high life change score may be more prone to illness, either physical or mental or both. One of the most surprising findings though, was the fact that all changes whether positive (such as marriage or promotion) or negative (such as divorce or job loss) potentially caused illness to occur.

Life Event		Value	Check if this applies
1	Death of spouse	100	☐
2	Divorce	73	☐
3	Marital separation	65	☐
4	Jail term	63	☐
5	Death of close family member	63	☐
6	Personal injury or illness	53	☐
7	Marriage	50	☐
8	Fired at work	47	☐
9	Marital reconciliation	45	☐
10	Retirement	45	☐

Figure 6.2 Extract from the Life Change Scale (Holmes and Rahe, 1967)

But, interestingly, not all individuals react to such changes in the same way. As we mentioned above, some people react to change in a positive way and seem to thrive on the challenges it brings whereas others find it hard to accept and are thrown into turmoil at the slightest change. Human behaviour is a complex area of study and there is no objective reality. Individuals behave according to the way in which they perceive the situation to be and as we know these perceptions vary greatly. This is simply because individuals approach the same situation with different attitudes. You may have heard the expression 'one man's meat is another man's poison'. Changes which may appear reasonable and straightforward to some may to others be intolerable and cause a huge amount of reaction and stress.

Time to reflect

 Activity

Think about how you react to changes in your personal and professional life. Write down the feelings and thoughts that accompany change and determine how they affect the way in which you behave. Reflect on how this has a positive or negative effect upon you and then write some notes on how you might change your thought processes to a more positive perspective.

As health professionals we need to be able to understand these behaviours as normal outcomes of the change process. By doing so, we can avoid over-reacting to the behaviours of people who may seem to be resistant to change or who find it difficult to tolerate.

2 Explain the positive and negative changes that may be experienced by people with mental health problems and carers, family, friends and others in the individual's network and describe how to support individuals to become more independent

Most change brings up the notion of something happening which we know nothing about. It represents a fear of the unknown and even though it may be a positive event, such as getting married or promoted, it still causes us to react as if this were a threat to us.

We can identify the reaction as a six-stage process.

Stage 1 – Shock

This is similar to grief and is the time when an individual needs to take stock of what has happened. At this time the person will need to consider what is happening and get used to the situation. They may feel overwhelmed and stressed during this time.

Stage 2 – Denial

In this stage you may find the person denies the impact of the change and you might hear them rationalising what is happening. You may have heard fellow workers commenting that 'the changes being brought in don't affect my department'.

Stage 3 – Anger

This is one of the major reactions you may have experienced with both clients and fellow workers. In this stage there is constant questioning as to why things need to change and some individuals will resist or attack the change. This is a destructive phase as anger can completely destroy positive intentions. For your clients, this is the stage that needs careful handling.

Stage 4 – Acceptance

When the anger dissipates the fourth stage sees acceptance of the change and a sort of resignation to the change sets.

Stage 5 – Exploration

This is where there is exploration of what might take the change forward.

Stage 6 – Moving forward

Stage 6 is the final stage and is the challenge of moving forward and ensuring that the change leads to improvement.

When anything negative happens in life, such as losing a job or the onset of financial problems or even a death, an individual will pass through the above stages and go into a sort of crisis and this can lead to feelings of depression and anxiety. For your clients, the onset of a mental health condition will inevitably lead to changes in lifestyle and in their relationships and this may well exacerbate the problems. As their care worker you can do much to recognise what they are experiencing and help them through the various stages.

You may well encounter resistance to their changed condition and some individuals may become extremely negative and closed-minded, unable to accept what is happening to them. Although it is difficult in the case of a mental health condition to see a positive outcome to what is happening, the individual may be helped to see that with treatment and good support and care they will be able to engage in a normal life and be able to continue with their work.

Change happens and may be the result of positive and negative factors. Any change requires us to adapt and this adaptation process is likely to cause some level of stress. This is a result of having to change a habit or familiar situation or even our lifestyle.

Encouraging independence in somebody who has endured a change in their lives requires careful and sympathetic handling and needs to be done gradually. In order to facilitate recovery the health professional, the family and informal carers need to be aware that at some point the individual will need to take more responsibility in their daily lives and start to do things on their own. This process will require a step-by-step approach and may take time. The setting of short-term and then longer-term goals can help the person to manage their lives in their own way and gradually the carers may start to take a step back from the care, providing support more and more at a distance.

Evidence Activity

6.2 **Activity**

Describe the effects of a change one of your clients has had to adjust to and demonstrate how they were helped to work through the change process. Did they exhibit signs that they were experiencing the stages as shown above? Give examples.

Explain how you supported them to deal with the changes and encouraged them to adopt an independent approach.

3 Explain how change may impact on mental health workers

In healthcare, change happens for various reasons. Recently an amendment to the Mental Health Act has led to new ways of working in mental health and changes to policies and regulations. Inevitably, new research in practice means further changes to the way in which we deliver care.

Any change is a challenge and causes anxiety for some, so health workers need to be aware of how to minimise this and keep focused. Managing change requires a planned and systematic approach to ensure that the team's motivation is maintained.

We may not always agree with what we are expected to do in healthcare work, and occasionally there are decisions made at national level which impact on local delivery of care and over which we will have no control. Cutbacks in budgets in the public sector have left many organisations with fewer resources at their disposal and little option but to reduce the number of staff to save money. These sorts of decisions lead to a stressed work force and strained team relationships. Change is uncomfortable, and this discomfort leads to resistance as well as emotional responses that can cloud objectivity. It is normal to feel sad when a co-worker leaves the team whether through choice or redundancy and on a similar note we may feel anxious when a new manager starts. In the midst of these sorts of feelings we often fail to see the how such changes may be a force for the positive and may try to resist what is happening.

To cope with the stress associated with change in an effective way it is important to recognise that we can control the way in which change affects us. If we have a tendency to view all change in a negative way this will lead to stress. We prefer to live and work in a stable and secure sort of environment, but when things stay the same for a long time there may be a tendency to become complacent. If, however, we can look at enforced change as an opportunity for positive outcomes we might overcome our resistance to it and accept it without becoming stressed.

Our ability to take a mental step back to check whether we are automatically resisting the change and putting up barriers without scrutinising what the change may actually mean for us is crucial here. If we can examine the change for positive outcomes this will do much to help us accept what is happening. The personal positive outcome here is the lowering of our stress level.

Activity

Consider a recent change to your working environment. Discuss with your colleagues how they reacted to the change and what their thoughts and feelings were when it was first introduced. Describe how the change impacted upon the individuals and identify the different responses they showed.

4 Explain how a theory about the impact of change may help us to understand the different ways in which people respond to change

John P. Kotter's (1995) 'eight steps to successful change' provides a useful model for managing the impact of change. Through each stage, Kotter recognises how individuals respond to and approach change, and identifies this through how we see, feel and then act towards change.

Kotter's change model can be summarised in eight steps:

- **Increase urgency** – Inspire people to move, make objectives real and relevant.
- **Build the guiding team** – Get the right people in place with the right emotional commitment and the right mix of skills and levels.
- **Get the vision right** – Get the team to establish a simple vision and strategy, focus on the emotional and creative aspects necessary to drive service and efficiency.
- **Communicate for buy-in** – Involve as many people as possible, communicate the essentials simply, and appeal and respond to people's needs. De-clutter communications – make technology work for you rather than against you.
- **Empower action** – Remove obstacles, enable constructive feedback and lots of support from leaders – reward and recognise progress and achievements.
- **Create short-term wins** – Set aims that are easy to achieve, in bite-size chunks. Have manageable numbers of initiatives. Finish current stages before starting new ones.
- **Don't let up** – Foster and encourage determination and persistence. Ongoing change – encourage ongoing progress-reporting – highlight achieved and future milestones.
- **Make change stick** – Reinforce the value of successful change via recruitment, promotion, new change leaders. Weave change into culture.

(www.businessballs.com/changemanagement.htm)

Kotter's model shows how individuals may be motivated to 'buy' into the change by 'owning' it and this is the important element of any successful change.

We can reduce the model above down to four major factors:

- the urgency factor
- the vision factor
- the resource factor
- the action factor.

The urgency factor

The pressure to change is on the organisation and you need to get the team behind you to ensure successful outcomes.

The vision factor

A clear shared vision is imperative and necessary to ensure that team members are with the change and not against it. Motivation is the key here and there are various things which motivate people.

Some individuals take huge pride in the work they do, but if this goes unrecognised, motivation drops. These individuals are more likely to perform well and provide new ideas for improving the organisations wellbeing if they do not feel they are being taken for granted.

Being happy in work is also a motivating force and treating others as we would wish to be treated ourselves is likely to improve relationships between everyone at all levels in the organisation.

Some individuals thrive on being given responsibility as this demonstrates to them that they are trusted.

Being valued and feeling as though you are part of the organisation's success is a huge motivating force. Think about the last time somebody thanked you for your contributions and for a job well done.

The resource factor

The resources needed to implement change have to be identified before changes are made. Without the necessary tools, you and your team cannot be expected to do the job.

The action factor

When everything else is in place, the next part of any change is to act. Having planned for change, and implemented it, you then need to check that it is working and act if it is not.

If the change is working, maintaining the effectiveness and appropriateness of the change is good practice. By monitoring and analysing the data produced you are in a position to evaluate its success or otherwise and to keep the team informed of progress.

The evaluation phase of any project involves a sequence of stages that includes:

- **forming** objectives, goals and hypotheses of the project;
- **conceptualising** the major components of the project, the participants, the setting, and how you will measure the outcomes;
- **designing** the evaluation and giving **details** of how these components will be coordinated;
- **analysing** the information, in both qualitative and quantitative ways;
- **using** what is learned through the evaluation process.

(adapted from Tilmouth et al., 2011)

Another model for change is that proposed by Kurt Lewin (1947). Although the theory has been criticised for being too simplistic, and a lot has changed since it was originally presented in 1947, it remains a useful model for understanding change. He proposed a three stage theory of change which is referred to as Unfreeze, Change, Freeze (or Refreeze).

Stage 1: Unfreezing

The first stage is about preparation for change and is an important stage to understand. Unfreezing is about readiness to change and perhaps creating a situation in which we and others want the change.

If we can help others to see that the change is necessary we are more able to motivate others to want it. By introducing a deadline we also introduce the idea of urgency to make the change and this has the effect of getting others behind the change. The closer we get to the deadline date, the more likely we are to get the task started. With a lack of deadline there is a lack of motivation and individuals become less likely to make the change.

In this stage the unfreezing is about getting motivated for the change and weighing up the 'pro's' and 'con's'. Lewin called this process the 'force field analysis', which is a way of way of looking at the different factors (forces) for and against the change and analysing the need for it. If the factors for change outweigh the factors against change, only then is the change made. If not, then this is likely to lead to low motivation and change will be difficult.

This first 'unfreezing' stage involves motivating teams and businesses towards change.

Stage 2: Change (or Transition)

Change is a process, not an event, and processes require transition. This stage is about the journey we need to make towards the change and also in reaction to the change. It is also the most alarming part of the process. When we are learning something new we need time to understand and work through the changes. At this time support is really important and can be given in the form of training and coaching. A useful thing to do is to keep reminding individuals of how the change will benefit them so that they have clear picture of how the change will be when it occurs.

Stage 3: Freezing (or Refreezing)

However this stage is referred to, it is the time in the process when the changes have been accepted and become the norm. This is when a new stability emerges. This is where the model has been criticised since change happens so frequently there is little time to settle into new routines and patterns. Freezing therefore offers a too rigid approach where change is seen as a more continuous and chaotic process.

The model has therefore evolved to now be seen with this final stage as being more flexible.

Lewin's model is a good one to frame a process of change. Each stage can be expanded to aid better understanding of the process and by applying the concepts of force field analysis we can gain a greater insight into how we deal with change.

> ### Evidence Activity
>
> **Activity**
>
> Write a reflective account of a recent change you have been forced to make as a result of funding cuts in the public sector.
>
> How did you manage the change and, on reflection, what might you do differently next time? Were you aware of any of the stages in either of the two models above being used?

5 Apply an active approach to enable service users or carers to manage change and explain how mental health problems may affect an individual's ability to cope with and manage change

The onset of mental illness is alarming for both the individual sufferer and family and friends. There may be an initial denial about what is happening followed by relief when the acute phase has passed.

The changes experienced during these times can be particularly difficult and families and the individual need to be provided with support to help them adapt. There may be a tendency, once the initial symptoms have subsided, to believe that this is the end of the problem and that the sufferer is now free of the condition. Even if the family accept that the individual has an illness that will have an ongoing effect on all of their lives, this can lead to tensions and relationship difficulties.

One way in which a family and the sufferer themselves can be helped to adapt to the change is to educate them about the illness. Knowledge about mental health conditions is so limited that some people may think the condition is totally disabling, needing a lot of support. This is not, however, the case in most instances. The family need to be able to take control of what is happening and be enabled to manage the illness and plan for the future. As a mental health worker you can do much to help the family find sources of information that help them to understand how the illness affects their loved one. In addition they can be given information about the types of treatment available and the ways in which they can support themselves.

A rather more difficult area to come to terms with is the stigma surrounding mental ill health that is felt by both the sufferer and the family and friends. This may lead to reluctance to discuss the condition with friends or employers since they may feel their reaction could damage relationships.

The myths and misconceptions surrounding mental illness continue even in these more enlightened times. In mental health conditions it is the lack of knowledge about the condition that causes fear and this may lead others to avoid the sufferer and family at the very time they require support. For example, a person with schizophrenia may start to act irrationally and exhibit bizarre behaviour traits which others find confusing and shocking. The unpredictable nature of the condition may result in others avoiding contact and also cause the family to limit visitors to the home thus exacerbating the isolation. There is also the tendency for others to blame the family for the sufferer's condition believing it to be a result of a poor family background. The result of stigma is that the family becomes more and more withdrawn in an attempt to protect themselves and their loved one. This is in contrast to the case of a physical illness such as cancer when the sufferer is likely to be inundated with help and support. Mental health workers therefore need to be aware that this is happening and encourage the integration of the sufferer and the family into normal life through help groups and activity.

The stress associated with the major changes occurring in the sufferer as a result of their behaviour is both exhausting and frightening and can cause a serious rift in family life. Families may believe that the person will be 'cured' when they are on medication only to become frustrated by the changes they need to make to accommodate a new routine.

Family life becomes unsettled and difficult and plans for family outings or holidays simply need to be put on hold as the needs of the person suffering the episode become all important. This has an effect on other members of the family, and with the focus solely on the sufferer for a time, they can feel neglected and forgotten.

A mental healthcare worker can be very helpful in working with the whole family to deal with their anxiety at this time. With a good knowledge of mental illness and community resources at the families' disposal the worker can help them to identify resources for their loved one and themselves. One resource is the Carer's Trust, a new charity formed in April 2012, with the remit to

'Work(s) to improve support, services and recognition for anyone living with the challenges of caring, unpaid, for a family member or friend who is ill, frail, disabled or has mental health or addiction problems. With our Network Partners, we aim to ensure that information, advice and practical support are available to all carers across the UK.'

(www.carers.org/about)

The trust came about as a result of the 'Partners in Care' campaign and the merger of two bodies working with families and carers. When it was launched in January 2004 the campaign aimed to:

- highlight the problems faced by carers of people with different mental health problems and learning disabilities;
- encourage true partnerships between carers, patients and professionals.

Peter Tihanyi (2004) of the Princess Royal Trust for carers stated that:

> 'The Partners in Care campaign helps to develop a dialogue on vital issues that affect the mental health and well-being of some of the most vulnerable people in Britain, including the carers themselves. We hope that the campaign will leave a legacy of better mutual understanding and improved care.'

Further information for carers has been produced by the College's Partners in Care campaign which is available online.

Evidence Activity

 Activity

Prepare a resource for carers and service users on how they can manage the changes brought about by mental health problems.

6 Explain how to help service users and carers take an active approach to managing change by: encouraging openness; exploring options; identifying losses and gains; exploring obstacles; problem solving; goal planning; identifying sources of support; finding ways of keeping motivated; maintaining hopefulness; acknowledging and anticipating setbacks; reinforcing achievements

This chapter has so far shown how change due to mental illness has an effect not only on the sufferer themselves but also on their family and friends. In helping the individual to cope with change there are a number of professionals who can contribute to this

When seeking treatment the GP is likely to be the first person who is contacted; alternatively the person may be taken into hospital and referred immediately to a psychiatrist. This first contact with the Mental Health team will do much to encourage the family and the sufferer to be *open* about the illness and how it is affecting them. In addition the health professional can start to help the family *explore options* available to them with respect to treatment and lifestyle changes. The changes being experienced not only by the sufferer themselves but also the family will require full exploration on the part of the team and the support being offered needs to be clearly outlined to all involved.

The GP can give support, prescribe medication or refer the individual to a counsellor or psychotherapist. If it is thought the condition may require different treatment there may be a referral to the CMHT or a psychiatrist.

The psychiatrist is a medical doctor with special training in mental illnesses and emotional problems and they may also have a psychotherapy background.

There are so many things that may be the cause of the mental illness that support may need to come from different areas of the mental health team and the *sources of support* are many and varied.

Whatever the cause – trauma, relationship difficulty, drug and alcohol problems or dependency, even unemployment causing stress – no one person in the team will be trained to deal with all these areas. This is why it is imperative that a whole-team approach is adopted so that the person may have access to other support when needed.

The key worker is the main link for the individual within the wider team and is responsible in the first instance to develop a helpful and supportive partnership with the individual and the family.

In *exploring obstacles, problem solving and goal planning* the key worker should be instrumental in getting to know the person really well and becoming aware of the difficulties they are experiencing. This member of staff needs to be able to give counselling and advice and guidance about resources available to them and their family and should also develop a care plan to ensure that any *setbacks* are dealt with efficiently and positively.

The care plan should include:

- the actual problem (or problems);
- the risks involved (if any);
- the person's strengths;
- what needs to be done to aid recovery;
- a list of staff who should be helping in the recovery;
- the person's own views.

There are other staff in the wider team who may be called upon to provide support and they can be instrumental in helping the sufferer and their family to maintain a positive outlook, to keep them *motivated* and hopeful. These may include outreach workers, benefits workers, support workers, recovery workers, vocational therapists, arts therapists and psychotherapists. In addition there are those who have specialist knowledge and skills who may work in other areas of health but can also be a useful support. These include people who have had mental health problems and therefore can give a service user perspective or even act as advocates. Staff who work in day centres and housing organisations provide a different type of service but one that nonetheless can be instrumental in helping the individual and their family remain motivated and positive.

Families and carers need support and encouragement but also often want to help in some way. As a health worker you need to ensure that they are provided with information and can attend regular support groups. Although there is a confidentiality issue here the CMHT will encourage the family to be involved and will therefore seek permission from the sufferer to enable information to be shared with their family.

> **Evidence Activity**
>
> **Activity**
>
> Choose four of the following areas and reflect upon how you have actively helped a service user in your care to approach and adapt to change and how others contribute to facilitating change:
>
> a. Encouraging openness
> b. Exploring options
> c. Identifying losses and gains
> d. Exploring obstacles
> e. Problem solving
> f. Goal planning
> g. Identifying sources of support
> h. Finding ways of keeping motivated
> i. Maintaining hopefulness
> j. Acknowledging and anticipating setbacks
> k. Reinforcing achievements

Summary

This chapter has summarised how dealing with the changes that we all encounter from time to time is often accompanied by feelings of stress not only from the service user's point of view but also for family, friends and care workers. Unexpected or even expected change can lead to all sorts of alterations to our lives that impact upon our mental wellbeing. The different ways in which change impacts upon individuals and how health professionals can help to support service users and carers through a change process have been demonstrated. In addition we have looked at the myths and misconceptions surrounding mental illness which tend to cause fear leading others to avoid the sufferer and family at the very time they require support. Health workers, then, are a crucial link to the support services for the family and sufferer in times of change.

References

Holmes, T and Rahe, R H (1967) The Social Readjustment Rating Scale. *Journal of Psychosomatic Research*, 11; 2: 213–18.

Lewin, K (1947) Frontiers of Group Dynamics. *Human Relations*, 1: 5–41.

www.carers.org/about

Tilmouth, T, Davies-Ward, E and Williams, B (2011) *Foundation Degree in Health and Social Care*. London: Hodder Education.

Toffler, A (1970) *Future Shock*. New York: Bantam Books.

Care and support planning and risk management in mental health

This chapter will provide the knowledge and understanding of the key processes involved in the planning of care and the support of clients with mental health issues. While reviewing risk assessment practice and the stages of the care assessment process you will be helped to understand how crucial such processes are in this field of work. We look at the risk factors involved in mental health care and describe the suicide reduction strategy for the United Kingdom.

The reading and activities in this chapter will help you to

1. Explain the following key principles and values which underpin effective care and support planning and describe the key features of models of mental health needs and care:
   a. person-centred
   b. needs-led
   c. holistic approach
   d. collaboration and full participation
   e. building on strengths
   f. anti-discriminatory practice
   g. promoting social inclusion and overcoming barriers to accessing services
   h. recovery-focused
   i. effective record keeping.
2. Describe the tasks associated with each stage of the care including the stages of a basic mental health assessment and support process and the key principles and values that should be implemented at each stage of the care and support process:
   a. assessment of need
   b. planning goals
   c. monitoring progress
   d. reviewing plans.
3. Explain how to enable service users and carers to take an active part in the care planning process.
4. Explain how and why agencies need to work together within the care planning process.
5. Describe three possible differences or conflicts that may occur between those involved in the care planning process and identify ways of overcoming these, including where to get additional support and advice.
6. Explain how to keep effective accurate records and describe how to respond to complaints.
7. Explain what a risk assessment is and the key principles and values that underpin effective risk management as well as how these contribute to the protection of individuals:
   a. positive risk-taking in addition to risk of harm
   b. considering a range of types of risks
   c. evidence-based approach
   d. forward planning to reduce the risk of harm
   e. specifying warning signs
   f. contingency planning

g. specifying roles and responsibilities
h. anti-discriminatory practice
i. regular review.
8. Explain how and why agencies need to work together in the risk management process.
9. Explain how to involve carers and families in the risk management process.
10. Describe the range and categories of risk factors that should be considered during risk assessment for an individual in different types of risk situations:
    a. risk of harm to self
    b. risk of harm to others
    c. risk of being harmed by others
    d. risk of being harmed by mental health services.
11. Describe the role of suicide reduction strategies and explain how they can inform actions within a risk management process.

Assessment criteria covered in this chapter

Reading this unit and completing the activities will provide you with the knowledge, understanding and skills required to meet the assessment criteria listed below.

City & Guilds Level 3 Diploma in Mental Health Care (QCF) (600/5241/7)		
Understand care and support planning and risk management in mental health (R/602/0167)		
Learning Outcome 1 Understand how to work within the care and support planning process		
Assessment Criteria	Page reference	Activity

1.1 Explain the following key principles and values which should underpin effective care and support planning:
  a. person-centred
  b. needs-led
  c. holistic approach
  d. collaboration and full participation
  e. building on strengths
  f. anti-discriminatory practice
  g. promoting social inclusion
  h. recovery-focused
  i. effective record keeping
	p.142	Evidence activity 7.1, p. 147

1.2 Describe the tasks associated with each stage of the care and support planning process:
  a. assessment of need
  b. planning goals
  c. monitoring progress
  d. reviewing plans
	p. 147	Evidence activity 7.2, p. 148

1.3 Explain the key principles and values that should be implemented at each stage of the care and support planning process:
  a. assessment of need
  b. planning goals
  c. monitoring progress
  d. reviewing plans
	p. 147	Evidence activity 7.2, p. 148

1.4 Explain how to enable a service user to take a full and active part in the care planning process	p. 149	Evidence activity 7.3, p. 149

(Continued)

(Continued)

1.5 Explain how to enable carers and family members to take an effective and appropriate part in the care planning process	p. 149	Evidence activity 7.3, p. 149
1.6 Explain why and how agencies and workers should work together within the care planning process	p. 149	Evidence activity 7.4, p. 150
1.7 Describe three possible differences or conflicts that may occur between those involved in the care planning process and identify ways of overcoming each of these differences or conflicts	p. 150	Evidence activity 7.5, p. 154
1.8 Explain how to keep effective, accurate and concise records of the care planning process	p. 152	Evidence activity 7.6, p. 154
Learning Outcome 2 Understand how to work within a risk management process		

2.1 Explain the key principles and values that should underpin effective risk management and how these contribute to the protection of individuals:
  a. positive risk-taking in addition to risk of harm
  b. considering a range of types of risks
  c. evidence-based approach
  d. forward planning to reduce risk of harm
  e. specifying warning signs
  f. contingency planning
  g. specifying roles and responsibilities
  h. anti-discriminatory practice
  i. regular review
  j. effective record keeping
	p. 154	Evidence activity 7.7, p. 156

2.2 Explain why and how agencies and workers should work together within the risk management process	p. 156	Evidence activity 7.8, p. 157
2.3 Explain how to involve carers and family members effectively and appropriately in the risk management process	p. 157	Evidence activity 7.9, p. 157

2.4 Describe the range of risk factors that should be considered during risk assessment for an individual in different types of risk situations:
  a. risk of harm to self
  b. risk of harm to others
  c. risk of being harmed by others
  d. risk of being harmed by mental health services
	p. 158	Evidence activity 7.10, p. 159

2.5 Describe the role of suicide reduction strategies and explain how they can inform actions within a risk management process	p. 159	Evidence activity 7.11, p. 162

NCFE Level 2 Award in Understanding Working with People with Mental Health Issues (QCF) (500/9956/5)		
Approaches to care and management in mental health (K/601/2950)		
Learning Outcome 1 Understand the key features of the care planning process		
Assessment Criteria	Page reference	Activity
1.2 Outline the stepped approach to care	p. 147	
1.3 State the key principles of care planning	p. 142	Evidence activity 7.1, p. 147

(Continued)

(Continued)

Learning Outcome 2 Understand aspects of good practice in the care planning process		
2.1 Describe the key features of models of mental health needs and care	p. 142	Evidence activity 7.1, p. 147
2.2 Explain what a risk assessment is	p. 154	Evidence activity 7.7, p. 156
2.3 Outline the importance of carrying out a risk assessment with a person who may have mental health problems	p. 154	Evidence activity 7.7, p. 156
2.4 Identify categories of risk and the key components of a risk assessment when working with a service user	p. 158	Evidence activity 7.10, p. 159
2.5 Describe the stages of a basic mental health assessment	p. 147	Evidence activity 7.2, p. 148
2.7 Explain how to report and record work activities	p. 152	Evidence activity 7.6, p. 154
2.8 Explain the importance of accurate record keeping	p. 152	Evidence activity 7.6, p. 154

City & Guilds Level 3 Diploma in Mental Health Care (QCF) (600/5241/7)		
Principles for implementing duty of care in health, social care or children's and young people's settings (R/601/1436)		
Learning Outcome 1 Understand how duty of care contributes to safe practice		
Assessment Criteria	Page reference	Activity
1.1 Explain what it means to have a duty of care in own work role	p. 154	Evidence activity 7.7, p. 156
1.2 Explain how duty of care contributes to the safeguarding or protection of individuals	p. 154	Evidence activity 7.7, p. 156
Learning Outcome 2 Know how to address conflicts or dilemmas that may arise between an individual's rights and the duty of care		
2.1 Describe potential conflicts or dilemmas that may arise between the duty of care and an individual's rights	p. 150	Evidence activity 7.5, p. 152
2.2 Describe how to manage risks associated with conflicts or dilemmas between an individual's rights and the duty of care	p. 154	Evidence activity 7.7, p. 156
2.3 Explain where to get additional support and advice about conflicts and dilemmas	p. 150	Evidence activity 7.5, p. 152
Learning Outcome 3 Know how to respond to complaints		
3.1 Describe how to respond to complaints	p. 152	
3.2 Explain the main points of agreed procedures for handling complaints	p. 152	

1 Explain the key principles and values which underpin effective care and support planning and describe the key features of mental health needs and care

We all come to the care process with differing values and beliefs. In effective care and support planning it is essential for care professionals to adopt shared principles and values in order to provide fair treatment.

Principles, which are based on values, refer to basic guidelines about the right way to behave. They refer, then, to your own personal code of conduct. Values on the other hand are beliefs about what is important to us as individuals, and our beliefs about what is morally right and wrong.

We learn our principles and values from all sorts of influences – parents, school, society, the media – and they change as we grow. The attitudes we display are linked to our values and affect how we react to others. It is important, however, especially when working in healthcare, that we value others who may not share the same beliefs as ourselves. We come into contact with people from all walks of life and it is so important to develop a tolerance of their differences and promote understanding of the different cultures we come into contact with. One of the ways in which we do this is through the adoption of general standards of behaviour in the work place which are set up through the policies and procedures of the service. By following such policies the care worker can support the service user in a professional way.

In supporting clients in mental health services there are a number of approaches and care models which have been identified and trialled. In recent years the emphasis has been to provide 'personalised care planning' to address an individual's full range of needs, namely: health, personal, social, economic, educational, mental health, ethnic and cultural background and circumstances. In the past the focus was on medical needs only and this meant other aspects of the person's life were neglected. Two models that arose to support this approach were:

a) Person-centred care and d) Collaborative and partnership care

The term 'person-centred care' often applied to elderly people and those with disabilities. Although it has not been defined sufficiently in the literature the term is now used to describe care which is user-focused, promoting independence and autonomy. Collaborative and partnership approaches to care often also use the term 'person-centred' to describe their ethos (Innes, 2006).

In 2004 Stephen Ladyman, former Parliamentary Under-Secretary of State for the Community, described person-centred practice as:

> 'a move away from mass-produced services. Services that too often created a culture of dependency and move towards a future that seeks to develop the potential that is in every single individual'

> (Ladyman, 2004)

Personalising the services offered to individuals is about building systems of care that are tailored to meet their own individual needs and designed with their full involvement. Historically, a 'one size fits all' approach to care was practised, and this meant the individual having to fit into and access already existing care services, whether they were appropriate or not. Person-centred practice is a way of caring for a person as an individual with unique needs and differences.

It is an empathetic type of care since you are caring for an individual by being aware of how they might be feeling, and is very different from treating everybody the same. The care is based upon collaboration and partnership.

b) Needs-led

The needs-led approach to care has been based upon a number of theories about human need.

The development of Maslow's original's hierarchy has moved it away from a hierarchy and towards 'an emergent collection of human development essentials'.

Theorists see needs as based upon such areas as:

- safety and security
- love and belonging

- self-esteem
- personal fulfilment
- identity
- cultural security
- freedom
- justice
- participation.

For Bradshaw, the needs approach to care refers to four types of need. He identifies:

- normative needs
- perceived/felt needs
- expressed needs
- comparative needs.

Normative needs refer to the needs which the health professional defines and which are based upon an 'expert' view.

Perceived/felt needs are those which the individuals themselves feel and are referred to as 'wants' rather than needs.

Expressed needs are those which are demanded when the person seeks assistance and **comparative needs** refer to a comparison made with others in defining their needs. This can be seen in our understanding of poverty. In some cases we may compare what we have with what others have and consider ourselves to be poor. This does not always, however, link to real poverty and is not a good measure (Bradshaw, 1972).

In care work this approach has been favoured as it clearly identifies giving the care the individual needs, but it is not without its critics. One of the problems is that the identification of 'needs' is a highly subjective one. Also, working with clients in a needs-led approach meant that professionals focused on the immediate situation and supported the requirements that would be provided by the care professional. Another problem with focusing on 'needs' is that they change over time, and there is no specified point at which the work can be said to have been achieved. The work frequently lacks direction and purpose and it is almost impossible to measure success or failure. Needs have a tendency to become moveable feasts in that, once they are identified, others also become apparent and there appears to be no end to the work being done for the client.

c) Holistic approach

Holistic care focuses on the whole individual. All needs including physical, mental, social, environmental and spiritual are viewed as of equal importance and, in determining the care needed, individuals who have all these needs met within one care package seem to have more positive outcomes.

The No Health Without Mental Health outcomes strategy (DoH, 2011b) aimed to promote physical and mental health as equal components and to shift society's perception of 'health' towards a more holistic understanding. In addition, Section 1 of the Health and Social Care Act 2012 emphasised the importance of mental health alongside physical health. To this end joint working initiatives between social services and CAMHS have reported positive outcomes when practitioners have extended their therapeutic role to include family therapy and other multidisciplinary work.

e) Building on strengths

Most people are aware of the benefits of living a healthier lifestyle and making more of an effort to change their diets and increase their exercise. Yet when it comes to mental health not many people think about making changes to improve their mental wellbeing. In Chapter 1 we looked at the idea of resilience, a trait that some people possess in abundance and yet others have no concept of. So, when life brings about the inevitable ups and downs they have not developed the strength to cope. For these individuals, strengthening themselves to deal with the negative aspects of life is essential and building their resilience is one way in which to do this. When we find ourselves experiencing bad times in our lives resilience means we are able to cope with the grief, anger and pain that happens. It is not about ignoring the feelings we have or even adopting a 'stiff upper lip' approach. It is about making a huge effort to recognise what is going on and seeking help and support. The organisation MIND is a useful resource to which individuals may turn to get some help.

By staying involved with others and developing strong relationships, maintaining a strong hope for the future and ensuring that the individual is encouraged to maintain their physical health, these things can help to build the strength to cope with mental problems.

f) Anti-discriminatory practice

In order to challenge discrimination and to practise in an anti-discriminatory way, we need to understand what discrimination is and how it manifests itself. Simply put, discrimination means distinguishing differences between one or more things, though this rather benign definition does not seem to confer anything negative. However, when used in the context of inequality, it is associated with a negative attribution (Thompson, 2011), and is used to discriminate against someone. This implies disadvantage or oppression of an individual which impacts negatively upon their self-concept, their dignity, their opportunities or their ability to get social justice. Discrimination can take many forms, such as stereotyping and marginalisation, and common categories of discrimination include race and racism, gender and sexism, age and ageism, educational disadvantage, economic disadvantage and mental and disability discrimination.

Figure 7.1 Discrimination can take many forms

Negative discrimination occurs when the identification of difference results in someone being treated unfairly on the basis of that difference.

In promoting practice which is truly anti-discriminatory, organisations must develop, implement and monitor policies that support this. All Codes of Practice for care workers must include statements about the requirement to treat others equally and fairly and to engage in non-judgemental and anti-discriminatory practice. Such policies and guidelines help to raise awareness about unacceptable behaviours and provide a structure for individuals to challenge such behaviours.

The term 'dignity' is often used in care work and it is important that all the people we care for are treated with respect. In this way, good practice demands that we protect our clients and patients from discrimination and oppressive practices. Recognising the diverse nature of practice and the fact that some individuals are disadvantaged just because they are different has led to the terms anti-discriminatory or anti-oppressive practice being used.

g) Promoting social inclusion and improving access to services

People are excluded when they have few links to social networks such as education, employment, family and friends due to ill health – whether physical or mental – and unemployment, and this can lead to difficulty in maintaining relationships as the opportunity to engage in activity in the community suffers. In this way the socially excluded individual becomes powerless to make changes.

Governments in the UK have worked hard to try to rectify these effects by introducing welfare improvements, and the service we deliver as healthcare workers can have a far reaching effect on the client's self-esteem and will go a long way to improving the treatment of these groups. We have shown in other chapters how people with mental health problems face problems in sustaining and preserving social contacts and social networks and those individuals who live in live in isolated rural areas and small communities where the service provision is limited are at an even higher risk of isolation. Drop-in and day centres have been an important development in reducing the isolation felt in such communities. Improving access to service has been effective in overcoming the barriers we so often see in mental ill health and has been instrumental in reducing the stigma attached to mental illness.

In promoting social inclusion much improvement has been made to practice. With the government's No Health Without Mental Health strategy there has been a concerted effort to ensure that a multidisciplinary approach to care involving a number of agencies is in effect. Social networks and transport issues are being targeted to help individuals integrate further into the community. In addition to this, links with community projects, community centres and schools have been strengthened to increase levels of social contact. There has also been a move to improve the involvement of individuals in their own care planning.

h) Recovery-focused

In mental health 'recovery' has two meanings. In a traditional sense 'recovering' from any illness means we return to some normality. In mental health services this might mean when the symptoms have gone. This is sometimes referred to as 'clinical recovery'. This can be more fully explained if we look at schizophrenia. Many individuals do experience full clinical recovery after one episode of psychosis and yet others may continue to have symptoms throughout their lives.

Figure 7.2 Isolation

The second definition of recovery is about regaining quality of life, whilst still having symptoms and not experiencing a full clinical recovery. This really goes back to the resilience we mentioned previously and is the ability of an individual to build a satisfying, fulfilling and enjoyable life, despite continuing to have symptoms of an illness. It is about control and taking decisions that are beneficial for the individual themselves.

Both meanings change the way in which support is given to sufferers. The mental health service in the past has aimed to achieve clinical recovery by treating symptoms and thus preventing relapse. In recovery-focused care a different approach is favoured which demands a different type of support. Whilst there is still a need for mental health professionals to prescribe medication and offer therapy the individual has a choice as to whether they want this sort of treatment. This means that mental health professionals need to work much more closely with their clients making joint decisions about what treatment is appropriate, rather than adopting the expert-led type provision of the past.

In recovery-focused services, it is the client who is deemed to be the expert in their own care and the health professional takes on a more passive role, listening to what they need for their own recovery. In this way the role of mental health professionals is to help each individual achieve goals and a whole new thought process as to how this is achieved is therefore required. With the development of community-based teams called 'recovery and support' teams we can see that practice is already beginning to change.

A major research project that aims to transform NHS mental health services is that provided by a team of researchers at the Institute of Psychiatry, King's College London. It began in 2009 and plans to run for five years. The REFOCUS trial:

'describes an intervention aimed at increasing the focus of community adult mental health teams on supporting personal recovery. The intervention is in addition to standard care and has two components: Recovery-promoting relationships and Working practices.'

The trial demonstrates that in recovery-promoting relationships the working relationship between staff and service users is central to personal recovery and in developing this relationship there needs to be:

- A shared team understanding of personal recovery.
- An exploration of values held by individual workers and in the team.
- Skills training in coaching.
- Team planning and carrying out a partnership project with people who use the service.
- A raising of the expectations held by people who use the service so that their values, strengths and goals will be prioritised.

(Adapted from the executive summary of the REFOCUS document.)

A further project called the 'Implementing Recovery through Organisational Change' (ImROC) programme is run by the NHS Confederation's Mental Health Network and the Centre for Mental Health. This started in 2011 with 30 NHS organisations taking part. The inclusion of people with personal experience of mental health problems working alongside mental health teams is a major part of this particular project. In addition there is also the development of so called 'recovery' colleges which offer individuals with mental health problems the opportunity to access education and training programmes to help them on their road to recovery. It is hoped that the courses delivered in the recovery colleges will help people become experts in self-care.

Evidence Activity

 Activity

Explain the key principles and values which underpin the care and support planning within your own setting. Say how you might incorporate at least two of the above categories in developing your support for your clients.

2 Describe the tasks associated with each stage of the care and support process including the stages of a basic mental health assessment and the key principles and values that should be implemented at each stage of the care and support process: assessment of need; planning goals; monitoring progress; reviewing plans

In assessing needs the Social Care Institute for Excellence has this to say about assessment:

'Although assessment has been recognised as a core skill in social work and should underpin all social work interventions, there is no singular theory or understanding as to what the purpose of assessment is and what the process should entail'

(SCIE, 2003)

This is interesting since, with no one theory to support it, the process of assessment becomes a huge subject and one which potentially differs with each service. This situation could lead to fragmentation of a client's care with many different approaches to assessing their needs being used at the same time. It becomes imperative then to determine how we as care providers will assess the client and simplify the process.

The care planning process is a good place to start and in any assessment of a individual with mental health needs the following 'basic helping cycle' as suggested by Taylor and Devine (1993) is useful (see Figure 7.3).

This basic cycle gives an opportunity to the client and care professional to work together to assess the needs of the client. The care necessary to meet those needs is then planned and put into action at the third stage and finally evaluated or 'reviewed', starting the cycle again. In all care planning processes assessment of need must be followed by goal planning. Monitoring progress should be an ongoing practice and during the evaluation stage there should be a review of the goals. The cycle should then start again if further needs are identified.

Figure 7.3 Basic care planning process

Thompson's (2005) ASIRT model of care planning identifies the following stages.

- AS – Assessment phase or the start of the process and the first part of an action plan leading onto the
- I – the Intervention stage when aims and objectives for the intervention area are selected.
- R – Review when the evaluation of what has happened takes place before finally
- T – Termination, when the intervention is no longer needed and can be stopped. (Thompson, 2005)

NICE break the care planning process down into a number of steps. See http://www.dwp.gov.uk/publications/specialist-guides/medical-conditions/a-z-of-medical-conditions/obsessive-compulsive-disorder/nice-ocd.shtml for an example.

The whole process of care planning is just one part of actual assessment. In research by Smale et al. (1993) three different models of assessment were suggested. These were:

- The Questioning Model – which is a service-led model and one in which the care professional leads the process by questioning and listening, before processing the information.
- The Procedural Model – which requires information to be gathered by the care professional who then makes a judgement as to 'best fit' for the service. This is criterion based and a range of checklists are used to determine which service is best for the client.
- The Exchange Model – which is where the care workers view their clients as the expert in their own care needs. This is really the most person-centred approach of the three. This model seems to describe the most holistic form of assessment, with the care professional managing a more client-centred approach (Smale et al., 1993). It would also seem to be more in line with the recovery-focused models currently being trialled.

Of course, the types of assessment mental health professionals carry out will differ according to the setting they are in or according to the type of needs the person has. For example, if the person living in their own home has difficulty with personal care, they may require support through a community care assessment of their needs. For individuals with mental health problems, assessments are carried out under the 'Care Programme Approach', which undertakes to assess the following areas:

- risk and safety
- psychiatric symptoms and experiences and
- psychological thoughts and behaviours. ·

> **Evidence Activity**
>
> **Activity**
>
> Using one of your clients as a case study (be mindful of confidentiality here) describe the care and support process you have undertaken showing each stage of the process.

3 Explain how to enable service users and carers to take an active part in the care planning process

It is the service user in any care planning process who needs to be the central figure in negotiating care, and this is certainly the main focus of the REFOCUS project we covered in the first section. This is recognised in legislation as being the optimum process for care planning. The NHS and Community Care Act (1990) and the Carer Recognition Act (1995) led the way in this type of care planning. The 'care professional knows best' way of operating takes away choice and limits the client's ability to make their own decisions and should therefore be a thing of the past. Any care plan that is developed without the client is meaningless since it is the client who experiences the discomfort of their condition and has the expert opinion of what they need.

To aid the client in the assessment process the best way to proceed is to ask the questions: what do you want, what do you need, and how are you feeling at the moment? By actively encouraging the client to voice their needs, concerns and wants with respect to their care, a good rapport is developed and the client will feel actively involved in all decisions.

Occasionally though we may find that the client is not fully able to engage with the process due to conditions that prevent understanding or sensory impairments which may make the process difficult. In this case, an advocate or the individual's carer or family member needs to be called in to act on behalf of the client and to ensure that they are fully represented.

> **Evidence Activity**
>
> **Activity**
>
> On the case study you started in the previous section, show how you ensured that your client had a full part in the care assessment process. Show the paperwork for one client, ensuring that confidentiality is maintained.

4 Explain how and why agencies need to work together within the care planning process

All care agencies need to work together so that the assessment and resultant care plan is effective and coordinated. The Single Assessment Process (SAP) was introduced in the National Service Framework for Older People (2001), in Standard 2: person-centred care, the aim of which was to ensure that the NHS and social care services treat older people as individuals enabling them to make choices about their own care.

Many older people have wide ranging needs and, in recognition of that, care must be holistic and centre on the whole person. The requirement to develop a Single Assessment Process was based on just this fact: to provide a person-centred health and social care framework, which includes entry into the system, holistic assessment, care planning, care delivery and review.

According to the National Service Framework for Mental Health the assessment process needs to cover:

> 'psychiatric, psychological and social functioning, risk to the individual and others, including previous violence and criminal record, any needs arising from co-morbidity, and personal circumstances including family or other carers, housing, financial and occupational status.'

As such, it demands a multi-agency approach. The standards go on to state that:

> 'Care planning and the delivery and regular review of a comprehensive package of services for people with severe mental illness is a multi-agency endeavour ...'.

Different systems of assessment, care planning, delivery and review have been developed. In social services, care management provides the framework for needs assessment and the organisation of a package of care. In the NHS, the CPA has established a similar framework for assessment, care planning and review by a designated care coordinator.

In working with partners to deliver care there is always the potential for repetition of work and overlap of delivery. SAP aims to ensure that the individual's needs are assessed thoroughly and accurately, without duplication by different agencies.

By sharing the information appropriately between all relevant agencies SAP coordinates the assessment and ensures effective delivery care.

Joint working necessitates the effective sharing of information and there are a range of approaches to implement electronic SAP (e-SAP) across the country that are currently being looked at. The Health and Social Care Integration Programme, an NHS Connecting for Health project, is working to enable the sharing of electronic records between the NHS and social care systems, subject to the individual's consent.

There is also a National SAP Resource available which has been commissioned by the Department of Health to create and host an online resource for health and social care professionals implementing SAP. This free resource holds material to assist multi-agency working and aims to provide access to information to enable the sharing of good practice and reduce duplication of effort.

Figure 7.4 Care agencies need to work together

To download information on this resource go to: www.cpa.org.uk/sap.

Evidence Activity

 Activity

Write a short reflective piece on how you currently work with partners when assessing clients.

5 Describe three possible differences or conflicts that may occur between those involved in the care planning process and identify ways of overcoming these, including where to get additional support and advice

Conflict within multi-agency teams is a common occurrence and can disrupt performance in a major way. The fact that conflict exists, however, is not necessarily a bad thing: as long as it is resolved effectively, it can lead to personal and professional growth of the team. If managed well, conflict can be creative and productive and creative solutions to difficult problems can often be found through positive conflict resolution. However, at all times conflict within the team or amongst staff should not impact upon the wellbeing of the service user.

Difference or conflict may involve:

- Task-based conflict – disagreements in relation to approaches to work, processes and structural issues within the teams and the organisation.
- Relationship-based conflict – conflicts between individual members of the team that generally stem from differences in personal values and beliefs.
- Conflict with carers and service users over service decisions.

Whatever the cause of the conflict, the emotions that arise can be quite damaging to the care being delivered and if badly managed ineffective care emerges. People may start to avoid each other and rifts then develop as teams take sides. In the midst of this happening the service user suffers as care starts to disintegrate into ineffectiveness.

Larson and LaFasto (1989) developed a CONNECT model for resolving conflict by conversation and this can be used whatever the cause of the conflict.

- **Commit** to the relationship – individuals should begin by discussing the relationship, and not the problem causing concern. Each person should say why they feel change should occur and what they hope to gain. This is a very positive approach.
- **Optimise** safety – both parties must commit to maintaining confidentiality and creating an atmosphere of trust.
- **Neutralise** defensiveness – in order to prevent a defensive response each person should explain what they have observed, how it made them feel, and the long-term effects of the other person's actions.
- **Explain** each perspective – each person should have the opportunity to explain their view of the issue.
- **Change** one behaviour – each person should commit to changing one behaviour.
- **Track** the change – the individuals will decide how improvements will be measured and agree to meet to discuss whether changes have been successful.

They suggest that the most effective way of solving conflict in a team is for the people concerned to have constructive conversation. This will allow each person to see the perspective of the other and to gain some understanding about the way the other person feels about the situation. The conversation must result in each party committing to making improvements in the relationship.

These conversations might be initiated by the people themselves or they may require the services of a neutral facilitator. Additional support in the cases of conflict within the team may be to involve the manager or a person from another team who can provide a non-biased view of events and help to establish a mediation process.

Thompson (2006) provides another approach and recommends the RED approach to managing conflict. He states that situations involving conflict tend to have a high degree of tension associated with them.

- R stands for **R**ecognise the conflict; do not sweep it under the carpet.
- E stands for **E**valuate the conflict; to see how detrimental it would be if it was allowed to develop.
- D stands for **D**eal with the conflict; keep open communication.

Thompson suggests that we need to avoid the two destructive extremes: either pretending the conflict does not exist or over-reacting.

In conflict resolution it's only when people's needs are discovered that a solution can be found and it is best, if possible, not to compromise but to find a solution. Compromise means that people's needs are still not fully met and this can lead to resentment and anger.

6 Explain how to keep effective, accurate records and describe how to respond to complaints

All of the situations we have covered in this chapter require documenting in some form or another and one of the issues arising here is the question of where the information is to be stored and whether it is required to be confidentially maintained.

Any records maintained need to be:

- accurate
- ordered
- up to date
- safe.

The last point is one of the most important to remember since it is a legal requirement to protect any data we may have on our clients or staff and maintain it in a confidential way. Any use of such information in an unsuitable way or any breach of confidentiality needs to be dealt with promptly and must be reported to the person in charge. The security of information is a safeguard for vulnerable clients and any breach of that security can be detrimental to clients.

Compliance with the Data Protection Act (1998) is imperative. This act gives individuals the right to access their records whether they are stored as paper files or on computers.

It is worth revisiting the eight principles concerning data that the act refers to.

- Data must be secure.
- Data must be not be kept for longer than necessary – you will need to check the requirements in your own organisation for the length of time. (For example antenatal records are kept for 25 years.)
- Data must be accurate.
- Data must be fairly processed.
- Data must not be transferred without protection.
- Data must protect individual's rights.
- Data must be processed for limited purposes only.
- Data must be adequate, relevant and not excessive.

We live in a highly litigious society and we are accountable for care we give. As such, we need to be aware of the place records have. If a complaint were to be made against us we would be hard pushed to defend ourselves if we had inadequately prepared records. If negligence is suspected in any care setting any records and statements pertaining to the case will be taken and scrutinised.

Dimond (1997), a legal writer, highlighted some of the major areas of concern in care reports which have been inadequately prepared. She revealed that in many records there were major omissions including:

- no dates
- illegibility

- use of abbreviations
- caller's and visitor's names not included
- no signatures
- inaccuracy with respect to dates and times
- delays in record writing
- inaccuracies about clients
- unprofessional language used.

Our responsibility with respect to record keeping is clear. We need to create records on clients and patients but the way in which we use and store that information is paramount.

We must handle all information effectively and be aware of the need to maintain the confidentiality of that information.

Complaints

Occasionally you may have to deal with a complaint from either a service user or a member of their family and it is imperative that certain procedures are followed in order to address this. Individuals complain for a variety of reasons and it is important that you have a good grasp about what it is they want. They may want an apology from a member of staff or for an action they feel was unwarranted. It may be that they feel the service is less than adequate and do not want others to suffer. Dissatisfaction is at the heart of every complaint and it can help you to improve what you do. It is important to take the following steps to ensure that the complainant feels they are being listened to:

- acknowledge the complaint
- resolve it with the person then and there if possible
- reassure the complainant
- ensure that you use your policy and follow its guidance
- provide a full response in writing to show that you take the complaint seriously and have covered all the relevant points.

The government, in a statutory instrument 'The Local Authority Social Services and National Health Service Complaints (England) Regulations 2009', has provided guidelines to enable the process to be dealt with effectively and your own policy should take into account this guidance. The section for handling complaints is shown in the box below.

Arrangements for the handling and consideration of complaints

3.—(1) Each responsible body must make arrangements ("arrangements for dealing with complaints") in accordance with these Regulations for the handling and consideration of complaints.

    (2) The arrangements for dealing with complaints must be such as to ensure that—

        (a) complaints are dealt with efficiently;

        (b) complaints are properly investigated;

        (c) complainants are treated with respect and courtesy;

        (d) complainants receive, so far as is reasonably practical—

            (i) assistance to enable them to understand the procedure in relation to complaints; or

            (ii) advice on where they may obtain such assistance;

        (e) complainants receive a timely and appropriate response;

        (f) complainants are told the outcome of the investigation of their complaint; and

        (g) action is taken if necessary in the light of the outcome of a complaint.

Activity

Undertake an audit of your current record keeping and reflect on how effective the records are.

Do you need to make any changes to bring them into line with recommendations in the box above?

7 Explain what a risk assessment is and the key principles and values that underpin effective risk management as well as how these contribute to the protection of individuals

A risk is anything that might potentially cause harm to somebody. A risk assessment determines what the risk might be, estimates how likely a risk is to happen and what the consequences might be for ourselves, our clients or for other visitors to the work place.

The risks posed by mental health service users to others has been brought to our attention by the government and media as inquiries into serious incidents suggest that the care services have failed in the risk management process. In this section we also address the risks associated with the individuals themselves and how health professionals deal with this.

Specifying roles and responsibilities

Risk assessment and risk management are an essential part of care but it is often difficult to balance empowerment with the duty of care we owe our clients. When we refer to 'duty of care' we mean:

> 'the extent to which a healthcare provider must reasonably ensure that no harm comes to a patient under the provider's care'

> (http://legal-dictionary.thefreedictionary.com/duty+of+care).

If individuals are to be enabled to lead independent lives, then they need to be able to take the risks they choose to take, but this constantly needs to be weighed against the likelihood of significant harm arising from that choice. Our attitudes to risk are likely to be different when it comes to risking our own personal safety, but as care professionals, we are bound by law and this is likely to change our attitude to risk management. We may be more careful when dealing with clients and take the view that as 'vulnerable adults' they need to be protected in some way. We may occasionally take a 'safety first approach' and focus upon what the client cannot do.

The responsibility for risk assessment lies with the individual in care and the care worker who is undertaking the care assessment and remains a core function of the mental health practitioner.

Considering a range of types of risks/forward planning to reduce risk of harm

In assessing the seriousness of risk, the following areas need to underpin your practice:

- The sorts of factors that increase exposure to risk, such as environmental, social, financial, communication and recognition of abuse.
- The existence of support to minimise risk.
- The nature, extent and length of time of the risk.
- The impact the risk may have on the individual and on others.

By assessing the type of risk that the client is under, the care professional can plan to reduce the likelihood of it occurring.

In addition to the above, care workers are also bound by law as stated in section 3(1) of the Health and Safety at Work etc. Act 1974, which clearly states:

> 'It shall be the duty of every employer to conduct his undertaking in such a way as to ensure, so far as is reasonably practicable, that persons not in his employment who may be affected thereby are not thereby exposed to risks to their health or safety.'

Unfortunately, this can make us risk averse and will undoubtedly lead to a lack of choice for clients, together with a loss of control and independent living leading to an adverse effect on care. A recent news report commented upon the growing 'paranoid' culture in which middle-class children are finding themselves. A psychologist reported seeing increasing numbers of children with anxiety disorders who lack 'emotional resilience' and are afraid of failure. She believes her findings are due to parents being risk averse and not allowing children the freedom to take normal risks in the course of their daily lives (BBC News, 6 December 2012).

Care settings and housing vary in type and the risks associated with them will differ. The rights of individuals in our care can occasionally be in conflict with health and safety issues and we need to be prepared to address such occasions.

Specifying warning signs and contingency planning

Whilst the client is clearly not imprisoned in the home, occasionally we may have concerns as to the client's safety when they are not in our care. The CSCI document Rights, Risks and Restraints: An Exploration into the Use of Restraint in the Care of Older People (2007), although concerned mainly with how some older people have been restrained in some care settings, does, however, make some useful points.

Respecting people's basic human rights to dignity, freedom and respect underpin good-quality care. People may need support in managing their care and making decisions but they have the right, whether in their own home or in a care setting, to make choices about their lives and to take risks.

Mental care services have responsibilities to keep people safe from harm and to ensure their safety. It is this need to balance people's rights to freedom and to make choices with ensuring people are safe that is at the heart of this exploration into the use of restraint in the care of the individual with mental health issues. A recent report by the Joseph Rowntree Foundation in 2007 commented that:

> 'Some negative outcomes, including violence, can be avoided or reduced in frequency by sensible contingency planning. Risk, however, cannot be eliminated. Accurate prediction is never possible for individual patients. While it may be possible to reduce risk in some settings, the risks posed by those with mental disorders are much less susceptible to prediction because of the multiplicity of, and complex interrelation of, factors underlying a person's behaviour.'

(JRF, 2007)

Evidence-based approach/effective record keeping/regular review

When determining risk, the care professional will collect evidence through the assessment process and document the specific signs they believe actually warn of risk and make plans to address these. Risk assessment then determines how to manage and reduce risks and will be used not only for the individual who is suffering from a condition who may be at risk, but also for others who may need support. In this instance, risk assessment is carried out to protect others from individuals that could cause harm.

Unfortunately, there is a danger in this approach of focusing on the person's mental health problems and how these may pose an additional risk to self and others. In doing so, there may be a risk of ignoring other needs. Treatment of this kind may lead to loss of self-esteem and denies the right to choice and an increase in independence. In this way, there is a danger that the care worker becomes more controlling of the client and person-centred approaches become less of a reality. The Department of Health agrees with this. In their paper of 2007, Independence, Choice and Risk: A Guide to Best Practice in Supported Decision Making, they make the point that a 'safety first approach' may 'not be necessarily the best option for the person and may be detrimental to quality of life and a risk to maintaining independence'.

Risk in this instance is thought of in terms of danger, loss, threat, damage or injury and the positive benefits of risk-taking are lost; therefore a more balanced approach needs to be adopted.

In the last section we talked about the importance of assessment. Risk assessment is no different and is equally subject to planning, implementing and review.

Positive risk-taking in addition to risk of harm

In Titterton's 'Positive Risk Approach', risk is seen as positive and enhancing, and recognises the needs of individuals. It demonstrates that choice and autonomy are important and promotes the rights of vulnerable people. Steve Morgan (2004) summarises the approach:

> 'Positive risk-taking is: weighing up the potential benefits and harms of exercising one choice of action over another. Identifying the potential risks involved, and developing plans and actions that reflect the positive potentials and stated priorities of the service user. It involves using available resources and support to achieve the desired outcomes, and to minimise the potential harmful outcomes. It is not negligent ignorance of the potential risks … it is usually a very carefully thought-out strategy for managing a specific situation or set of circumstances.'

If we are to provide real choice and control for our clients, we need to enable individuals to take the risks they choose, with support from the staff. This means allowing the individuals using our service to define their own risks and to plan and monitor any activity they wish to undertake which may entail some form of risk.

Evidence Activity

 Activity

Write a short reflective piece outlining how you maintain an environment that is safe and secure but still manage to promote freedom and choice.

8 Explain how and why agencies need to work together in the risk management process

The Laming Report (2003) into the death of Victoria Climbié paved the way for some far-reaching changes not only to the care of children but to other parts of the health sector.

The key findings focused on in the report concern the:

- 'failure of communication between different staff and agencies'
- 'inexperience and lack of skill of individual social workers'
- 'failure to follow established procedures'
- 'inadequate resources to meet demands'.

In particular the Laming Report was concerned with ways in which:

> '*all the agencies involved* (four social services departments, three housing departments, two specialist child protection teams in the Metropolitan Police, two different hospitals, and the NSPCC) ... had failed to communicate and interact with each other.'

As a result of this report the subsequent recommendations were 'geared towards improving the system as a whole' and this led to a shaping of the current systems within the NHS, bringing together multi-agency working and professionals from all disciplines into teams that work together for the service user's benefit.

It is true that each professional in a discipline within the mental health team will approach the care of an individual from their own perspective. There may also be the use of different types of assessment processes and risk assessment tools for different situations. But it is the sharing of information and findings from these different forms of assessment with the wider team that ensure the individual is kept safe and that efficient care is forthcoming.

Evidence Activity

 Activity

Put together a flow chart to show the multi-agency nature of your own setting and reflect on how this improves care.

9 Explain how to involve carers and families in the risk management process

In the guidance paper Promoting Quality Care. Good Practice Guidance on the Assessment and Management of Risk in Mental Health and Learning Disability Services (2009), working in partnership with families of service users was hailed as 'one of the most important elements in effective risk assessment and risk management planning'.

To have positive working relationships collaboration is key, and in mental health work – where the service user may have difficulty engaging fully in an assessment process – the family and carers should be involved. Family members and carers know the individual best and have first-hand information about his/her history, behaviours and situation. These need to be discussed and worked through so that agreement is reached as to the acceptable risks for the particular individual (DoH, 2007a).

A paper published by the Royal College of Psychiatrists entitled 'Rethinking risk to others' makes the suggestion that risk management be conducted 'in a spirit of collaboration between the mental health team, the service user and carers', with the process being as 'trusting as possible' (RCP, 2008). The college suggests that the role of service users in identifying their own triggers that might precipitate crisis has been increasingly recognised and that service-user personal safety plans should be encouraged as useful tools. In the case of families and carers the findings were less constructive and many reported that their concerns about an individual's deteriorating condition were often ignored. The suggestion that families have access to the staff who work with the individuals whenever they feel the need to raise concerns should be implemented.

Evidence Activity

 Activity

Write a short piece to show how service users and their families are involved in the risk management process in your work place.

10 Describe the range of risk factors that should be considered during risk assessment for an individual in different types of risk situations

Risk of harm to self

According to the Mental Health Foundation 142,000 patients self-harm and present themselves to hospital emergency departments each year. This in no way gives the full picture since there are almost certainly a greater number of people who self-harm without seeking medical help. It appears that the most common group of those who self-harm are those between the ages of 11 and 25, with 1 in 12 young people deliberately harming themselves. This type of behaviour is termed 'parasuicide' as it is not always an attempt at suicide. Most individuals who deliberately harm themselves do not intend to kill themselves, but equally are not always aware of the dangers of what they are doing. Unfortunately, though, a person who self-harms is 50–100 times more likely to attempt suicide than someone who does not.

The Rethink Mental Health factsheet highlights the following information for those at risk:

'A mental health specialist can help by providing:

Support.

Practical help to deal with the situations that led or could lead to self-harm.

Help understanding the things that lead to harm and the motivation for self-harm.

An evaluation of the short-term risk of suicide.

Psychiatric assessment to identify mental health difficulties.

Treatment of mental health difficulties.

Access to talking therapies such as cognitive behavioural therapy and psychotherapy.

Access to problem solving therapy/training.'

(http://www.rethink.org/living_with_mental_illness/coping_in_a_crisis/suicide_self_harm/index.html)

Risk of being harmed by others

A recent study carried out by Bellis et al. (in Hughes et al 2012) reported the incidence of violence against mentally ill people as being four times more likely than other occurrences, and mental health charities have said that, despite public fears, 'people with mental illness were much more likely to be a victim than a perpetrator'.

With 24 per cent of people reporting violence against them in the previous year, evidence continues to support the notion that mental health issues are more likely to subject the individual to harm by others. The reasons given in the study include difficulty with personal relationships, substance abuse, homelessness, living in poverty and being imprisoned, all of which raise the risk of becoming a victim. The Mental Health Foundation and the charity Mind, commenting on the study, expressed concern that it was the stigma and discrimination against people with mental health problems that continues, with individuals being victimised in their communities and in their own homes.

Risk of harm to others

Against a backdrop of fear about mental health sufferers carrying out murders and violence and the suggested failure of health professionals to manage such risks, the RCP was concerned that a culture preoccupied with risk to others was prevalent within the UK. They therefore commissioned a report about the risks posed to others by mental health sufferers in an effort to 'stimulate further debate and research as well as most importantly, improvements in clinical practice and patient and public safety'.

Five key findings emerged as shown in the box below.

---

1. The concern that a culture preoccupied with risk to others has emerged has had a negative impact on mental health professionals, professional practice, service users and the public.

2. Risk management is complex and although some negative outcomes, including violence, can be avoided or reduced in frequency risk, they can never be wholly eliminated. Accurate prediction for individual patients is never possible since the risks posed by those with mental disorders are complex.

3. Risk assessment instruments must be understood as an assessment of a current situation, not as a predictor of a particular event. Their critical function is to group people into a low, medium or high risk category, which will help identify the appropriate care and risk management strategy.

4. Improvements for training and continuing professional development in risk assessment and management need to be undertaken. Core competencies should be identified for psychiatric training.

5. Cooperation with patients and carers in assessing and managing risk should be fostered through care planning.

Source: ENDORSED BY College Central Policy Committee and the Central Executive Committee (RCP, 2008).

Risk of being harmed by mental health services

In terms of the risk associated with the mental health services, criticism has been directed towards failures within the health service to manage risk effectively, and although some research suggests that there have been no significant improvements in training (Davies et al., 2001), as we noted in the above section more emphasis is being placed upon the role of risk assessment to improve the services offered.

Evidence Activity

 Activity

Using the four headings from Section 10 compile a resource for other staff in your area which describes the range of risk factors that should be considered during risk assessment.

11 Describe the role of suicide reduction strategies and explain how they can inform actions within a risk management process

The National Suicide Prevention Strategy for England supported the Saving Lives: Our Healthier Nation target of reducing the death rate from suicide by at least 20 per cent by 2010. Designed as an ongoing, coordinated set of activities, it set out to be comprehensive and evidence-based and was delivered as a core programme of the National Institute for Mental Health in England (NIMHE).

This has now been superseded and currently there are three key strategy documents that take a public health approach to improve mental health and wellbeing and reduce suicides across the whole population. These key strategies are:

- Healthy Lives, Healthy People: Our Strategy for Public Health in England (2010);
- No Health Without Mental Health: A Cross-government Outcome Strategy for People of all Ages (2011); and
- The Department of Health's Consultation on Preventing Suicide in England.

There were 4215 suicides recorded in 2010 and over the last ten years the general trend has been a decrease in the overall rate. For the 2008–10 period the average rate was 7.9 suicides per 100,000 general population which was 17.9 per cent lower than in 1998–2000.

The government's new draft suicide prevention strategy adopts a different tack to those previously in place and rejects the top-down approach of the past. In developing outcome strategies, focus is directed toward the individual and how they can be empowered to 'lead the lives they want to lead and to keep themselves and their families healthy'. The major change has been the recognition that partnership working achieves more than working in isolation. Integrated pathway working builds on existing joint working across central government departments.

In this draft strategy the government makes it clear that there is no single approach to suicide prevention but rather it:

> 'needs a broad co-ordinated system-wide approach that requires input from a wide range of partner agencies, organisations and sectors. People who have been directly affected by the suicide of a family member or friend, the voluntary, statutory and private sectors, academic researchers and government departments can all contribute to a sustained reduction in suicides in England.'

To achieve this, the strategy sets out six key areas for action.

- Area for action 1: Reduce the risk of suicide in key high-risk group.
- Area for action 2: Tailor approaches to improve mental health in specific groups.
- Area for action 3: Reduce access to the means of suicide.
- Area for action 4: Provide better information and support to those bereaved or affected by a suicide.
- Area for action 5: Support the media in delivering sensible and sensitive approaches to suicide and suicidal behaviour.
- Area for action 6: Support research, data collection and monitoring.

In assessing the risk of suicide there are a number of tools which might be used. However, many writers urge caution with the use of any assessment tool unless used within a comprehensive clinical assessment process.

One such tool is the Suicide Risk Factor Checklist (shown in Figure 7.5) which enables a systematic consideration of risk factors.

Others include self-administered scales such as the SIS or the Suicidal Intent Scale which is an interview-based or self-administered scale designed to assess the intention to die among people who have attempted suicide (www.beckinstitute.org) and the BHS or the Beck Hopelessness Scale which measures an important suicide/self-harm risk factor (www.harcourt-uk.com).

A further tool – the SSI or the Scale for Suicide Ideation – is a 21-item scale that can be self-administered or completed through an interview and is designed to assess the intensity of a person's attitudes with regard to suicide and their behaviours and plans to complete suicide over the past week (www.harcourt-uk.com/).

STORM is a suicide prevention training package which covers assessment, crisis management, crisis prevention and problem solving when working with potentially suicidal service users. As well

Early Intervention Suicide Risk Factor Check-list

Name:

Date:

Put a 'Y' for 'yes' 'N' for 'no' in the appropriate box

Current Risk Factors		Historical Risk Factors		Future/Potential Risk Factors	
Preoccupation with morbid/suicidal thoughts	☐	Previous suicide ideation	☐	Service disengagement and refusing help	☐
Suicidal intent/plans	☐	Previous suicide attempts or serious self-injury	☐	Service transitions or transfer of staff	☐
Suicidal behaviour: e.g. researching the subject, storing up medication	☐	Long duration of untreated psychosis (DUP)	☐	Protracted recovery	☐
Hallucinatory content/commands	☐	Previous depressive episodes	☐	Depression	☐
Distressing symptoms/experiences	☐	History of abuse or bullying	☐	Social rejection/loss of relationship	☐
Prominent guilt, hopelessness and self-reproach	☐	History of impulsiveness and/or other high-risk behaviour	☐	Relapse of psychosis	☐
Acutely depressed or labile mood	☐	History of harmful/persistent substance misuse	☐	Assertive action to reduce immediate suicide risks and MDT review of care plan	☐
Agitation or motor restlessness	☐	Family history of suicide	☐		
Impulsive/unpredictable behaviour or bizarre risk-taking decisions	☐	Friend or acquaintance committed suicide	☐	Care plan for current risk factors and remain vigilant for future risk factors	☐
Recently admitted or discharged from hospital	☐				
Relapse/first relapse of psychosis	☐				
Slow or incomplete recovery/poor treatment response/fear of mental disintegration	☐				
Poor/non concordance with prescribed medication	☐				
Problematic engagement and refusing help	☐				
Significant personal stress or loss e.g. debts, job, relationship, abuse	☐				
Critical family environment/high expressed emotion	☐				
Social isolation: single/separated/living alone	☐				
Unemployment/inactivity	☐				
Recent contact with police/criminal justice system	☐				
Serious physical health problems, terminal illness, pain, intolerable side effects	☐				
Harmful/persistent substance misuse	☐				
Access to lethal means	☐				

RISK STATUS

HIGH Assertive action to reduce immediate suicide risks and MDT review of care plan

MODERATE Care plan for current risk factors and remain vigilant for future risk factors

LOW Remain vigilant for future risk factor

Figure 7.5 Suicide risk factor checklist

as an adults pack there is also a Children's & Young Person's version (www.medicine.manchester.ac.uk/storm/).

The Department of Health's Best Practice in Managing Risk Principles and Evidence for Best Practice in the Assessment and Management of Risk to Self and Others in Mental Health Services (2007) is a comprehensive guide to the sorts of risk assessments that are in place.

Evidence Activity

 Activity

Evaluate the risk assessment tool favoured by your setting and compare it to one of the tools mentioned in the 'best practice' document. Say which you prefer and why.

Summary

In summary, responsibility for managing the process of suicide risk assessments rests with senior mental health professionals, but all members of the multidisciplinary team should be able to recognise and assess standard suicide risk. In doing so it is crucial that as much information as possible about historical and current suicide risk factors is gathered from the individual, the family, carers and the referrer. In addition, the risks should be reviewed regularly, and awareness of potential risk factors for the future if circumstances change must be noted. Changes in mood, anxiety or substance use, major stressful life events such as serious rejection or loss, deterioration in psychosis, and refusing help or disengaging from service use should indicate a need to re-evaluate the individual in terms of the risk they pose to themselves.

References

Bird, V, Leamy, M, Le Boutillier, C, Williams J and Slade, M (2011) *REFOCUS Promoting recovery in community health services. Rethink recovery series: volume 4.* London: Section for Recovery, Institute of Psychiatry, King's College.

Bradshaw, J (1972) The concept of social need. *New Society*, 496: 640–3.

Bradshow, J (1972) 'A taxonomy of social need' in Mclachlan, G (ed) *Problems and Progress in Medical Care* 7th series, NPHT/Oxford University Press.

Burton, J (ed.) (1990) *Conflict; Human Needs Theory*. London: Macmillan.

CSCI (2007) Rights, Risks and Restraints: An Exploration into the Use of Restraint in the Care of Older People. London: Commission for Social Care Inspection.

Davies, S, Amos, T and Applby, L (2001) How much risk training takes place in mental health services? A national survey of training and policies. *Psychiatric Bulletin*, 25, 217–19.

Dimond, B (2008) *Legal Aspects of Nursing 5th edition*. Pearson Education: England.

DoH (2007a) Best Practice in Managing Risk: Principles and Evidence For Best Practice In The Assessment And Management Of Risk To Self And Others In Mental Health Services. London: National Risk Management Programme.

DoH (2007b) Independence, Choice and Risk: A Guide to Best Practice in Supported Decision Making. London: HMSO.

DoH (2011a) Consultation on Preventing Suicide in England: A cross-government outcomes strategy. London: Department of Health.

DoH (2011b) No Health Without Mental Health. Outcomes strategy. London: HMSO.

The Free Dictionary (n.d.): Duty of care. Available at: http://legal-dictionary.thefreedictionary.com/duty+of+care (accessed 6/12/12).

National Institute for Health and Clinical Excellence (NICE) (2004): *Self Harm: the short-term physical and physiological management and secondary prevention of self-harm in primary and secondary care. Practice Guideline Number 16*, p. 25. Available at: http://www.nice.org.uk/nicemedia/live/10946/29421/29421.pdf (accessed 23/11/11).

HM Gov. (2009) The Local Authority Social Services and National Health Service Complaints (England) Regulations. No. 309; London: National Health Service.

HM Government (2011) *Consultation on preventing suicide in England. A cross-government outcomes strategy to save lives.* London: Department of Health.

House of Commons (2003) *Sixth Report: The Victoria Climbié Inquiry Report. Report and formal minutes together with oral evidence.* London: HM Government.

Hughes K, Bellis M A, Jones L et al. (2012) Prevalence and risk of violence against adults with disabilities: a systematic review and meta-analysis of observational studies. *The Lancet.* (Early online publication.)

Innes, A, Macpherson, S and McCabe, I (2006): Promoting Person-Centred Care At The Front Line. York: Joseph Rowntree Foundation/SCIE.

Ladyman, S (2004): 'Health and social care advisory service: new directions in direct payments for people who use mental health services' (speech). London: Department of Health, 18 May.

Langan J and Lindow V (2004): *Living with risk: Mental health service user involvement in risk assessment and management.* Bristol: The Policy Press.

Larson, C E and LeFasto, F M (1989) *Teamwork: What must go right/What can go wrong.* London: Sage Publications.

Mental Health Foundation (2006) Self Harm: *What is Self Harm?* Available at: http://www.mentalhealth.org.uk/information/mental-health-a-z/self-harm/ (accessed 23/10/11).

Morgan, S (2004) *Positive risk taking. An idea whose time has come.* Available at: Practicebasedevidence.squarespace.com/storage/pdfs/OpenMind-PostiveRiskTaking.pdf

RCP (2008) *Rethinking risk to others in mental health services: Final report of a scoping group.* London: Royal College of Psychiatrists.

SCIE (2004) *Leading Practice: A development programme for first line managers.* Available at: www.scie.org.uk/publications/guides/guide27/files/lp-participants.pdf

www.selfharm.net/ Secret shame (self-injury information and support) *What self injury is* (1998)

Smale, G, Tuson, G, Biehal, N and Marsh, P (1993): *Empowerment, Assessment, Care Management and the Skilled Worker.* London: HMSO.

Taylor, B and Devine, D (1993) *Assessing Needs and Planning Care in Social Work.* London: Arena Press.

Thompson, N (2005) *Understanding Social Work: Preparing for practice.* Basingstoke: Palgrave Macmillan.

Thompson, N (2006) *People Problems.* Basingstoke: Palgrave Macmillan.

Thompson, N (2011) *Anti-discriminatory Practice.* Palgrave Macmillan.

Effective team working and collaboration within the mental health setting

What are you finding out?

Team working is not only about taking responsibility for your own work, but respecting the contributions of all your colleagues, and working in a manner that develops a supportive and positive culture in the work place. Staff in the immediate team and in the agencies that work alongside it need to be supportive of a shared vision to meet the agreed objectives for the individual using the mental health care service.

Good communication is essential to the effective team.

In this chapter you will learn how to contribute to effective teamwork within your care setting and will be introduced to the key elements of successful teamwork. In addition, you will also learn about the barriers that undermine good teamwork and how to overcome these.

The most important person in the whole process will be the individual who uses the service, and the way in which that service is delivered will impact on that individual either positively or negatively depending upon how effective we are as health professionals working together.

The reading and activities in this chapter will help you to:

1. Explain the contribution of effective working relationships in promoting the wellbeing and mental health of:
   a. service users
   b. carers
   c. workers.
2. Explain how the following key elements contribute to an effective team working environment:
   a. effective and accessible policies and procedures and clear aims and objectives
   b. clear job descriptions and defined boundaries of role
   c. supervision and support, regular review of team working and continuous development for workers
   d. effective communication systems
   e. access to current information on best practice, help and guidance
   f. audit and quality management.
3. Explain how an individual worker can contribute to an effective team working environment.
4. Explain common barriers to establishing and maintaining effective working relationships arising from:
   • differing values and approaches
   • conflicts of interest and group/power dynamics
   • differing systems and procedures and access to resources
   • poor systems for communication.
5. Explain how to overcome common barriers to effective working relationships between individuals within a home team, in a multidisciplinary context and between agencies.
6. Apply a strategy to promote effective team working within either a home team, multidisciplinary or multi-agency context.

Assessment criteria covered in this chapter

Reading this unit and completing the activities will provide you with the knowledge, understanding and skills required to meet the assessment criteria listed below.

City & Guilds Level 3 Diploma in Mental Health Care (QCF) (600/5241/7)		
Effective team and joint working in mental health (D/602/0172)		
Learning Outcome 1 Understand how to contribute to an effective team working environment		
Assessment Criteria	Page reference	Activity

1.1 Explain the contribution of effective working relationships in promoting the wellbeing and mental health of:
  a. service users
  b. carers
  c. workers
	p. 166	Evidence activity 8.1, p. 166

1.2. Explain how the following key elements contribute to an effective team working environment:
  a. effective and accessible policies and procedures
  b. clear job descriptions
  c. defined boundaries of role
  d. clear aims and objectives
  e. regular review of team working
  f. continuous development for workers
  g. supervision and support
  h. access to current information on best practice, help and guidance
  i. audit and quality management
  j. effective communication systems
	p. 167	Evidence activity 8.2, p. 171

1.3 Explain how an individual worker can contribute to an effective team working environment	p. 171	Evidence activity 8.3, p. 173
Learning Outcome 2 Apply strategies to promote effective team and joint working		

2.1. Explain common barriers to establishing and maintaining effective working relationships arising from:
  a. differing values
  b. differing approaches
  c. structures and systems
  d. power dynamics
  e. access to resources
  f. group processes and dynamics
  g. interpersonal conflicts
  h. communication channels
  i. differing pressures and demands
  j. physical environment
	p. 173	Evidence activity 8.4, p. 177

2.2 Explain how to overcome common barriers to effective working relationships between individuals within a home team, in a multidisciplinary context and between agencies	p. 177	Evidence activity 8.5, p. 179
2.3 Apply a strategy to promote effective team working within either a home team, multidisciplinary or multi agency context	p. 180	Evidence activity 8.6, p. 181

1 Explain the contribution of effective working relationships in promoting the wellbeing and mental health of: service users; carers; workers

A team is a group of people who work together and a group is a collection of two or more people who communicate together because they have interests in common. From the beginning of time, people have used work groups to get things done and to generate new ideas (Wheelan, 2005).

Effective teams work together towards common goals and objectives.

The individual with a mental health issue presents with a very complex set of problems, often a combination of physical, mental or social conditions all contributing to their ill health. To help such an individual there needs to be collaboration between several different health professionals who all need to function as a team.

Mental health problems often impact upon different parts of an individual's life and they may therefore require help with all sorts of issues, from help with medication, relationship and family problems, housing or with finances and benefits. In addition to which the treatments they may require or help with accessing services may also be problematic.

In dealing with these sorts of problems a variety of health professionals will work together in order to bring a variety of skills into play. It goes without saying that with several people all working on one person's care programme, success can only be achieved where there is effective teamwork and good communication between the workers.

The professional skills each team member possesses mean they will be able to offer support and encouragement from several different perspectives and by working closely together they can ensure that the service user has the best type of help. In an effective and close knit team the staff who work together often know a great deal about how the other professions work, and this means they are able to deal with many social and work-related problems. For example, whilst the individual in your care may never see an occupational therapist, it is quite likely that the key worker in their case may have a good knowledge about the work of this professional and be able to give the individual some information about resources they may need and can access.

With up to as many as 16 different people in the CMHT engaged in the care of one service user, the effective team will have one goal in mind and that is to promote the health and wellbeing of that service user. In the sections that follow we address in more detail how this can be managed.

 Time to reflect

Describe the team you work with and put together a chart showing all the other agencies involved in the care of one individual in your work setting. How many make up the team?

Evidence Activity

 8.1 Activity

How successful do you think your extended team is in promoting the wellbeing and mental health of:

- service users
- carers
- workers?

Write a reflective account.

2 Explain the key elements that contribute to an effective team working environment

When we are coordinating the work of a large group of health professionals, there must be a set of shared goals. All staff, whether in the immediate team or in agencies working alongside that team, need to be working towards a common aim, namely the care of the service user. Members of the team must be able to communicate and collaborate effectively to function well and one of the ways in which this is accomplished is through the use of shared policies and procedures where possible.

a) Effective and accessible policies and procedure and clear aims and objectives

Policies and procedures provide the link between what the service aims to achieve and its day-to-day operations.

As a written guide on how to handle issues should they arise, a policy equips a worker with a course of action they need to take in order to come to a decision. Boundaries are identified and accepted practice and how to handle situations is highlighted.

Policies generally:

- are rule driven;
- state their aims and objectives;
- state when the rule applies;
- describe who is covered by the policy;
- describe the consequences of not following the policy;
- are described using simple sentences and paragraphs.

Procedures, on the other hand, provide a plan of action to carry out the policy and one which is well written will also identify job responsibilities and boundaries for the health professional.

Procedures:

- identify actions and when to take them;
- describe alternative and emergency procedures;
- include warnings and cautions;
- give examples;
- show how to complete forms.

When there is a need to be consistent in practice, policies and procedures can perform that function and will ensure that the team in a setting are all working towards the common goal and meeting its aims and objectives. The use of these documents in the wider team setting will also ensure that all staff are aware of how the team can work together effectively for the good of the service user.

b) Clear job descriptions and defined boundaries of role

We often take these documents for granted and if you took part in the reflective activity here you may have taken some time to even find your job description! But job descriptions are important because they highlight the roles and responsibilities of a position within an

Time to reflect

Take a look at your own job description and that of your manager. Compare the two and say what you can learn from it about team working.

organisation and list the tasks the person is responsible for performing. They also indicate where that role stops, its boundary.

In addition a job description should state to whom the person will be reporting and may also indicate who the post relates to within the team structure and outside of the team. In effective team working this an important consideration to ensure that the correct communication channels are maintained and not bypassed.

Job descriptions communicate the competencies and skills required by an employee in a particular role and clearly state what is expected of the person. Without them there may be confusion about what is expected of the employee and this can lead to poor communication within the team.

c) Supervision and support, regular review of team working and continuous development for workers

Your job description is likely to have described the process of supervision and named your supervisor and manager. It may also outline the process of appraisal.

Figure 8.1 Supervision

Supervision is the process whereby a manager or supervisor oversees, supports and develops the knowledge and skills of a supervisee. It is the way in which a manager can enable a worker to carry out their role in an effective way.

The purpose of supervision is to ensure that there is a quality service in place. Supervision ensures that practice is reviewed and good practice is shared. Performance that falls below that which is expected or desired can be dealt with and coaching can be undertaken to help the supervisee to improve.

The purpose of this practice is to improve the quality of the work we do in order to achieve agreed objectives and outcomes, as well as to ensure that all individuals who use our service are in receipt of good up-to-date care. It also ensures that staff themselves feel supported in their work and have recourse to a system of help should they require it.

But how does it help to improve teamwork? By engaging with the process of supervision the team member is reminded of the aims and objectives of the organisation and the work they engage in. They are able to voice their views on practice and can also access support and information on further training. Having the opportunity to discuss their roles and responsibilities will also enable the worker to feel empowered with respect to decisions made about their work and the team as a whole and any limitations they have come across as a result of their work. Hawkins and Shohet (2009) suggest supervision is an important part of taking care of the team members. It is an opportunity to review their own direction in their role and encourages healthy environments for communication.

Appraisal, alongside supervision, is another strategy for managers to assess performance and needs against organisational requirements and aims. It is a formally constituted, annual activity that should take place with all staff.

As a vehicle for structured, personal development planning, the appraisal process can have positive outcomes for both individuals and the organisation and it can also help develop a strategy for an individual to meet personal goals and objectives, both short and long term. Ideally, appraisal is a shared activity that is conducted in partnership and it should result in some kind of individual personal development planning (Tilmouth et al., 2011).

To summarise then, supervision and appraisal involve education, support, self-development and self-awareness, the main advantage of which is that team members are able to continue to learn and move forward at work.

d) Effective communication systems

In the development of effective team working, positive relationships with a wide range of staff from different disciplines are crucial and this requires that staff communicate effectively with people at all levels within the organisation. Poor communication is an area which is consistently held up as a reason for underperformance and can also lead to conflict (Yoder-Wise, 2003).

Effective communication requires the use of a variety of inter-personal techniques and by definition:

> 'involves the reciprocal process in which messages are sent and received between two or more people.'

> (Bazler Riley, 2008)

And

> 'is something we do in our internal world of thoughts and in our external world by speaking, writing, gestures, drawing, making images and symbols or receiving messages from others.'

> (Crawford, Brown and Bonham, 2006)

If we are to send meaningful messages which are received and understood there must be a matching of the appropriate communication with the individual to whom we are speaking and the circumstances in which the interaction takes place. For example, speaking to a young child requires a different way of communicating than speaking to a member of staff. They are not interchangeable as there would be a distinct lack of understanding on the part of the child and, if the situation were reversed, a feeling of being patronised for the member of staff!

Whatever the communication need or type, a good working relationship is essential where there is trust and the ability to be able to talk openly and honestly. In the course of your work you will undertake a variety of roles and will need to adjust your communication to each circumstance. In the mental health setting you may deal with individuals who find it difficult to communicate with clarity due to the condition they present with, so the ability to adapt your communication style to the situation and respond in a sensitive and empathetic way to the needs of that individual is paramount.

Empathy is the ability to understand the client's frame of reference, by putting yourself in their shoes, so to speak. Active listening skills are the best way to show this. Empathy is not about showing sympathy, which might make a person feel pitied.

By accepting and valuing the people with whom we interact, with expressions of warmth and a non-judgemental attitude, we will improve our communication skills no end. This is sometimes difficult to achieve, particularly when we dislike what they are saying or doing. However, this sort of situation needs to be dealt with in an honest way that shows that, although we may disagree with a point of view, an action, or a behaviour, we still value the individual.

In the CMHT the geographical boundaries which exist where staff are working in different centres can make communication a difficult process. However, developments in electronic communication have had a significant impact on how team members and different teams interact, although the communication will differ from teams who regularly communicate face to face.

To summarise this section, have a look at the some of the following points which are useful to cultivate in developing skill in communication.

- Empathy. Have we really considered what it feels like to be in the shoes of the particular team worker with a problem? By having a greater depth of understanding about the problems others in the wider team may have we can start to communicate in a more effective manner.
- Do we listen and seek clarification to make sure that we fully understand the other person's position and their needs? Listening is a skill and sometimes we only hear what we *think* is being said or what we *want* to hear. Learning to listen with integrity and clarity will go a long way to improving our interpersonal skills.
- Are we calm or taking things personally? Occasionally, we may come under some criticism and it is how we react to this that can make or break a relationship. If we can deal with it in a calm manner we may be able to learn from it and make successful changes to the way in which we work.

Successful communication is linked to assertiveness and being open and flexible in order to achieve a successful outcome, and an effective team is reliant upon people who can work together effectively and with a high level of inter-personal and communication skill.

e) Access to current information on best practice, help and guidance

In order to ensure staff remain up to date with new practice it is imperative that a cycle of continuous professional development (CPD) is in place.

The RCN (2007) in a joint statement for continuing professional development for health and social care practitioners set out the CPD requirements for health and social care practitioners from a range of settings in accordance with the statutory training requirements under *The Health and Safety at Work etc. Act 1974* (HMSO, 1974). The expectation of all staff is to meet the requirements of their own regulatory body and those working in the NHS must meet the Knowledge and Skills Framework (KSF) requirements by undertaking CPD. They further recommend that six days (45 hours) per year should be the minimum time to facilitate CPD.

In your own setting you need to ensure that you are aware of what you are required to undertake in terms of additional training to meet these statutory regulations.

f) Audit and quality management

The Chartered Quality Institute defines quality management as:

> 'an organisation-wide approach to understanding precisely what customers need and consistently delivering accurate solutions within budget, on time and with the minimum loss to society.'

> (http://www.thecqi.org/Knowledge-Hub/What-is-quality [accessed on 30/12/12])

In order to ensure this in your own setting you need to have in place policies that identify service users' needs and wants from the service as well as detailed structures to show how you will deliver the service and how you will measure the quality of that service. The performance of staff also needs to be regularly assessed and how service users rate the service should also be a part of your quality management cycle.

The key to a good-quality service means paying attention to the following areas:

- service-user satisfaction
- continual improvement of working methods
- efficiency of work procedures to reduce waste and cost
- care and responsibility

When identifying areas for improvement and recommending change you need to consider the following:

- What has changed in legislation or what recent innovations in care practice require the construction of new policies or procedures?
- Are all staff fully aware of the health and safety procedures within the work place or is more training needed to ensure they have up-to-date knowledge?
- How will you go about recommending the changes needed and what will you need to do to ensure the change is accepted?

By undertaking a review of your processes or auditing what you do on a regular basis, you are in a good position to identify weak points and potential areas for improvement. In this way you can ensure that the policies you have in place are effectively protecting the individuals who come into contact with your setting.

Evidence Activity

 Activity

1. Write a reflective account of your own team and say how effective it is with respect to the following points.
   a. effective and accessible policy and procedure and clear aims and objectives;
   b. clear job descriptions and defined role boundaries;
   c. supervision, regular review and appraisal and continuous development for workers;
   d. effective communication;
   e. access to current information on best practice, help and guidance
   f. audit and quality management.
2. Say how you would improve the above to increase the effectiveness of your team across the wider CMHT.

3 Explain how an individual worker can contribute to an effective team working environment

The ideal team members who contribute to making a team effective are those individuals who work constructively with others and have a willingness to grow and develop within the team. The ineffective team member is the sort of individual who seeks to maintain their position by protecting their experience, or who prefers to work alone and unaided and is not willing to discuss their assumptions, negotiate options or explain solutions (Tilmouth, et al., 2010).

Effective teams recruit people who:

- commit to a shared goal;
- listen and respond to others in an objective and productive way;
- are willing to take on different roles in the group in order to accomplish shared ends;
- are open and honest with their ideas, concerns and values;
- avoid carrying hidden agendas into team meetings.

Effective teamwork requires that all team members relate well to each other. Belbin's research (1981) on the various roles of team members is worthy of note here. The study looked at determining how problems could be predicted and avoided in teams by controlling the dynamics of the group.

The results revealed that the difference between success and failure for a team was not dependent on factors such as intellect, but more on the behaviour of the group member. The research team began to identify separate clusters of behaviour, each of which formed distinct team contributions or team roles (www.belbin.com).

Belbin (1981) found that good teams consisted of individuals who had the ability to adopt different roles and that in selecting people for jobs, eligibility by way of qualifications and experience did not necessarily reflect suitability. Other qualities such as aptitude and versatility were seen to be more fitting. So-called personality clashes at work, which often lead to conflict in the setting, were remarked to actually be 'role' clashes.

The text which follows highlights the roles as outlined in Belbin's work.

Plant

These people tend to be highly creative and good at solving problems in unconventional ways. As lateral thinkers and problem solvers, they often find new ways of tackling a problem and better ways of doing things. If somebody, however, favours this role they may have lots of energy at first but when boredom sets in, be unable to carry things through. This may well lead to not following standard procedures because of boredom and becoming a rebel.

The monitor evaluator

These are logical, objective people who weigh up the team's options in a dispassionate way but with a tendency to disregard the emotions in the team. In team meetings this person can bring the team back to the task, enabling the team to focus. They are unlikely to be side-tracked by the emotions involved in the situation.

Coordinators

These are the people who delegate work appropriately and have an ability to draw out team members and focus on the team's objectives. With facilitator and leadership qualities, they have a skill in bringing people together, recognising that every member of the team has a skill. They acknowledge diversity and make sure that everyone's opinions are heard. They know a lot of people and are good at networking.

Resource investigator

If the team is isolated and inwardly focused, this is a good person to have since they will investigate the world outside in order to obtain knowledge about what is happening locally and nationally.

Implementer

This is the person in the team who carries out strategies as efficiently as possible and takes forward and gathers the ideas that have come from the team. This person gets the task done.

Completer finisher

This is the person in the team who polishes the job to the highest result. They may be the perfectionist in the team. If they become too involved at the beginning of the task, they may be interested in getting to the detail but may make the task laborious and over long. Getting them involved at the end of the task to go over the detail, eradicating the typing errors, is a good use of their skills.

Team workers

These are the frontline soldiers who carry out the work. Team workers are given an idea and they turn it into action immediately.

Shaper

These are very task-focused people who cannot abide meetings that go on and on as they just want to get out and do the work. They will challenge a team to keep moving and recognise when an idea has had its day and the team need to try another tack. They have an idea of the bigger picture.

Belbin came up with the final, ninth, team role called the **Specialist**. Specialists in their particular fields, for example, are those who focus on their own subject only. They can be seen as more independent and not really part of the team.

Each role has its strengths and weaknesses and by being aware of the roles each of your staff exhibit and assigning them duties that fit that role, effective performance can be assured.

(Tilmouth et al., 2010.)

Evidence Activity

 Activity

In developing teams it is important to consider not only individuals' technical skills, knowledge and experience but also their ability to coordinate actions and their interpersonal qualities as potential members. What qualities do you possess that contribute to your team's effectiveness?

---

4 Explain common barriers to establishing and maintaining effective working relationships

Differing values and approaches

We all hold our own values according to our beliefs and the culture in which we have been brought up. A value is a deeply held view on something that acts as a guiding principle. In the work place differing values can lead to barriers to good working relationships as well as a lack of consistency in the way in which the team works.

In defining the values as they apply to your work place, you may choose the following as being the most important:

- integrity
- quality of service
- respect for others
- innovation.

However, if these values differ from others in the team and are not shared then you may have conflict. For example, if you prioritise your work according to delivering a high-quality service and you take pride in how you do your job, a person who does not value this approach may be a source of conflict for you and this can cause work to become stressful.

The culture in the work place can be defined as the way things are done. If the culture or approach to the way a service is being delivered and the values are different then there is the risk of a lack of openness and a lack of trust may start to develop.

In addition to the culture within the work place, we also need to be aware of the wider team. Working in the health sector requires that we 'foster equality and diversity' and respect the differences of all the individuals we may come across. This is not just about cultural differences but also about the differences in values that people hold as this can have a huge impact on our ability to communicate.

It is most important to be culturally aware in our interpersonal interactions because we live in a multi-cultural society. Miller (2006) says that defining the term culture is complex. Often discussions we may have about race become confused with the terms ethnicity and culture. Ethnicity, gender and social class, should additionally include religious beliefs, sexuality, rationality, skin colour and experience of oppression (Miller, 2006) and by developing a respectful curiosity about the beliefs and practices within all service users' lives, we are able to communicate in a more meaningful manner.

The challenges to team working in multi-agency settings are many and varied. Being separated by geographical boundaries, and working in external settings, can create communication boundaries and status inequalities, all of which can become a source of conflict. They can be frustrating and make the completion of tasks difficult. In addition, the mismatch of cultures, behaviours and understanding of services in the setting can also be challenging and may affect the work we do.

We may also find that there is a lack of understanding of each other's roles within the immediate and the wider team and a lack of clarity regarding management roles and responsibilities, all of which may lead to unrest in the team and conflict.

Conflicts of interest and group/power dynamics

Another source of tension in the work place is when a conflict of interest arises, and this can lead to a disruption in performance and upset within the group dynamic. By definition conflict refers to a state of disagreement which might be caused by opposition of some sort. We might experience conflict within ourselves or at the hands of others but either way it can disrupt working relationships. Occasionally power struggles may arise in the work place and these usually occur when we try to control the environment or others within it. This situation may lead to conflict if somebody disagrees with what is happening.

There are two types of conflict: those which revolve around the disagreements in relation to approaches to work and those conflicts which may arise between individual members of the team stemming from differences in personal values and beliefs.

If badly managed, conflict will inevitably lead to ineffective teamwork and individuals may start to avoid each other. This means that rifts in relationships start to develop, leading to ineffectual and poor care of service users, clients and patients. Any situation that is causing conflict may cause us to have negative feelings about a person or a group of people.

Conflict is often viewed as a negative issue and becomes a problem when it affects our work, or causes individuals to behave in an inappropriate manner. This leads to low morale in the work place and impacts negatively on the work force and the clients.

In Section 8.5 we look at how we can rectify this.

Differing systems and procedures and access to resources

When new teams start to work together it is inevitable that there will be different systems for working and procedures in place. In working towards an effective team it is imperative that there is a shared view of how the service will be delivered and how resources and staffing are to be allocated.

When new teams come together the overall barrier to effectiveness is how to help a diverse group of professionals to work together and establish themselves as a coherent group.

You may be familiar with Tuckman's (1965) theory on how groups develop over time and the process of forming a team. His system for common stages of group development is:

- forming
- storming
- norming
- performing
- mourning or adjourning.

Forming

In this first stage the members of the team are new to each other and the wider group and at this time there is a general wariness of each other. Initially individual roles are unclear and the team leader is relied upon for direction and support. Being too directive at this time may result in team members not 'forming' together as a team, thus slowing down the process towards team cohesion.

Storming

As team members become more familiar with each other personality clashes and differences of opinion may occur and the atmosphere within the group changes and may well start to feel uncomfortable.

Although storming is uncomfortable it is a most important stage since without it the next stage of norming is protracted and drawn out.

Norming

Here the team begins to find some mutual direction and consensus. The ideas which may have been voiced during the storming stage start to come together and a more harmonious state of affairs begins. This is the time when the team starts to feel positive and more together.

Performing

This is the stage when the work gets done and the team members start to apply themselves to the job in hand. Because they now have a better knowledge of members of the wider team, individuals start to feel safe to take on different roles and activities.

Mourning/adjourning

This fifth stage was added later in Tuckman's theory and occurs when a team comes to an end. This may happen within your team when committees are set up to work on certain projects. Individuals leaving the team for other jobs and new members joining may lead to a stage of mourning. You may look back and review events from the past and you will look forward to future challenges. At this stage it is natural to experience negative feelings for the team as a way of coping and feeling better about leaving it.

In established teams a different set of issues may exist. The major challenge is to ensure that the team continues to work towards the objectives of the work place as set out in your strategic plan. Everyone in the team needs be working together to keep operations running smoothly, and this requires keeping the team together and the communication lines open (adapted from Tilmouth et al., 2011).

Communication channels

Poor communication is often cited as one of the reasons why a job does not get done. Perhaps you yourself have remarked about ineffective channels of communication making your job more difficult?

These are some of the reasons you may have identified as communication barriers:

Time to reflect

Think for a moment about a time when you felt your message just wasn't being received. List the factors both internal and external that may have been reasons for the blocks or barriers in communication.

- Differences in culture and values.
- Becoming upset about what you are hearing, leading to conflict.
- Having negative feelings about the person you are speaking to.
- Anxiety about areas of your own life, making it difficult to concentrate.
- Feeling unsafe, due to the other person's behaviour.
- Not listening effectively.
- Feeling unwell or tired.
- Noise or being in an inappropriate environment.

These are all problems we may have with one-to-one communication or within the team in which we work. In our wider working environment the sorts of issues which arise with communication are to do with the problem of working across environmental and interagency boundaries. It is about getting the message across to a more diverse group of people and ensuring that the channels of communication are effective.

In two major reports Ritchie (1994) and Davies (1995) cited the failure of care provision leading to tragic outcomes as being due to poor communication in the delivery of care.

In a further high profile case, the Laming inquiry into the death of Victoria Climbié (2003) established the circumstances leading to and surrounding the death of this young person. Part of the inquiry was concerned with how social services, health services and the police cooperated and communicated with each other and local education and local authorities. For full details of the report please refer to www.publications.education.gov.uk. Recommendations 14, 15, 16 are all concerned with team working, communication and interagency working.

This inquiry found that the ability to work effectively across organisational boundaries within social care was lacking and improvements to the way information was exchanged within and between agencies was imperative if children were to be adequately safeguarded.

The NHS plan (2000) suggested a more integrated way of working, with the patient at the centre of the team being given new powers and more influence over the way the NHS functions. The NHS plan is thus promoting greater collaboration with other agencies in joint teams and to implement such arrangements will require clear communication between the wider team. In the next section we look at ways to remove these barriers.

Activity

Using each of the headings:

- differing values and approaches
- conflicts of interest and group dynamics
- differing systems and procedures and access to resources
- poor systems for communication

write a case study of your own experience in your work place and comment on how these barriers have affected your own team working.

5 Explain how to overcome common barriers to effective working relationships between individuals within a home team, in a multidisciplinary context and between agencies

Having looked at some of the things that cause conflict within the team we now turn our attention to the methods we might employ to deal with these issues.

An effective team works towards the same goals and the team members will cooperate with the decisions made.

The organisation which promotes openness and creativity, and encourages the team members to share information in an effective way is on the way to being successful. Providing a positive climate in which to work, to innovate and take calculated risks, and with proper management, teamwork improves processes and produces results quickly.

Wheelan provides a useful list of characteristics of high-performing teams.

The characteristics of high-performing teams

1. Members are clear about and agree with the team's goals.
2. Tasks are appropriate to team versus individual solution.
3. Members are clear about and accept their roles.
4. Role assignments match members' abilities.
5. The leadership style matches the team's development level.
6. An open communication structure allows all members to participate.
7. The team receives, gives and utilises feedback about its effectiveness and productivity.
8. The team spends time defining and discussing problems it must solve or decisions it must make.
9. Members also spend time planning how they will solve problems and make decisions.
10. The team uses effective decision-making strategies.
11. The team implements and evaluates its solutions and decisions.
12. Task-related deviance is tolerated.
13. Team norms encourage high performance, quality, success and innovation.
14. Subgroups are integrated into the team as a whole.
15. The team contains the smallest number of members necessary to accomplish its goals.

16. Team members have sufficient time together to develop a mature working unit and to accomplish the team's goals.
17. The team is highly cohesive and cooperative.
18. Periods of conflict are frequent but brief, and the group has effective conflict management strategies.

(Wheelan, 2005, p.40 as cited in Tilmouth et al., 2010)

But how do we strive to become such a highly performing team? As mentioned above having effective conflict strategies in place can help.

In dealing with any conflict, four key steps can be identified:

1. Describe and define the actual conflict.
2. Listen to all parties to fully understand the issues.
3. Secure the commitment of all parties to resolve the conflict by emphasising the benefits of finding a way forward and the consequences of not doing so.
4. Reaching an agreement.

In dealing with conflict Thompson's (2006) RED approach to managing conflict is for situations with a high degree of tension associated with them:

- R – Recognise the conflict and do not ignore it.
- E – Evaluate the conflict to see how detrimental it would be if it was allowed to develop.
- D – Deal with the conflict; keep open communication.

The two destructive extremes, either pretending the conflict does not exist or over-reacting to the situation, are according to Thompson best avoided.

A further method comes from John Adair in his book *Effective Teambuilding* (2000). He came up with the following five strategies for dealing with conflict:

1. **Competing** – forcing your own ideas through because you believe your way is right.
2. **Confronting/collaborating** – by bringing all the issues into the open and exploring all feasible options you are showing an openness to change.
3. **Compromise** – negotiating halfway.
4. **Avoid** – opt out altogether and avoid taking up any position.
5. **Accommodate** – allowing the change to happen in order to not hurt feelings.

The reality of modern mental health and social services is that the care we get depends as much on how health and social care employees work with each other as on their individual competence within their own field of expertise and conflict is inevitable at certain times in the course of our work (Tilmouth et al., 2010).

Conflict may often arise when there are changes to the way in which we work and this may raise issues within the work force.

With effective communication that encourages the team to accept and understand the reasons for the change, you can move to a new way of working that is embraced by everyone.

In dealing with communication barriers we refer to environmental and cultural barriers. The environment where we engage with visitors and staff when we communicate bad news or have supervision and team meetings needs to be looked at with critical eyes. If you feel uncomfortable in this setting, then the chances are that your staff and visitors will feel likewise (Tilmouth et al., 2010). In dealing with individuals who are in crisis with their mental health this can be a very important consideration.

These sorts of issues can be dealt with by making changes to the actual fabric of the environment and improving the general layout of the place in which communication is to occur.

Cultural barriers are about recognising that everybody is different. In your own settings you may have noticed that some care workers fail to respond to some clients in appropriate ways simply because they lack an understanding of the condition or culture of the client. For example, an individual who is suffering from depression may be excluded from certain social activities or a client who wishes to practise their religion is not given the opportunity to do so. Raising awareness of cultural and religious differences in your work force may, for some individuals, require more training or revisiting the anti-discriminatory policy.

For staff in the team to respond to the differences of their clients, they need to be aware of the responsibilities they have to *all* individuals in the setting and you may need to revise and update your policy to ensure that all staff are aware of how they can use it in their practice and how they should address issues of cultural sensitivity and diversity.

Another area of communication focuses on the emotions and feelings within us and how they affect our dealings with others. Being aware of how we present and portray ourselves can only come about if we reflect on our own skills in communication and this can be uncomfortable. We sometimes need to move out of our comfort zone and identify areas for our own self-development in terms of how we communicate. Donnelly and Neville (2008) comment that being aware of oneself enables us to review our personal values against the professional standards that we are now expected to work within. This awareness is invaluable in mental health care. In dealing with clients who may present with confusion or delusional outbursts the way we react and communicate with the individual can be the difference between escalation of a problem or calmness returning to the situation. We therefore need to be acutely aware of our own strengths and weaknesses with respect to how we communicate.

We learned previously about the sorts of challenges we might meet with respect to teamwork. Newly formed teams need to go through a development process, and well-established teams have to be motivated to perform in roles to which they comfortably fit. Effective teams are those which comprise groups of people who complement each other in the roles they undertake within the team and who are managed and led in an efficient way.

Singh (2000) in the article 'Running an effective community mental health team' comments that:

> 'Building and maintaining an effective team requires commitment, clarity of purpose, a shared vision and frequent review of team operations.'

As community mental health teams are going to constitute a large part of the metal health service in the future, there needs to be a

> 'team consensus on targeting serious mental illness, using evidence-based practice and equity of case-load to improve effectiveness and that basic knowledge and core skills necessary for providing effective mental health care should be developed early in the training'

(Singh, 2000)

Evidence Activity

 8.5 Activity

Using the case study from Evidence Activity 8.4, show how you have overcome each of the issues raised.

6 Apply a strategy to promote effective team working within either a home team, multidisciplinary or multi agency context

Individuals within a home team and in a multidisciplinary and multi-agency context

Effective teams, whether they are a small group of members or the larger CMHT, display certain features and the following list is of eight characteristics of effective teams identified by Larson and LaFasto (1989) in their book *Teamwork: What Must Go Right/What Can Go Wrong.*

1. The team must have a clear goal.
2. The team must have a results-driven structure.
3. The team must have competent team members.
4. The team must have unified commitment.
5. The team must have a collaborative climate.
6. The team must have high standards that are understood by all.
7. The team must receive external support and encouragement.
8. The team must have principled leadership.

Effective teams are cohesive, sharing goals and visions and operating in an atmosphere of openness and cooperation. With multi-agency teams and those involving members from a variety of settings and professional disciplines, the meeting is the most popular forum with which to communicate information.

A meeting is an opportunity to communicate with the whole team present and can be a useful vehicle to encourage the staff to discuss the overall aims of the team with the shared vision in mind. They also enable team members to get to know each other and open discussions and make action points. But we have all attended badly managed meetings, where the start and end times are not adhered to, or where some people talk a lot and others just sit silently. If there is little or no control about what is happening or indeed what is being accomplished members may come away wondering what the meeting actually achieved.

Figure 8.2 Multi-agency working

Some useful pointers for ensuring meetings are useful and effective follow.

- Be prepared for the meeting.
- Attend the meeting on time.
- Start and end the meeting on time.
- Respect and value the diversity of team members.
- Participate in the meeting.
- Actively listen to the discussions.
- Make decisions by consensus.

(Tilmouth, et al., 2011.)

The success of the CMHT will largely depend on its ability to bring together people with diverse skills and knowledge.

Your team will also work with other members of wider groups of professionals and you may find yourselves liaising with and calling on the services of those who work in social work, community mental health crisis teams, the justice system and education staff.

In the past, groups of staff from the same discipline rarely communicated with other specialists around patient issues and this led to a number of problems in service provision. The push towards multidisciplinary team working has been encouraged over the last 20 years or so, and as we saw earlier in the chapter the Laming Report (2003) highlighted the importance of working closely with people from other professional groups and agencies

One of the advantages of teamwork is the abundance and quality of ideas. However, some teams can start to think in the same way and ideas from individuals then become subsumed in the team view. For the team to perform successfully, it is essential that they do not become side-tracked with unimportant issues or take too much time discussing small details or get caught up in team conflict. An effective team supports its individual team members and recognises that the skills and knowledge of each team member, although varied, are of equal value.

A three-year multidisciplinary project (2008–2011) that aimed to generate national guidelines for effective team working in mental healthcare in the NHS was described and led by Professor Walid El Ansari. Entitled 'Effective Team Working in Mental Health' the research surveyed NHS staff and found that as that as many as 50 per cent of the staff in mental health trusts were working in groups that did not display all the characteristics required for good team working.

Clearly there is a need to improve the way in which the CMHT work together to provide a quality service and to demonstrate effectiveness in the mental health sector.

> **Evidence Activity**
>
> **Activity**
>
> Write a reflective account of the effectiveness of your own team in working with the wider community. Show evidence in your portfolio of meetings and shared policy and procedure.

Summary

In this chapter we have addressed how effective team performance requires the development of a positive and supportive culture in an organisation, and seen how it is only in this way that can we expect staff to be supportive of a shared vision to meet the agreed objectives for a CMHT.

How teams function and the roles that members adopt have been examined, together with a variety of models of leadership relevant to the health and care sector. The strategies for effective team working and leadership have been reviewed through the activities you have been requested to undertake for your portfolio.

Team working means taking responsibility for your own work, as well as respecting the contributions of all your colleagues, and good communication is essential to effective team working.

References

Bazler Riley, J (2008) Communications in Nursing. Missouri: Mosby Elsevier.

Belbin, M (1981) Management teams: why they succeed or fail. London: Heinemann.

Carroll, M (2007) One More Time: What is Supervision? Psychotherapy in Australia 13 (3). Available at: www.supervisioncentre.com/docs/kv/one%20more%20time.pdf (accessed 20/10/12).

Crawford, P, Brown, B, Bonham, P (2006) Communication in Clinical Settings. Cheltentham: Nelson Thornes.

Davies, N (1995) Report of the Inquiry into the Circumstances Leading to the Death of Jonathan Newby. Presented to the Chairman of Oxford Regional Health Authority. London: HMSO.

Donnelly, E and Neville, L (2008) Communication and Interpersonal skills. Exeter: Reflect Press.

El Ansari, W (2011) Effective Team Working in Mental Health. Available at: http://www.abs.aston.ac.uk/newweb/research/projects.asp#Effective

Hawkins, P and Shohet, R (2009) Supervision in the Helping Professions (3e). Berkshire: Open University Press.

Larson and LaFasto (1989) Teamwork: What Must Go Right/What Can Go Wrong. London: Sage Publications.

Miller, L (2006) Counselling Skills for Social Work. London: Sage Publications.

RCN (2007) Joint Statement for Continuing Professional Development for Health and Social Care Practitioners. London: RCN.

Ritchie, J H (1994) The Report of the Inquiry into the Care and Treatment of Christopher Clunis. London: HMSO.

Royal College of Psychiatrists' Public Education Editorial Board (2009) A checklist for psychiatrists: working in partnership with service user and carers. London: RCP.

Singh, Swaran P (2000) Running an effective community mental health team. Available at: http://apt.rcpsych.org/content/6/6/414.full

Thompson , N (2006) People Problems. Hampshire: Palgrave Macmillan.

Tilmouth, T, Davies-Ward, E and Williams, B (2011) Foundation Degree in Health and Social Care. London: Hodder Education.

Tilmouth, T and Quallington, J (2011) Level Five Diploma in Leadership and Health and Social Care and Children and Young Peoples Services. London: Hodder Education.

Wheelan, S A (2005) Creating Effective Teams: A guide for members and leaders (2e). London: Sage.

Yoder-Wise, P S (2003) Leading and Managing in Nursing (3e). St Louis, Missouri: Mosby.

Promote and implement health and safety in health and social care

What are you finding out?

Every time you set foot into your work place you are subject to a number of hazards with respect to the environment and the people with which you work. This may sound dramatic but think about it for a moment. How safe are you from infection, hazardous substances, fire, visitors, intruders or faulty equipment? When we consider the dangers which we come into contact with on a daily basis the list seems endless. In this chapter we will discuss how we keep ourselves, and others, safe in a potentially hostile environment, and outline who is ultimately responsible for the safety of all who you come into contact with the setting.

> ## The reading and activities in this chapter will help you to:
>
> 1. Understand your own responsibilities, and the responsibilities of others, relating to health and safety:
>   - 1.1 Identify legislation relating to health and safety in a health or social care work setting
>   - 1.2 Explain the main points of health and safety policies and procedures agreed with the employer
>   - 1.3 Analyse the main health and safety responsibilities of:
>   - self
>   - the employer or manager
>   - others in the work setting
>   - 1.4 Identify specific tasks in the work setting that should not be carried out without special training.
> 2. Be able to carry out your own responsibilities for health and safety:
>   - 2.1 Use policies and procedures or other agreed ways of working that relate to health and safety
>   - 2.2 Support others to understand and follow safe practices
>   - 2.3 Monitor and report potential health and safety risks
>   - 2.4 Use risk assessment in relation to health and safety
>   - 2.5 Demonstrate ways to minimise potential risks and hazards
>   - 2.6 Access additional support or information relating to health and safety.
> 3. Understand procedures for responding to accidents and sudden illness:
>   - 3.1 Describe different types of accidents and sudden illness that may occur in your own work setting
>   - 3.2 Explain procedures to be followed if an accident or sudden illness should occur.
> 4. Be able to reduce the spread of infection:
>   - 4.1 Explain your own role in supporting others to follow practices that reduce the spread of infection
>   - 4.2 Demonstrate the recommended method for hand washing
>   - 4.3 Demonstrate ways to ensure that your own health and hygiene do not pose a risk to an individual or to others at work

5. Be able to move and handle equipment and other objects safely:
   5.1 Explain the main points of legislation that relate to moving and handling
   5.2 Explain principles for safe moving and handling
   5.3 Move and handle equipment and other objects safely.
6. Be able to handle hazardous substances and materials:
   6.1 Describe types of hazardous substances that may be found in the work setting
   6.2 Demonstrate safe practices for:
     • storing hazardous substances
     • using hazardous substances
     • disposing of hazardous substances and materials.
7. Be able to promote fire safety in the work setting:
   7.1 Describe practices that prevent fires from:
     • starting
     • spreading
   7.2 Demonstrate measures that prevent fires from starting
   7.3 Explain emergency procedures to be followed in the event of a fire in the work setting
   7.4 Ensure that clear evacuation routes are maintained at all times.
8. Be able to implement security measures in the work setting:
   8.1 Demonstrate use of agreed procedures for checking the identity of anyone requesting access to:
     • premises
     • information
   8.2 Demonstrate use of measures to protect your own security and the security of others in the work setting.
9. Describe common signs and indicators of stress:
   9.1 Describe signs that indicate your own stress
   9.2 Analyse factors that tend to trigger your own stress
   9.3 Compare strategies for managing stress.

Assessment criteria covered in this chapter

Reading this unit and completing the activities will provide you with the knowledge, understanding and skills required to meet the assessment criteria listed below.

City and Guilds Level 3 Diploma in Mental Health Care (QCF) (600/5241/7)		
Promote and implement health and safety in health and social care (F/601/8138)		
Learning Outcome 1 Understand own responsibilities, and the responsibilities of others, relating to health and safety		
Assessment Criteria	Page reference	Activity
1.1 Identify legislation relating to health and safety in a health or social care work setting	p. 186	
1.2 Explain the main points of health and safety policies and procedures agreed with the employer	p. 187	Evidence activity 9.1, p. 188
1.3 Analyse the main health and safety responsibilities of: • self • the employer or manager • others in the work setting	p. 187	Evidence activity 9.1, p. 188
1.4 Identify specific tasks in the work setting that should not be carried out without special training	p. 188	Evidence activity 9.1, p. 188

(Continued)

(Continued)

Learning Outcome 2 Be able to carry out own responsibilities for health and safety		
2.1 Use policies and procedures or other agreed ways of working that relate to health and safety	p. 188	Evidence activity 9.2 Activity 1, p. 188
2.2 Support others to understand and follow safe practices	p. 188	Evidence activity 9.2, Activity 1, p. 188
2.3 Monitor and report potential health and safety risks	p. 189	Evidence activity 9.2 Activities 2, 3, 4 and 5, p. 190
2.4 Use risk assessment in relation to health and safety	p. 189	Evidence activity 9.2 Activities 2, 3, 4 and 5, p. 190
2.5 Demonstrate ways to minimise potential risks and hazards	p. 189	Evidence activity 9.2 Activities 2, 3, 4 and 5, p. 190
2.6 Access additional support or information relating to health and safety	p. 190	Evidence activity 9.2 Activities 2, 3, 4 and 5, p. 190
Learning Outcome 3 Understand procedures for responding to accidents and sudden illness		
3.1 Describe different types of accidents and sudden illness that may occur in own work setting	p. 190	Evidence activity 9.3, p. 199
3.2 Explain procedures to be followed if an accident or sudden illness should occur	p. 190	Evidence activity 9.3, p. 199
Learning Outcome 4 Be able to reduce the spread of infection		
4.1 Explain own role in supporting others to follow practices that reduce the spread of infection	p. 199	Evidence activity 9.4, p. 201
4.2 Demonstrate the recommended method for hand washing	p. 200	Evidence activity 9.4, p. 201
4.3 Demonstrate ways to ensure that own health and hygiene do not pose a risk to an individual or to others at work	p. 199	Evidence activity 9.4, p. 201
Learning Outcome 5 Be able to move and handle equipment and other objects safely		
5.1 Explain the main points of legislation that relate to moving and handling	p. 201	Evidence activity 9.5, p. 202
5.2 Explain principles for safe moving and handling	p. 202	Evidence activity 9.5, p. 202
5.3 Move and handle equipment and other objects safely	p. 202	
Learning Outcome 6 Be able to handle hazardous substances and materials		
6.1 Describe types of hazardous substances that may be found in the work setting	p. 203	Evidence activity 9.6, Activity 1, p. 203
6.2 Demonstrate safe practices for: • storing hazardous substances • using hazardous substances • disposing of hazardous substances and materials	p. 203	Evidence activity 9.6, Activity 2, p. 204
Learning Outcome 7 Be able to promote fire safety in the work setting		
7.1 Describe practices that prevent fires from: • starting • spreading	p. 204	Evidence activity 9.7, Activities 1 and 2, p. 204
7.2 Demonstrate measures that prevent fires from starting	p. 204	Evidence activity 9.7, Activities 1 and 2, p. 204
7.3 Explain emergency procedures to be followed in the event of a fire in the work setting	p. 205	Evidence activity 9.7, Activities 3, p. 205
7.4 Ensure that clear evacuation routes are maintained at all times	p. 205	

(Continued)

(Continued)

Learning Outcome 8 Be able to implement security measures in the work setting		
8.1 Demonstrate use of agreed procedures for checking the identity of anyone requesting access to: • premises • information	p. 205	Evidence activity 9.8, p. 207
8.2 Demonstrate use of measures to protect own security and the security of others in the work setting	p. 205	Evidence activity 9.8, p. 207
Learning Outcome 9 Know how to manage stress		
9.1 Describe common signs and indicators of stress	p. 207	Evidence activity 9.9, p. 208
9.2 Describe signs that indicate own stress	p. 207	Evidence activity 9.9, p. 208
9.3 Analyse factors that tend to trigger own stress	p. 207	Evidence activity 9.9, p. 208
9.4 Compare strategies for managing stress	p. 208	Evidence activity 9.9, p. 208

1 Understand own responsibilities, and the responsibilities of others, relating to health and safety

1.1 Identify legislation relating to health and safety in a health or social care work setting

The main piece of legislation is the Health and Safety at Work Act 1974 (HASAWA) often referred to as an 'umbrella act' since it describes various regulations which make up the whole. These are:

● Manual Handling Regulations 1992
● Control of Substances Hazardous to Health Regulations 2002 (COSHH)
● Reporting on Injuries, Diseases, and Dangerous Occurrences Regulations 1995 (RIDDOR)
● Health and Safety First Aid Regulations 1981
● Management of Health and Safety at Work Regulations 1999.

COSHH and RIDDOR

These two pieces of legislation are likely to be the ones you will become most familiar with the course of your work.

The Control of Substances Hazardous to Health Regulations (2002) requires all settings to do the following:

● Identify the substances specific to the setting and risk posed by these to health.
● Decide on precautions to take when working with these substances.
● Control any exposure to substances where it is unavoidable.
● Ensure safe procedure is followed at all times.
● Monitor exposure if unavoidable.
● Carry out health assessments.
● Prepare a plan of action should an accident occur.
● Ensure all staff are trained and supervised and that a COSHH file is available in the work place detailing where the substances are stored, how they are to be labelled, what their effects might be, safe exposure times and how to deal with an emergency if one arises.

The Reporting of Injuries, Diseases and Dangerous Occurrences Regulations (RIDDOR) is a legal requirement and all major injuries, accidents and outbreaks of disease need to be reported to the Incident Contact Centre which was set up in 2001. These occurrences are then logged and passed on to either local environmental agencies or the HSE. Anything which may have occurred which has the potential to be dangerous must also be reported.

1.2 Explain the main points of health and safety policies and procedures agreed with the employer

The National Minimum Standards for Care no. 11.2 sets out the requirements for each work place, where there are more than five employees, to have a written Health and Safety Policy in place. It states that:

'The agency delivering the care has a comprehensive health and safety policy and written procedures for health and safety management defining;

individual and organisational responsibility for health and safety;

responsibilities and arrangements for risk assessments under the requirements of the Health and Safety at Work Regulations (1999) (management regulation).'

(DOH, 2000)

The main points in any policy are:

- A commitment to ensuring the safety of all employees, patients/clients and visitors to the organisation.
- A statement of intent to that purpose.
- An implementation plan which shows how this will be achieved.
- A list of procedures with respect to action to be taken in the event of accidents or need to evacuate premises.

In addition Health and Safety posters should also be displayed giving details of the staff who are designated safety officers and first aiders.

Figure 9.1 A health and safety poster

1.3 Analyse the main health and safety responsibilities

Self

As an employee your responsibility in the work place is to take care of your own safety and that of others and to cooperate with your employer on all aspects of Health and Safety.

The HSE (Health and Safety Executive) is part of the government Health and Safety Commission (HSC) and these bodies are responsible for the control and monitoring of the risks within the work place to ensure that workers remain safe. The belief that 'prevention is better than cure' informs their mission statement which is:

'… to protect people's health and safety by ensuring that risks in the checking workplace are properly controlled.'

(www.hse.gov.uk)

The employer or manager

The main responsibility of an employer or manager is to protect the health, safety and welfare of all employees and visitors to the organisation and one of the ways in which this is accomplished is by carrying out risk assessments for the premises and then putting in place risk control measures. They also need to make sure that they are complying with the Safety Representative and Safety Committee Regulations (1977) and the Health and Safety Consultations with Employees Regulations (1996).

In addition the employer is duty bound to make sure that everyone is aware of the risks in the work place and that training about how to deal with the risks and how to protect yourself is given.

Others in the work setting

Just as we are responsible for own safety and for following procedures to ensure this, others who enter our work place should be encouraged to do the same. A visitor book for signing on entering the premises and signs which show what to do in the case of any emergency should be available around the premises to ensure that those who are unfamiliar with the setting can access information to prevent harm to themselves.

1.4 Identify specific tasks in the work setting that should not be carried out without special training

For this section you need to have a copy of your conditions of service or contract available to you and the code of conduct. Practising in a safe manner means you should only be undertaking tasks for which you are trained and should not be expected to take on anything new to you without being supervised and shown what to do. There are some specialist tasks such as taking blood, or administering medications for which training needs to be undertaken.

Your code of conduct is a set of guidelines to which you agree when you sign your contract. Working outside of that code means you might be subject to disciplinary action.

Evidence Activity

9.1 Activity

1. Write a reflective account to show what your understanding of your own and others responsibility relating to health and safety is.
2. Look at your contract and code of conduct and identify areas for professional development with respect to specialist tasks you could train for. Is there anything you currently undertake which is not covered in your contract? Do you need to discuss this with your manager?

2 Be able to carry out own responsibilities for health and safety

2.1 Use policies and procedures or other agreed ways of working that relate to health and safety

2.2 Support others to understand and follow safe practices

Policies and procedures provide the link between what the service aims to achieve and its day-to-day operations. Your health and safety policy is a translation of the legislation that needs to be in place in order to ensure safe working practice and safe delivery of care.

As a written guide on how to handle issues should they arise, a policy equips a worker with

Evidence Activity

9.2 Activity 1

Using the health and safety policy for your work place prepare and undertake a staff training session to ensure that all staff are aware of their responsibilities and roles with respect to health and safety.

a course of action they need to take in order to come to a decision. Policies are rule driven and state aims and objectives, as well as describing who is covered by the policy and the consequences of not following the policy.

2.3 Monitor and report potential health and safety risks

The Health and Safety Executive outline guidance for monitoring this activity in the workplace and state that 'Monitoring and reporting are vital parts of a health and safety culture' (http://www.hse. gov.uk/leadership/monitor.htm).

The HSE makes the point that there are certain things that an organisation needs to be monitoring in order to maintain good practice. They suggest that by monitoring sickness absence and work place health the management team can be advised of any underlying problems that might result in long-term illness.

Any data that is collected regarding aspects of health and safety can also be used to measure the organisation against others in the area. By undertaking regular audits the organisation is then in a position to make changes and to introduce new ways of working to ensure that effective risk management and control are in place. This makes for a safer environment for all.

2.4 Use risk assessment in relation to health and safety

2.5 Demonstrate ways to minimise potential risks and hazards

We may view risk assessment as a somewhat onerous task but we need to carry out such an assessment prior to any activity being undertaken. The key stages within the process seek to address the following areas:

Step One: Looking for hazards

An investigation of the premises, activity or procedure needs to be undertaken. As we mentioned earlier in the chapter the hazards identified will depend very much on the type of work being carried out.

Step Two: Identifying who could be harmed and how

This seeks to show special arrangements for the types of hazards that people may come into contact with through their daily work in an area or even as clients. We are all familiar with hard hats being worn by anybody entering a building site, but have you thought about the risks you may face during a span of duty?

Step Three: Evaluating the risk

In this part of the assessment you are making a judgement as to the arrangements already in place for dealing with a potential problem area. An example might be simply changing storage arrangements to free up the fire exit or identifying safer ways to transport clients to outpatient appointments.

Step Four: Recording the findings

A record needs to include checklists identifying the hazards, the people likely to be at risk, and arrangements to reduce the hazard.

Step Five: Assessing the effectiveness of the precautions in place

Following any dangerous occurrence staff are expected to complete accident forms and sometimes to inform the HSE. If the same occurrence happens several times then clearly the risk assessment needs to be revisited and safer actions put into place.

2.6 Access additional support or information relating to health and safety

The Health and Safety Executive supplies the most up to date information with respect to health and safety and can be accessed online at: http://www.hse.gov.uk/leadership/monitor.htm.

In addition, managers may undertake further training and other staff can be encouraged to become health and safety officers in the work place.

Evidence Activity

 Activities 2, 3, 4 and 5

Undertake a risk assessment for one aspect of practice in your work place.

1. Use the five stages as outlined above.
2. Ensure that all processes are documented.
3. Publish the findings to staff via a staff meeting.
4. Reflect on whether your findings require a change in policy to ensure safe practice.

3 Understand procedures for responding to accidents and sudden illness

3.1 Describe different types of accidents and sudden illness that may occur in own work setting

3.2 Explain procedures to be followed if an accident or sudden illness should occur

Within the remit of this text it is only possible to give you a general overview of the sorts of situations that may arise in your care setting and which you may need to deal with as the first person on the scene.

Being faced with a potential emergency situation is a frightening experience and feelings and emotions can often escalate causing us to act in irrational ways. You will, of course, have been required to undertake some first aid training.

It is impossible to say what you may experience in your own work place as it depends very much on the setting. For example, if you work with elderly people you may experience falls and strokes (CVAs) whereas if you work with young people you may come across self-harm or drug/alcohol abuse.

In any situation when you are the first on the scene for an emergency situation you need to ensure that you do not put yourself in any danger. When you are sure you are safe you should then call for help and check that the person is breathing normally. You do this by listening and watching for ten seconds, checking that you can hear breathing and watching the chest rise and fall. If the person is breathing then you can be fairly certain that the heart is still beating also. This means that there is there is still circulation and you can then call for an ambulance and start to check to see if there are any other injuries that are evident such as bleeding or breaks. This is called the secondary survey and involves a check for other injuries and must be carried out quickly and methodically.

If you are happy that the casualty is breathing you can do the following.

Check for bleeding

If you do find a bleed then follow the correct procedure for controlling haemorrhage.

Head and neck

Check for swelling, deformity or bleeding. Other clues may be the surroundings and the environment, for example there might be a ladder nearby, an object that may have fallen onto them or an overturned chair.

Shoulders and chest

Carefully run your fingers along the collar bone (clavicle). Look at both sides to see if they are symmetrical – is there a distinct difference to indicate a break?

Do the ribs look normal?

Abdomen and pelvis

Check for breaks in bones or even swelling in the area.

Legs and arms

Is there a medic alert bracelet which might indicate a reason for the collapse? Do the legs and arms look as though they may have sustained a fracture?

Pockets

Are there any objects/tablets in the pockets? Make sure nothing can injure the casualty as you turn them into the recovery position.

Anything untoward found during this survey will now need to be treated in order to meet the casualty's needs and to prevent the condition from worsening.

Following this check you may wish to place the person into the recovery position (see Figure 9.2) to ensure that the airway stays open. Your aims as the first person on the scene are to:

- preserve life
- prevent the situation from getting worse
- promote recovery.

(Barraclough, 2008)

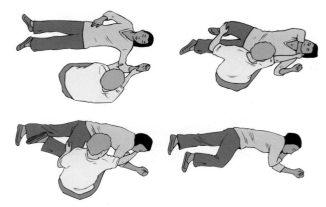

Figure 9.2 The recovery position

Now let's look in detail at the recovery position to remind ourselves how we can achieve this.

The Recovery Position

When a person lies on their back there is a potential for their airway to become blocked because the tongue tends to touch the back of the throat. If a person vomits in this position then the airway can also become blocked. To reduce both these risks turn the person onto their side.

Straighten both legs and bend the arm nearest to you outwards and at right angles. Palm uppermost.

Bring the casualty's other hand up to their face and lie the back of the hand across the cheek. This will act as a support and cushions the head. Remember you will have to hold the hand in place since a person who is unconscious will have no muscle control to do so.

Now with your other hand bring the far knee up, foot firmly placed on the floor and using the knee as a lever pull the casualty towards you placing the knee onto the floor. The casualty will now be on their side.

Figure 9.3 Step one recovery – arm nearest to you at right angles, lift knee and hand on shoulder

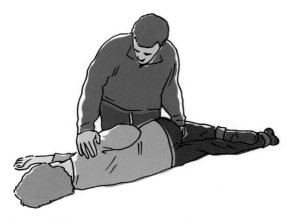

Figure 9.4 Step two – turn towards you

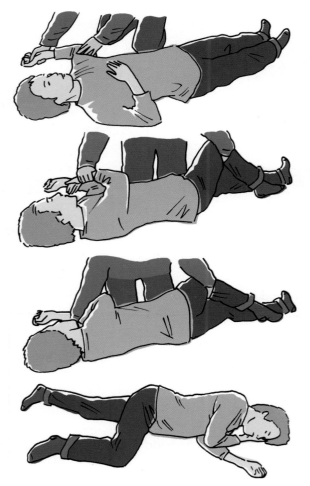

Figure 9.5 Procedure

You may find that a person in your care stops breathing altogether and this then requires a further response. This means that no oxygen is getting into the person's body which means the heart is likely to stop and brain cells will start dying off in minutes.

You now need to get help and ask somebody to dial 999 and say that the casualty has stopped breathing. It is then up to you to start resuscitation or CPR – Cardio-Pulmonary Resuscitation. You may be familiar with the new protocols advertised in the media: compressing the sternum to the tune of 'Staying Alive' and this is a useful guide. You are no longer required to breathe for the person, although if an airway is available you may employ such a device.

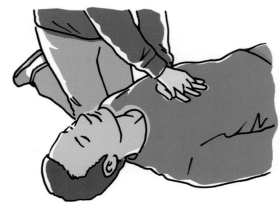

Figure 9.6 CPR

CPR

Place the heel of your hand onto the middle of the chest then interlock your fingers of the other hand over it. Keep your arms straight (not like they do on the films!) and press down on to the breast bone (sternum) to about 5 cm, then release and do this 30 times. What you are doing is pushing the rib cage down to squeeze the heart, allowing it to pump blood around the body.

When you have finished that cycle you need to tilt the head back, nip the patient's nose and then breathe two breaths into them. This gives them some oxygen for the heart to pump around to feed the tissues and brain cells. Watch the chest rise as you breathe in – if it doesn't do so then check you have cleared the airway sufficiently.

Every now and then you will need to check that the patient has not started breathing again or that the airway remains open and some oxygen is getting in.

CPR for Children

For children the rate can be the same as the adult rate – 30:2 – but five breaths are given before continuing with 30 compressions.

Modifications to the pressure used need to be made and a good rule is for children over 1 year use one hand for the compression and for babies use two fingers.

Unconsciousness is a sleep like state which disables the normal body reflexes and places the individual in danger of airway obstruction and subsequent lack of oxygen. You need to make sure the person is breathing, call for professional assistance and then try to ascertain what may be causing the unconsciousness. Some of the causes are listed below.

F – Fainting	
I – Imbalance of heat – heat stroke or even cold	
S – Shock	
H – Head injury	
S – Stroke	
H – Heart attack	
A – Asphyxia	
P – Poisoning	
E – Epilepsy	
D – Diabetes	

(You will notice that these are easy to remember as they form the mnemonic 'fish-shaped'.)

We shall now look at some of the likely conditions you may come across in the course of your work.

Fainting

A simple faint can occur for a number of reasons and is sometimes heralded by the person complaining of feeling 'woozy' or looking as if they are swaying. This may look like a case of shock and you may notice the person has cold clammy skin and the pulse is slow.

Action

- If the person is about to faint lay them down on the floor. Often this action will enable the blood to return to the vital organs, in particular the brain and heart, and the person will start to feel better.
- In the case of actual loss of consciousness you need to check breathing then place the person in the recovery position.
- Make sure the airway is maintained by tilting the head back and checking for breathing.
- Then carry out a secondary survey.

In all cases you should never:

- give anything by mouth (you may compromise the airway)
- leave the person alone (unless you have to go and get help).

Haemorrhage/bleeding

Any bleed from any injury requires prompt treatment to prevent severe shock.

The severity of the haemorrhage depends largely upon the type of injury and the vessels involved. We have three types of blood vessel and each type delivers blood to tissues in different ways.

Arteries – These are larger vessels which pump blood under pressure. A wound to an artery can cause the blood to 'spurt' out of the body at high speed and occasionally some distance. This means that the casualty will quickly lose a lot of blood volume which can be fatal. The blood is bright red in colour due to being highly oxygenated.

Veins – These vessels carry the same amount of blood as the arteries but are not under so much pressure so a bleed from a vein tends to come out much more slowly. The bleed from a varicose vein may be slow but is potentially very dangerous since a lot of blood can be leaked at one time.

Capilliaries – These are tiny vessels and any cut to these may at first be quite profuse but generally eases to a trickle after slight pressure is applied. You might recall cutting your finger and wondering if it will ever stop!

The effect of any blood loss therefore depends upon the size of the wound, the injury and the vessels involved but loss of blood over a prolonged time can cause severe shock and can be fatal.

Action

- You need to stop the bleed by applying direct pressure to the wound. Sometimes an internal haemorrhage occurs and the only indication you will have of this will be the casualty's shocked appearance and the symptoms that go with this (see below).
- If you can, elevate the part affected as this will have the effect of reducing the flow of blood to the area and will slow the bleed.
- You need to cover the wound to reduce the infection risk and to keep the pressure constant.
- Ensure you maintain your own safety by:
  - Checking for glass and embedded objects in the wound that might cut you.
  - If gloves are available wear them and then wash your hands thoroughly after treating. Any cuts on your own hands should always be covered when you are at work in order to provide a barrier from blood to blood contact.
- Call 999 if severe.

Do not:

- apply a tourniquet, which can cause long-term tissue damage
- secure the dressing too tightly.

Shock

If blood pressure falls low enough and there is inadequate blood getting to the tissues a condition known as shock is said to exist.

There are three types of shock:

- hypovolaemic
- cardiogenic
- anaphylactic.

Hypovolaemic shock occurs when there is a low (hypo) volume (vol) of blood (aemic) circulating and may be caused by internal or external haemorrhage.

Cardiogenic shock refers to the fall in blood pressure caused by heart and respiratory problems such as a heart attack (or myocardial infarction), heart valve disease or lung problems.

This type of shock is dealt with later.

Anaphylactic shock is an allergic reaction in which histamine is released in large quantities causing the blood pressure to drop and the heart to contract more slowly.

Recognising the person in shock

Initial stages of shock. In any shock condition the body responds by releasing adrenaline. You will remember the 'fight or flight' analogy in which faced with a dramatic event or stress we either make the decision to run away or stay and deal with the situation. Whatever we decide to do our body responds by releasing adrenaline, which has the effect of raising the pulse rate. Our skin will start to become pale and clammy.

Second-stage shock. As the condition gets worse our breathing becomes faster and shallower and the pulse starts to weaken. This has the effect of less oxygen getting to the tissues and will therefore cause a slight blueness around lips and nose (cyanosis) subsequent dizziness and perhaps vomiting.

Critical stage. This presents as a condition known as 'air hunger' which is characterised by deep sighing breaths. It leads to confusion and perhaps aggressive behaviour and finally unconsciousness.

Action

- Lay the person down and raise the legs (if there are fractures in the lower limb raise one leg). This will help the blood return to the brain and heart.
- Dial 999.
- Keep the person warm.
- Keep a close eye on breathing and respiration and be prepared to resuscitate.

Do not allow the person to eat, drink or smoke.

Seizures

A person who has been diagnosed with epilepsy may have regular seizures and will know exactly what to do in the event of one occurring. In this case your treatment is to ensure the safety of that individual during the actual seizure.

Seizures can vary from a momentary loss of consciousness or the appearance of day dreaming as in 'absence' seizures (formerly known as *petit mal*) or major seizures which can be very frightening to watch.

Action

- Help the person lie on the floor.
- Prevent injury by moving anything that may be in the way.
- Cushion the persons head.
- Ask bystanders to leave the scene.
- Check airway and breathing if possible to do so.
- Dial 999 if seizure continues for longer than three minutes, another seizure follows recovery or this is the person's first seizure.

Do not:

- restrict the person's movements in any way
- put anything in to their mouth during the fit stage.

Following the seizure, check the airway and the individual's breathing.

Keep casualty in recovery position until fully awake.

Febrile convulsions

These sorts of seizures can occur in children and babies who have a high temperature and may be the only time they suffer from a seizure. It is obviously very distressing and can also lead to a cessation in breathing.

The action needed here is to reduce their temperature by removing clothing and cooling the body. If a fit does occur then you need to deal with it as before.

Figure 9.7 Choking

Choking

When a person inhales food or a sweet they may be unable to tell you what they have done. The signs to look out for are:

- distressed look
- clutching and pointing to throat
- inability to speak or cough and pale skin leading to cyanosis and compromised breathing.

Action

Encourage the person to cough. If this is not successful:

- Shout for help and then bend the casualty forward and give five firm back slaps between the shoulder blades
- If still obstructed stand behind the casualty and grasp them around the waist.
- Make a fist and place it above the naval.
- With your other hand pull the fist sharply upwards five times (abdominal thrusts).
- If the casualty becomes unconscious you need to carry out CPR.

Anaphylaxis

This is a serious condition in which there is a sudden swelling of the face, tongue and lips. It is usually due to the ingestion of something that the patient is allergic to: peanuts, medication or other food stuffs. It may also be brought on in some people by wasp or bee stings. Whatever the cause, a rapid deterioration of the situation can lead to the airway being constricted and the breathing becoming compromised.

The person may have a rash on the skin, complain of itchiness and have a rapid, weak pulse.

Fast action is required.

Action

- Call 999.
- If the person has their own treatment with them due to previous knowledge of an allergy you may assist them. These treatments usually come in the form of adrenaline in an auto injector which is a little like a pen – hence the term epi-pen.
- Otherwise treat the airway and breathing as for an emergency and if the patient is faint lay them down.

Diabetes and the problems that may occur

It is becoming more common to deal with clients and patients who suffer from diabetes – a disorder caused by the reduced production of the hormone insulin, which is used by the body to break down sugar. Without insulin the body cannot use the sugar taken in and this has major health effects.

There are three types of diabetes.

- **Diet controlled**. Individuals with this type of diabetes can control their symptoms by reducing and monitoring the amount of sugar they ingest. Their bodies are producing some insulin.
- **Tablet controlled**. These individuals need to control their diets and take medications, which reduce the level of sugar in the body. Their supply of insulin is limited.
- **Insulin dependent**. With this type of diabetes the person has no insulin in their body or only a minimal amount and they need to inject insulin several times a day in order to keep their sugar levels under control.

Hyperglycaemia can occur if there is a mismatch of sugar and insulin. High (hyper) sugar (glyc) levels in the blood (aem) become quite toxic to the body. Acid builds up and sets up a chain of events that make the person ill. As the body tries to get rid of the acid build up they are likely to present with the following signs and symptoms.

- After a slow period of time, about 12–48 hours, the person will become increasingly drowsy and may even become unconscious.
- They will have a rapid pulse and are likely to breathe slowly and deeply. They pass a lot of urine and are constantly thirsty and hungry. Occasionally the breath smells of 'pear drops'.

As you will appreciate it is easy to put these symptoms down to other reasons so we need to be very aware of what is happening over time.

Action

The treatment for this condition is always to contact the emergency services and to carry out the airway and breathing protocols as above.

Hypoglycaemia

You are more likely to come across this condition in which there is a low (hypo) level of sugar (glyc) in the blood (aem). In fact you may have experienced this at some point yourself. It does not make you a diabetic it just means that you may have used the insulin in your body and not taken in enough, giving you a slight lowering of blood sugar levels. This sometimes happens if we do not eat enough and have taken lots of exercise and we may feel a little dizzy and weak. We can usually sort this out with a drink and something to eat. For the diabetic individual the same treatment generally applies although they are more likely to experience this type of episode more regularly.

The signs and symptoms are likely to be as follows:

- The onset is rapid and within minutes the person may exhibit weakness, lack of coordination, confusion and slurring of speech. They may also start to behave in a way that is aggressive and may become quite belligerent. The behaviour may be quite uncharacteristic and the person may seem to be a little drunk.
- If you feel their skin it will be cold and sweaty and their breathing is likely to be rapid as will the pulse.

Action

It is quite possible that the person may have had their insulin and then either forgotten to have breakfast or left it a little too late. As this condition occurs quickly you will notice that when you start to treat the person they will quickly return to their normal self.

- Sit them down and give them a sugary drink or some chocolate or a biscuit.
- If they are becoming unconscious you can still help them by rubbing something sweet onto their gums. This will have a slower effect but can be useful to try to get the casualty alert enough to then take a drink.
- If there is no response after ten minutes you need to contact 999.

Cerebrovascular accident/CVA/stroke

A cerebrovascular accident or 'stroke' is an emergency situation and the sooner the person is sent to hospital the sooner treatment can be given. First aid is limited in this instance.

A CVA occurs when there is a reduction of blood flow to the vessels in the brain. This may be due to a narrowing of the cerebral arteries or a blood clot actually blocking the flow altogether. This is easier to understand if you think about it being a bit like the flow of water in a blocked hosepipe. The water is unable to get to where it is needed, that is, your garden perhaps, and therefore the consequence is that the garden dies. This is similar to the blockage of blood flow of blood to parts of the brain. The blood will be unable to deliver nutrients that are needed to a part of the brain and the tissue will therefore cease to function. This means that part of the brain will not work sufficiently well if at all. Hence the variety of different effects that a stroke can have on a person.

For example, paralysis to one or other side of the body or speech problems or memory problems all indicate a specific area of the brain has been affected and you will only realise this once the individual has further tests at the hospital. However your quick action as a first aider in recognising what might be happening is crucial to recovery.

The signs and symptoms may vary but usually the person will complain of a headache and then may become confused and perhaps have sight and speech difficulties. You may notice they are unable to balance well and it is possible that if you get to look at their pupils you will see that they are different sizes.

If unconsciousness occurs then you need to call 999 F.A.S.T.

Angina

We used the analogy of a blocked hosepipe above and it can also be applied to angina and heart attacks.

Angina pectoris is a condition of the heart in which the flow of blood through the coronary arteries is reduced due to a narrowing of those arteries. The narrowing of the arteries is due to a build up of fatty acids and cholesterol (in the case of your hose pipe it might be due to clogging from soil or even a foreign body which has entered the pipe). This reduces the width of the artery and the casualty will notice this when the heart needs to work harder. The person with angina will therefore complain of pain when they exercise or at times of stress when the heart has to pump a little harder to get the tissues oxygenated. The lack of blood getting to the area means there is a smaller amount of oxygen getting through and it is this that causes the pain.

Action

Get the person to rest as this should result in a lowering of the heart rate and the pain will subside. If the individual knows they suffer from angina then they are likely to have medication to relieve the symptoms. If this is the first time they have had an attack then it is wise to get medical assistance.

Heart attack/myocardial infarction

The signs and symptoms of angina are similar to a heart attack but they subside with drugs or rest.

The person who is suffering from a heart attack will not get relief from rest and this is because the artery involved is totally blocked by a blood clot and no oxygen is being delivered to part of the heart muscle thus causing severe pain. This is an emergency situation and could result in the casualty's death if not treated efficiently.

The onset is sudden, and although the pain may be mistaken for indigestion it can also be so severe that the person complains of a crushing sensation in the chest. The left arm and shoulders may also be painful and the casualty will be very pale, sweaty and the pulse may be fast and irregular. They will be short of breath and very anxious. They may feel sick and may even feel as if they are going to die.

Action

The individual should sit down and you need to call 999 immediately. If they suffer from angina they should be encouraged to take their medication which may give some relief.

Although you are unable to prescribe medication it has been shown that aspirin chewed slowly has an anticoagulant effect and can help the casualty. You need to inform the person of this potential treatment and allow them the choice as to whether they will take it or not. You should however check that they are not already taking anticoagulants such as warfarin or heparin.

If the person becomes unconscious then check their breathing and act according to the emergency procedure.

There are a number of injuries and conditions which you may come across in the course of your day-to-day work and which are likely to occur in your own setting. You are advised to carry out a risk assessment of the common conditions you are likely to come across so that you can be prepared for any eventuality and staff can be trained to undertake the first aid needed for those conditions.

> **Evidence Activity**
>
> **Activity**
>
> Prepare a risk assessment which identifies the different types of accidents and sudden illness that may occur in your own work setting and explain procedures to be followed if an accident or sudden illness should occur.
>
> Prepare a document that shows the procedure to be followed.

(The above text was adapted from Tilmouth, T, Davies-Ward, E and Williams, B (2011) Foundation Degree in Health and Social Care, London, Hodder Education.)

4 Be able to reduce the spread of infection

4.1 Explain own role in supporting others to follow practices that reduce the spread of infection

4.3 Demonstrate ways to ensure that own health and hygiene do not pose a risk to an individual or to others at work

Your role in infection control is to be aware of practice in the setting and to ensure that you practice in a safe way. To do this you need to ensure that you are trained in infection control and have a good knowledge of the ways in which your setting reduces the risk of infection. In addition, you need to ensure that the staff in the setting are adhering to protocol.

Health Care Associated Infections or HCAIs have proved problematic in care settings for a number of years and the need to control infection is high on the agenda of health care professionals. You will be aware of the rise of MRSA or Methicillin resistant *Staphylococcus Aureus* but also on the increase are VRE or Vancomycin Resistant *enterococci,* E. Coli or *Escherichia Coli*, ESBL or Extended-spectrum beta lactamases and the *Clostridium difficile* or C. Diff infections.

Our daily exposure in health care settings to blood and bodily fluids places us at high risk of contamination and therefore we need to be vigilant in protecting ourselves and others in the work place. We are also duty bound to ensure that the patients and clients we come into contact with are not at risk from poor practice on our part.

Your own work place will have an infection control policy and it is most important that all staff are up to date with the procedures therein to prevent infection.

The core principles related to infection control can be summarised in the following:

- effective hand washing
- the use of protective clothing
- isolation nursing
- correct procedures for laundry and waste management
- cleanliness of the environment
- decontamination of equipment.

(Tilmouth and Tilmouth 2009)

Your own responsibility in infection control is to ensure that your own health and hygiene in no way pose a threat to others in the setting. For example, if you suffer from an illness such as a cough or a cold and continue to work, the more vulnerable clients may be exposed to viruses and bacteria that may be more damaging for them. If you have cuts or abrasions on exposed parts of your body these need to be carefully covered to protect yourself from further infection which may come from clients with wounds or other conditions.

It very much depends upon the type of setting you are working in but there will be guidelines in place which show what you need to do when you are ill or have a condition that may prove infectious, and you need to follow these procedures for the protection of your own health and others you come into contact with.

4.2 Demonstrate the recommended method for hand washing

Our hands are one of the foremost ways in which infection can be transmitted from patient to patient and, despite knowing this for years, the wealth of information and research about this simple procedure is testament to the fact that we still fall short in our compliance.

Think of it in this way. Our hands are heavily populated with micro-organisms which we acquire through various activities we undertake in the case setting. These micro-organisms survive on the hands and can then be transmitted to others when we carry out procedures in our daily activity. We can also pick up disease-causing organisms as well, so we are at risk of becoming ill ourselves. With good hand-washing techniques we can remove large numbers of these microbes.

Ayliffe et al. (1978) devised a useful six-step technique to ensure that all parts of the hand are washed efficiently.

Step One – Using soap and running water start with the palms.

Step Two – Right palm over back of hand and left palm over right back of hand.

Step Three – Palm to palm and interlace fingers.

Step Four – Backs of fingers to palms with fingers interlocked.

Step Five – Rotational rubbing of each thumb.

Step Six – Rotational rubbing with clasped fingers of right hand in left palm and vice-versa.

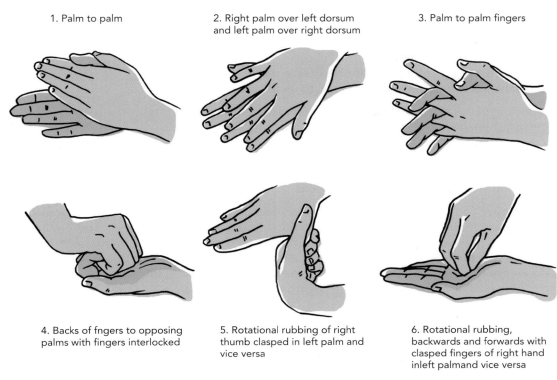

1. Palm to palm

2. Right palm over left dorsum and left palm over right dorsum

3. Palm to palm fingers

4. Backs of fngers to opposing palms with fingers interlocked

5. Rotational rubbing of right thumb clasped in left palm and vice versa

6. Rotational rubbing, backwards and forwards with clasped fingers of right hand inleft palmand vice versa

Figure 9.8 Correct hand-washing method

You will have noticed that hand rubs and alcohol have also been introduced into care settings and other establishments to try to address the risk of infection.

5 Be able to move and handle equipment and other objects safely

5.1 Explain the main points of legislation that relates to moving and handling

The website www.hse.gov.uk/healthservices/moving-handling.htm is a useful one to access as it highlights the main legislation which applies to moving and handling. This is:

- Health and Safety at Work etc. Act 1974 (HSWA)
- Manual Handling Operations Regulations 1992 (MHOR) (as amended 2002)
- Management of Health and Safety at Work Regulations 1999
- Provision and Use of Work Equipment Regulations 1998 (PUWER)
- Lifting Operations and Lifting Equipment Regulations 1998 (LOLER).

The main points to come out of these laws focus on the responsibility of the employer and the employee and highlight the need to avoid manual handling if at all possible.

> ### Evidence Activity
>
> **Activity**
>
> Write an account of your own role in supporting others to follow practices that reduce the spread of infection and show how you ensure that your own health and hygiene do not pose a risk to an individual or to others at work.
>
> Teach a new member of staff the recommended method for hand washing and ask your mentor/manager to observe and write a witness statement for your portfolio.

Employers are responsible for assessing the risks involved and need to do the following:

- evaluate the task
- assess the loads involved
- check the environment in which the task takes place
- assess the individuals who are expected to undertake the task.

The reduction of risk is the next step and the employer needs to take steps to ensure that if lifting is necessary then the risk of injury is minimal.

The HASAWA 1974 states that:

'It is the duty of the employer to ensure as far as is reasonably practicable the health, safety and welfare at work of all employees.'

As an employee you also have a responsibility as outlined in law and must ensure that you comply with procedures for lifting and handling as laid out in your employment policies. These will include instructions for the use of equipment and undertaking training. At times we may think it is quicker to dispense with the use of a hoist to move a client from bed to chair but in doing so you are putting yourself and the client at risk of injury and are working against the policy of your employer, which could result in disciplinary measures being taken against you.

5.2 Explain principles for safe moving and handling

There are a few principles for safe moving and handling, and everyone who works in the care setting is required to adhere to safe working procedures.

To reduce the risk of injury to staff and anybody using the service you are required to:

- assess and reduce the risks
- avoid manual handling tasks that could result in injury, where possible
- follow systems of work and use the equipment provided
- cooperate with the employer and provide information about any problems
- ensure actions do not place yourself or others at risk of injury.

5.3 Move and handle equipment and other objects safely

If it becomes necessary to move a person or an object then a risk assessment is the best way forward.

The following checklist will help to make the move as safe as possible.

- Ascertain what the person can do themselves and how they can participate.
- Assess other factors that might impact upon the move such as pain, disability, or immobility.
- Assess the equipment needed – such as handling equipment and type of hoist and sling needed or the type of bed, bath and chair that will be useful.
- Assess the assistance needed, including the number of staff.
- Assess the arrangements for reducing the risk of and for dealing with falls.

Evidence Activity

9.5 Activity

Write an account of your own setting's arrangements for moving and handling and attach a copy of the policy with highlighted areas showing the principles you work to and how this relates to legislation in this area.

6 Be able to handle hazardous substances and materials

6.1 Describe types of hazardous substances that may be found in the work setting

You will need to make an assessment within your own work place of the substances that you may be in contact with, but a hazardous substance is anything that might cause harm if used inappropriately. These sorts of substances include:

- Any substance that might be used in the course of your work, for example cleaning materials, paint, adhesives, medications.
- Any substance that may be generated during work activities, such as welding or paint spraying or replacing wound dressings which require you to handle soiled materials.
- Any naturally occurring substance such as dust or hair.
- Bacteria and other microorganisms.

6.2 Demonstrate safe practices

Storing hazardous substances

This is common sense really but you would be surprised at the number of people who fail to keep their own homes safe.

The first thing to remember is to keep hazardous substances in a safe place and out of reach of pets and children. If this means you need to move them to a high cupboard you must ensure that they can be safely removed without dropping them.

The next thing is not to decant the substances to other bottles or containers. By keeping them in the manufacturer's containers you reduce the risk of misidentification.

You should also be aware to keep incompatible chemicals away from other types and in cool, well-ventilated areas.

The final thing to remember is to ensure that all containers are clearly labeled and intact and not leaking.

Using hazardous substances

The HSE provides a very useful online resource to give guidance about the use of hazardous substances. Entitled Working with substances hazardous to health: A brief guide to COSHH, it outlines how to control hazardous substances at work and what needs to be done to comply with the Control of Substances Hazardous to Health (COSHH) Regulations 2002.

> **Evidence Activity**
>
>  **Activity 1**
>
> Go to http://www.hse.gov.uk/pubns/indg136.pdf and make short notes on using hazardous substances.

Disposing of hazardous substances and materials

Since July 2005 new regulations exist with respect to how we classify the waste we generate in care settings.

Hazardous and non-hazardous labelling now applies and the former refers to waste that is potentially disease causing. This waste needs to be incinerated and must be placed in yellow bags. Any other waste can be placed in black bags.

Sharp objects must be put into yellow sharps bins with wording on the side in black and red.

The use of chemicals to decontaminate various pieces of equipment carries a risk to care workers as well as client and patients. The COSHH regulations (2002) are in place to ensure that all substances used to disinfect areas are clearly labelled and safely stored.

Substances you may be familiar include: alcohol, such as methylated spirits, handrubs, chlorhexidine, gluteraldehyde, Hycolin and Jeyes fluid.

Evidence Activity

9.6 Activity 2

Carry out an assessment of all the hazardous substances that may be found in your work setting and describe how they are stored and disposed of.

7 Be able to promote fire safety in the work setting

7.1 Describe practices that prevent fires from starting and spreading

7.2 Demonstrate measures that prevent fires from starting

The government supplies guidance on fire safety for all care establishments in its booklet Fire Safety Risk Assessment for Residential Care Homes and details what needs to be done to comply with fire safety law and carry out a fire risk assessment, in addition to identifying the general fire precautions for a premises.

Your premises will have in place a Fire Safety Order which covers 'general fire precautions' the duty of which requires a 'responsible person' to carry out a risk assessment.

In the work place

The risk assessment needs to focus upon:

- those at special risk, such as disabled people (mobility impairment or learning disability)
- children and those who you know have special needs
- reference to any dangerous substance which may be kept on the premises.

To prevent fires from starting and spreading your work place must have guidance in place which ensures that all employees are informed of certain procedures. For example, there should be information available about how to contact the emergency services.

Equally, all employees must be trained about the fire precautions in place and they also need to be able to handle any equipment provided in connection with fire fighting and fire detection.

The emergency exits in the work place need to be clearly signposted and be kept clear of any equipment.

Evidence Activity

9.7 Activities 1 and 2

Describe the practices in your own work place that prevent fires from starting and spreading and write a short piece to show how these measures prevent fires from starting.

7.3 Explain emergency procedures to be followed in the event of a fire in the work setting

7.4 Ensure that clear evacuation routes are maintained at all times

Every organisation needs to have in place a PEEP or Personal Emergency Evacuation Plan which needs to cover the following information:

- what to do on discovering a fire
- what to do when you hear the fire alarm
- how to call the fire brigade
- how to evacuate the premises
- how to assemble following evacuation
- registering evacuated staff and service users.

> **Evidence Activity**
>
> **Activity 3**
>
> Obtain a copy of your PEEP portfolio and reflect upon its currency and any changes or additions you believe should be made to it.
>
> When your evaluation is complete discuss with your mentor or manager plans to present a professional development activity to all staff to present your findings.

8 Be able to implement security measures in the work setting

8.1 Demonstrate use of agreed procedures for checking the identity of anyone requesting access to premises and information

8.2 Demonstrate use of measures to protect own security and the security of others in the work setting

This is a shared responsibility between yourself and your employer and you are responsible for the safety of the people who use your setting and who visit it, whether they are trades people or the family of clients.

People may pose all kinds of threat to us and it is good practice to be aware of who is actually on the premises at any given time as well as those who might request information from us. We are aware of the threat to colleagues who work in settings such as emergency departments, who come across individuals who may be violent and aggressive towards them. But even in care home settings we may potentially have visitors who are unhappy about an aspect of care and can pose a threat should they become agitated. In addition, clients with mental health issues may present themselves to us when they are in crisis and this may result in a volatile situation.

These sorts of situations need to be dealt with in a specific manner and you need to think about how you would deal with any such issue that might arise.

In many settings there is open access for anyone and everyone to enter the premises and this can have major implications with respect to our own and our clients' safety. In larger organisations where identity badges are used it is fairly easy to identify the staff but smaller premises may not have this luxury and rely on staff to be vigilant about who is entering the premises.

A visitor signing-in system is a fairly good idea as then at least you have some idea as to who is on the premises. In fact, you will need this sort of information anyway, as if there were a fire you would be asked to account for people in the building. However, an intruder who presents a risk is unlikely to stop and sign the book.

In work settings where independence is encouraged this can prove very difficult to manage. Vulnerable individuals may be confined to their own homes or in schools and nurseries or even leisure settings where young children work and play, and in such settings a policy needs to be in place to provide protection.

Your setting may well have a policy in place, which gives guidelines as to how you are to proceed if an unknown individual gains access to your setting. Read this policy now to familiarise yourself again with the protocols.

Some of the golden rules are set out here.

- Challenge unknown individuals with a polite enquiry: 'How can I help you?'
- If they are a visitor, escort them to where they want to go. Don't just give directions.
- Make sure you are aware of new faces in the building.
- Do not tackle an intruder but raise the alarm.

Some care professionals work in settings where tensions run high and there is a danger of situations escalating and abusive behaviour poses a safety risk. Even the most pleasant of settings can be a potential trigger for verbal and physical abuse if individuals become upset and the situation is dealt with poorly.

Some of the things we have experienced are shown below:

- Teenagers losing their temper and behaving unreasonably.
- Visitors unhappy with aspects of care a loved one is receiving starting to shout.
- Being blamed by a colleague for something you did not do.
- A patient or client shouting and behaving in an aggressive manner.

Whatever your situation is, it is the way that you deal with it that will make the biggest difference to all concerned. There are many factors that can lead to the escalation of violence and abuse in a setting, but your interpretation of the event and the person's feelings may also contribute to the situation becoming worse or better.

There may well be differences in perspective about a particular situation, which can lead to different ways in which you would deal with the behaviour. For example, we may view a person's aggression as purely a way of seeking attention and demand that something should be done about the person. However an onlooker may believe that the person was provoked to behave in the way they did simply because of the response staff gave at the outset. Another response might be that the person was in fact dealing with pain or anxiety and a kind and caring response might well have improved the situation.

Time to reflect

Consider this for a moment.

If we describe behaviour in a negative manner we are likely to deal with it as such.

The term 'attention seeking' carries connotations of being negative, manipulative and just plain spoilt! But if we view it as a way of getting attention to a problem we might have a different reaction to it. The child who fails to understand the lesson being taught may behave badly and in a disruptive manner and be unable to ask the question they most need to ask. The teacher who recognises that behaviour will seek to help that individual in a different way and not just remove them altogether from the lesson.

By working out what the 'function' of the challenging behaviour is and what it helps the person to achieve in a given situation we can then start to help the individual to deal with the situation they find difficult in more constructive ways. For further reading see Lowe and Felce (1995).

Bissell et al. (2005) report the case of a man with learning difficulties whose behaviour became less violent following his dental problems being resolved. The point being made here is that challenging behaviour may be the only way a person can communicate at that time and it is important for us as care workers to find out what the 'function' of that particular behaviour is. For example the man who is shouting at staff in the emergency department may well be feeling pain, frustration, anxiety and even be very frightened. His behaviour is potentially dangerous to us, but by trying to understand what it is that behaviour is doing for that individual we can help to change the situation. It is easy to shout back or to manhandle somebody out of the department, but by standing back and trying to determine what led to the behaviour and what is actually being communicated by that behaviour we can go a long way to diffusing the situation.

Evidence Activity

9.8 Activity

What are the agreed procedures for checking the identity of anyone requesting access to your work place premises?

What about for those who request information?

What measures are in place in your own work setting to protect your own security and the security of others in the work setting?

9 Know how to manage stress

9.1 Describe common signs and indicators of stress

If we feel threatened in any way our bodies respond with the 'fight or flight' mechanism. Danger is recognised biologically and psychologically and our body responds by entering what is commonly regarded as a 'survival mode'. This state prepares us to defend ourselves or to fight and the body starts to secrete the hormone adrenaline to help us do so. This may become harmful to the body and mind if the body remains in this stressful state for lengthy periods of time.

Symptoms of stress include the following:

- problems with thought processes and only seeing the negative in life
- memory and concentration issues
- constant anxiety and worry
- irritability
- mood swings
- depression and isolation
- unexplained aches and pains
- upset digestive tract causing diarrhoea or constipation
- nausea, dizziness
- chest pain, rapid heartbeat
- loss of sex drive/libido
- frequent infections
- poor sleeping habits
- using alcohol, cigarettes or drugs to relax.

9.2 Describe signs that indicate own stress

9.3 Analyse factors that tend to trigger own stress

Only you can say how your own stress manifests itself and you need to be aware of the symptoms. Stress has a tendency to slowly accumulate so you are unaware of it actually happening until it is too late and you suddenly feel overwhelmed.

NHS Choices gives good advice as to how you might recognise your stress triggers and advocates keeping a diary to note down stressful episodes for two to four weeks.

Their website gives the following checklist of things you might include:

- the date, time and place of a stressful episode
- what you were doing
- who you were with
- how you felt emotionally
- what you were thinking
- what you started doing
- how you felt physically
- a stress rating (0–10 where 10 is the most stressed you could ever feel).

(http://www.nhs.uk/Conditions/stress-anxiety-depression/Pages/understanding-stress.aspx)

9.4 Compare strategies for managing stress

The NHS highlights ten stress-busting strategies, and you need to try the strategies to determine which are helpful for you. The main point made is that turning to an unhealthy behaviour such as drinking more alcohol or smoking more will not help and could make your stress worse (Cooper, cited in www.nhs.uk/Conditions/stress-anxiety-depression/Pages/understanding-stress.aspx).

By building ourselves up emotionally we can do much to develop good ways of dealing with stress; we covered this in more depth in Chapter 1.

Strategies include:

- being active
- taking control of the issue that is causing you stress
- seeking help and support from others
- taking some time for yourself – 'me' time
- setting yourself a challenge to help build confidence
- helping others and become a volunteer
- developing good time management at work and 'work smarter, not harder'
- be positive and appreciate what you have
- if you can't change something, accept it – change is not always possible so recognising this will help you to cope.

> ### Evidence Activity
>
> **Activity**
>
> Keep a diary for two weeks and using the checklist in the text above write down your stress triggers and how they make you feel. Write a reflective account of some of the ways in which you have helped yourself, stating your preferred stress-busting strategies.

References

Barraclough, N, (2008) *First Aid Made Easy*. Qualsafe Ltd.

Bissell, L, Phillips, N and Stenfert Kroese, B (2005) 'The experience of a man with severe challenging behaviour following a resettlement from hospital: a single case study design'. *British Journal of Learning Disabilities*, 33(4):166–73.

Cooper cited in www.nhs.uk/Conditions/stress-anxiety-depression/Pages/understanding-stress.aspx

Lowe, K and Felce, D (1995) The definition of challenging behaviours in practice. *British Journal of Learning Disabilities,* 23(3): 118–23.

Tilmouth, T, Davies-Ward, E and Williams, B (2011) *Foundation Degree in Health and Social Care*. London: Hodder Education.

Tilmouth T and Tilmouth S (2009) *Safe and Clean Care Infection Prevention and Control for Health and Social Care Students*. Exeter: Reflect Press.

Index

Mental Health Care
A Care Worker Handbook

Working, learning or training in mental health care? You don't have to go it alone!

Caring for people with mental health issues is one of the most challenging and rewarding roles in Health and Social Care. But with a range of awards and certificates available for work-based learners it can be a confusing area. That's why we've put together a one-stop handbook to support your training and continuing professional development in mental health care.

Here in one place is all the topic knowledge, assessment support and practical advice you will need for a range of mental health care qualifications. Core topics are linked to the specific competencies you need to demonstrate.

This book covers NCFE Level 1 Award in Mental Health Awareness, NCFE Level 2 Award in Understanding Working with People with Mental Health Issues and City & Guilds Level 3 Diploma in Mental Health Care.

It's also useful for candidates taking any of the Level 1, Level 2 and Level 3 awards, certificates and diplomas in mental health care. It's also a must have reference for those who want to brush up skills and knowledge from previous qualifications.

So whatever your level of specialism, give yourself the tools you need to survive and even flourish in mental health care.

Visit www.hoddereducation.co.uk for full details.

Also available:

Dementia Care
A Care Worker Handbook
(ISBN 9781444163223)

Learning Disabilites Care
A Care Worker Handbook
(ISBN 9781444163261)

End of Life Care
A Care Worker Handbook
(ISBN 9781444163247)

HODDER EDUCATION
www.hoddereducation.co.uk

KT-905-551

ISBN 978-1-4441-8379-5

9 781444 183795